ASSOCIATION FOR SCOTTISH LITERATURE

NUMBER FIFTY-FOUR

SETTING THE STAGE: NEW WAVE SCOTTISH DRAMA FROM THE 1970S AND 1980S

*

The ASSOCIATION FOR SCOTTISH LITERATURE aims to promote the study, teaching and writing of Scottish literature, and to further the study of the languages of Scotland.

To these ends, ASL publishes works of Scottish literature (of which this volume is an example); literary criticism and in-depth reviews of Scottish books in *Scottish Literary Review*; and scholarly studies of language in *Scottish Language*. It also publishes *New Writing Scotland*, an annual anthology of new poetry, drama and short fiction, in Scots, English and Gaelic. ASL has also prepared a range of teaching materials covering Scottish language and literature for use in schools.

All the above publications are available as a single 'package' in return for an annual subscription. Enquiries should be sent to:

ASL, Scottish Literature, 7 University Gardens, University of Glasgow, Glasgow G12 8QH. Telephone +44 (0)141 330 5309 or visit our website at **www.asls.org.uk**.

ASSOCIATION FOR SCOTTISH LITERARY STUDIES

SETTING THE STAGE

NEW WAVE SCOTTISH DRAMA FROM THE 1970S AND 1980S

Edited by Steven Cramer and John Corbett

GLASGOW

2025

*

Published in Great Britain, 2025
by the Association for Scottish Literature
Scottish Literature
University of Glasgow
7 University Gardens
Glasgow G12 8QH

ASL is a registered charity no. SC006535

www.asls.org.uk

ISBN: 978-1-906841-65-2

All rights reserved. No part of this book may be reproduced, stored in a retrieval system, or transmitted in any form or means, electronic, mechanical, photocopying, recording or otherwise, without the prior permission of the Association for Scottish Literature.

Introduction © Steven Cramer, 2025

Mary © Ian Brown
An Island in Largo © Sue Glover
White Rose © Peter Arnott
Playing With Fire © Jo Clifford
The Way to Go Home © Rona Munro

A catalogue record for this book
is available from the British Library.

Our authorised representative in the EU for product safety is
JGU Scotland HUB, Johannes Gutenberg Universität Mainz
Jakob-Welder-Weg 18, 55128 Mainz, Germany
scotland@uni-mainz.de

Set in Sabon

Typeset by ASL, Glasgow
Printed and bound by Ashford Colour, Gosport

CONTENTS

Acknowledgements vii
Introduction ix

Mary – Ian Brown 1
   Glossary 69
   Notes 73

An Island in Largo – Sue Glover 77
   Glossary 154
   Notes 155

White Rose – Peter Arnott 159
   Notes 204

Playing With Fire – Jo Clifford 207
   Notes 255

The Way to Go Home – Rona Munro 257
   Glossary 310
   Notes 312

ACKNOWLEDGEMENTS

Although this book has two editors, the collection would not have come together in its present form without the willing cooperation of many others, only several of whom is there space to mention here.

The plays collected in this volume represent formative and important work by playwrights who are now well established. We hope this volume will illuminate a period of dramatic and literary history that has been relatively neglected. First and foremost, we are grateful to the five playwrights who willingly and generously helped us to revisit their earlier work, and who graciously agreed to add a brief contextual note to each one.

The editors owe a debt to the members of the ASL Publications Board for suggesting this volume to us and supporting our venture with constant encouragement and sage advice that has kept us mostly, we hope, from error. The ASL Director, Duncan Jones, has, as ever, been a source of surprisingly comprehensive knowledge on a bewildering variety of subjects, as well as a patient and careful midwife to the production process. His contribution cannot be overstated.

Neither can we overstate the support and understanding of our respective partners, Augusta Alves and Rosalind McCaig, who have borne with good grace the necessary absences that volumes like these require of their editors. Our dearest hope is that readers will be inspired by this vibrant collection of plays to write, produce and support further 'new waves' of Scottish drama in the future.

INTRODUCTION

Steve Cramer

The term 'New Wave', describing a rapid increase in the production of Scottish Theatre texts from the years around 1970 onwards has sometimes been contested within Scottish letters. Randall Stevenson, for example, sees the phrase as neglectful of earlier work such as that of George Munro which pre-dated the socially conscious theatre of the early 1970s.[1] What remains undeniable, though, is that the quantity of plays exploring issues around Scottish language, identity and politics increased significantly around the latter time. The plays themselves addressed contemporary Scottish urban life on a scale that had not previously occurred. The texts within this volume might, then, be called a second flowering of this phenomenon, more often using history as a metaphor for the turbulent period this volume covers, and providing a more international view of Scotland by locating much of its storytelling in places beyond Scotland's borders. What all these texts have in common is their qualities as drama, leaving this reader astonished that they have not, until now, been published.

Ian Brown's *Mary* (1977) is chronologically the earliest play of this selection, and the only one where the action takes place wholly within Scotland. Even here though, there is an international flavour. The narrative tension is very much geared towards a woman who was a relative stranger to Scotland, Mary Queen of Scots, who returns to the country to

---

[1] Randall Stevenson, 'Home International: The Compass of Scottish Theatre Criticism', *International Journal of Scottish Theatre and Screen*, 2.2 (2001).

ascend to its throne having spent her life in France since infancy. Mary's story has so often been repeated through Scottish letters as a sombre morality tale, a glamorous romance or instructive but bloodthirsty story of political intrigue, chiefly because it allows the reader such multifarious possibilities for the imposition of meaning.

Brown's play makes this point, mainly through an ingenious approach to the technical possibilities of the theatre, showing many versions of Mary. As this author has pointed out in prior publication,[2] Brown employs a series of popular forms in telling his story, creating a *Verfremdung* that distances the audience from the action, focusing on the metatheatrical rather than straightforward realist storytelling by the employment of melodrama, farce, pantomime, Kailyard sentimentality and a bewildering array of other forms to tell us, less the story of Mary, than the narrational apparatus too often employed in the telling. There is even a nod to the sumptuous 1971 film production, *Mary, Queen of Scots*, starring Vanessa Redgrave, produced by Hal B. Wallis and distributed by Universal Pictures, in the character of a Sir Lew Grade figure, Lou G. Rade, as a producer planning the latest version of 'Mary':

> LOU G.: This is a strictly commercial story of human passion, love, lust, and frailty. A Highland Star is Born – *Roots* in Kilts.
> AIDE: Fantastic.
> LOU G.: What would you say to tall romantic, red-haired, short-sighted Vanessa Redgrave as the tall romantic red-haired . . . was she short-sighted?
> WRITER: No.
> LOU G.: That can be arranged . . . as the tall romantic red-haired, short-sighted, lovelorn highland queen. Whaddya say?
> DIRECTOR: I wouldn't say anything.
> LOU G.: Knew it would take your breath away. We'll need some Scotch actors. Find out the names of some. (p. 13)

The incidental satire of the ignorance of the English arts establishment adds to the sense of a tale told for the commercial viability of an orientalised romantic drama.

---

2 Steve Cramer, 'History, Ideology and Performance in Ian Brown's *Mary* and *A Great Reckonin*', *International Journal of Scottish Theatre and Screen*, 3.1 (2002).

Brown has already set the dark tone of his humour by this time, for early on, we see the trial of the rebellious Earl of Huntly for treason, a crime for which he must pay with his life. Huntly, though, was in fact already inconveniently dead, having been defeated by royal forces in battle in 1562, captured and dying soon thereafter of an apoplectic stroke. Nonetheless, under prevailing Scots law, his corpse had to be tried, as it indeed was, and judged guilty. Brown satirises this event amidst much toying with his corpse (pp. 7–10). This rather grim, Jacobean scene achieves the same tone as some of the work of Brown's English contemporary, Peter Barnes.

Perhaps the most effective and instructive form of audience alienation occurs through the multitude of characters who assume the role of 'Mary' throughout the play, often to comically ironic effect. Represented in drag by the squabbling Nobles around her, maids and even Mary Hamilton, the servant put to death for her dalliance with Darnley, the Queen's philandering wastrel second husband, these characters all perform 'Mary' as the figure they project upon her, rather than the woman herself. The real Mary remains enigmatic, but believable as a woman caught between the vast forces that envelop her. The structural role of this character is key to the play: she, a little like the figure in farce who represents the 'normal' world of the audience, sees the frenetic scenario around her with mounting perplexity and anchors the audience in their own rational world as the constructed world on the stage becomes increasingly bizarre.

Mary, in this incarnation, is represented realistically even in her language. Early in the play, she shows an uncertainty in both spoken English and Scots and questions those closest to her in order to understand the country she has been sent to rule.

> MARY: I do not understand always this country so well, David. I wish I could see the high bright sun again. This is a cold country and a grey city with the rain that drizzles on its grey streets.
> RIZZIO: It has a stern church and many brothels.
> MARY: I do not understand the women so well either. (p. 16)

Of the land she rules, she says 'I left it when I was six and expected never to see it again, never. I have forgotten it. It is no longer in my bones. It was to be a province of France.' Later, her vulnerability to the ruthless power-mongering nobles around her, as well as to the delicate balances between England and France and the related quandaries of Catholicism and Presbyterianism, is clear when she explains to Rizzio

> No. It is not the beautiful France. To think that I was to be a French princess and a French king's wife, and a French king's mother. Then Francis died. And I have come here to be a politician and learn to rule. Elizabeth was taught to be politic. I was taught to be a princess in a glittering court. (p. 40)

In this context, the historical metaphor of the play becomes clear, since the sense of vast changes taking place in the nation, of a historical turning point, pervades the play. At the time of its first production, this piece had seen the leadership of the Conservative opposition passed to Margaret Thatcher, and it had become clear that a new form of Conservatism had replaced the welfarist consensus form of Toryism that had lasted throughout the post-war generation. The catastrophic economic and social consequences of this change would be visited upon Scotland perhaps more than anywhere else in the UK, and it was apparent that Thatcher would not be open to compromise on its enforcement. It was the zealousness of her character, her absolute conviction of rectitude which finds echoes in the character of Knox, whose hostility to a Catholic Queen threatened the peace of the land and the compromise reached after much bloodshed.

> KNOX: What do you want to speak to me for?
> MARY: I wished to speak to you concerning some matters which have happened.
> KNOX: I'm not used to wasting my time in wandering round the main matter. I dinnae need humoured.
> MARY: Mr. Knox, your preaching is becoming intolerable. You interfere with my private matters, and incite my people to not like me.
> KNOX: There's none find the truth mair intolerable than they that lie.
> MARY: Why are you so proud, Mr. Knox? Why will you not listen?
> KNOX: I've only the pride of my faith, and the humility of my heart guarantees that.
> MARY: Why so fierce?
> KNOX: You're the woman at the head of the land, and that's not a woman's place, and you're a papist.

MARY: We must have peace.
KNOX: Then put away they that are liars and followers of Antichrist. (p. 20)

Knox's misogyny is hardly surprising, but the author of 'The First Blast of the Trumpet Against the Monstrous Regiment of Women', three years before Mary's reign commenced, is hardly alone in this. To nobles such as Moray, she is to be patronised ('Aye, ye're a gid lass, Mary.' p. 11), while to both Darnley and Bothwell, she becomes a wife in a loveless marriage intended to bring them closer to the throne. Bothwell tells her, 'Mary, ye're nae miracle in bed, bit ye're queen an A want ye. Whit ye are is powerless, bit whit ye mean is power.' (p. 58), in an echo of Darnley's equally brutal assessment. Attempting to operate in a world peopled almost entirely by men, she becomes quite literally objectified as a talisman of power. Her final reflection upon her life sums up the loss of self that became a tragic inevitability, given her circumstances:

> I sit and plot now to make pass the time. I can plot now for only the death. I am alone. Always I was alone. I have failed. I have made no-one happy. No-one has made me happy. I have done nothing. Nothing. All that blood, all that hope, and all that blood from my body in births. And the Scots call me whore, the English danger, and the Catholics they already call me martyr. They call me all these things and I am no-one. Who cares about me? I could be neither public nor private. Myself. I am nothing. All my life is this pain. (p. 68)

*

Sue Glover's *An Island in Largo* (1980) tells the story of another real person who would come to be fictionalised as a symbol of values unrepresented by his life. Outside of Scotland, the figure of Alexander Selkirk is largely unknown, yet a thinly fictionalised version of his story, Daniel Defoe's *Robinson Crusoe*, is almost universally understood. Glover uses a complex and heady mix of poetic monologue and realism in front of an abstract set, which represents the island of the title, as well as a series of urban and rural locations across both Scotland and England.

Her representation of Selkirk takes into account the many causalities that created a character who is, by turns childish, selfish and repellent but also sympathetic, because of the suffering imposed upon him by his impulsive but often astonishingly courageous choices. At the time of the production, a phrase such as Post Traumatic Stress Disorder was not in common usage, but the effects of this condition were well understood, and Glover's narrative explores its symptoms.

Glover creates a figure who is troublesome and stubbornly individualistic from childhood, instilling tensions between his siblings and marital strife between his adoring mother, Euphan, and staunchly Presbyterian father, Jock, by his determination to eschew the values of his bourgeois family of small business traders in favour of a life at sea, far beyond the fishermen of his hometown, Lower Largo in Fife.

> JOCK: You believe too much. Too easily. (*Suddenly very angry – with* ALEX.) His dreams told him that, did they? Dreams! Even the honest name Selcraig isn't good enough for him now. On, no, it's Alexander Selkirk he cries himself now. Makes us all a laughing stock.
> EUPHAN: Selkirk's a grand-sounding name. It has a fine ring to it.
> JOCK: Selcraig seemed a good enough name for you once. And an honest tanner seemed a good enough kind of a man.
> EUPHAN: I'm talking about my son!
> JOCK: Ay – your son! Since he could talk – and even before – he's darkened this house, divided it.
> EUPHAN: He's always been a loving son to me. He's a very loving son, in his way. You couldn't stand the sight of him, the sight of his cradle even . . . Maybe it was a daughter you wanted for the seventh.
> JOCK: It was you I wanted. You were a mother six times over, and still my loving friend til you bore Alexander.
> EUPHAN: I'm sure I always am your wife and friend.
> JOCK: You were my loving friend – til Alexander was born . . . (*awkward pause*) . . . But like he said – it's not wee fishing boats bobbing about in the Forth – it's galleons he's after, with cannons, sailing to the edge of the world. (p. 86)

Selkirk's Oedipal fixation with Euphan, who he imagines calling to him when marooned on his Caribbean island (p. 87) is carried through the text. This occurs as part of a wild poetic monologue delivered from the sands he has been marooned upon by Stradling, an incompetent English privateer captain. In it, he slaughters the seals and sea lions of the island with an axe, the only useful tool with which he has been left, in a kind of violent breakdown. At the end of this Selkirk begins to acquire the beginnings of a new relationship with his spiritual self, and a rejection of the Christian practice within which he has existed. After preparing stew from a slaughtered goat, he contemplates an offering:

> ALEX: So here I have prepared boiled cabbage palm, and goat stew. Flavoured with piemento nuts . . . (*very awkward*) . . . Lord:
> *He ladles out food into a bowl.*
> I have it in my mind to offer you . . . But Mr. Magill, the minister at Largo, would be fair affronted at the notion of an offering! . . . Papism! . . . But this is my land, and I must be my own minister. (p. 88)

What emerges after his rescue is his journey into a kind of pantheism through his long sojourn on the island. This spirituality allows him a certain sense of holiness, since, as he wittily observes, 'It's easy to obey the ten commandments when you live alone'. He attempts to explain this to his appalled father after his return to Largo:

> ALEX: At first my prayers were just mouthings. As my prayers at home had always been . . . God had sometimes given me dreams before, and they told me what to do and I believed in them. Because . . . other people did . . . But speaking to him – that's more difficult. God changes with the climates!
> JOCK: (*very shocked*) There is only one God.
> ALEX: One God? We worshipped on the top deck of our ship, and the Papists down below.
> JOCK: One God.
> ALEX: The Turks say that also. (pp. 119–20)

It should be added at this point that, as Tom Maguire has observed,[3] Glover's work has frequently dealt with individuals who in the course of long and enforced periods away from home, slip the moorings of

---

3 Tom Maguire, 'Women Playwrights from the 1970s and 80s', in Ian Brown (ed.), *The Edinburgh Companion to Scottish Drama* (Edinburgh University Press, 2011), pp. 154–64.

traditional religious practice and begin to identify with older forms of mystical ritual which draw strength from the land and alienate them from both family and social class. Seals, too, those frequent visitors to both Scotland and the Caribbean, play a role in this process in the case of *The Seal Wife* (1980).

Here though, Glover finds another apt historical metaphor for our times. Her target is less the character of Mrs Thatcher than the philosophy espoused by her and the new President of the USA, Ronald Reagan. The New Right – or as we now know it, Neoliberalism – had begun to flourish under these governments: its high priests Friedrich Von Hayek and Milton Friedman preached a philosophy of absolutist individualism. In the new age of the privateer, figures such as Selkirk were welcome and encouraged, despite his sister-in-law Maggie's charge: 'A buccaneer – that's all he is – a pirate! And a misfit!' (p. 127). This piracy earns Selkirk a fortune, in his day, of eight hundred pounds but he seems uninterested in wealth and fritters it away. In the era of Thatcherism, the tensions between Scottish culture and English were heightened by the poverty imposed upon Scotland as the City of London prospered. The difference in these ideological cultures is illustrated in Selkirk's consciousness of the inequalities created. The scene which leads to his abandonment sees him present a letter, signed by the ship's crew, to Captain Stradling:

> STRADLING: . . . "the reasons of our troubling you at this time are: we have good reason to believe that if what fortune we make this voyage should be carried to London, we should never receive half thereof . . . that the articles we signed at Plymouth were never read in our hearing . . . How dangerous is it for poor men to trust their fortune in the hands of the rich? . . . we make bold to present you with our due rights . . . that all plunder should be appraised and divided as soon as possible after the capture; also every person to be sworn and searched . . . That Captain Stradling should give the whole cabin-plunder to be divided . . .!" (*To* ALEX, *livid*) It was you drew up this letter. (p. 100)

Stradling's fury at the foiling of a cynical robbery of the crew's share of bounty is revealing in its identification of Selkirk's origins as a source of the problem 'Dreams! From a bull-headed, quarrelsome Scotch bastard who navigates by second-sight! ... and holds most at my men in the palm of his hand' (p. 103).

When Selkirk's attempts to recreate his former isolation in a cave above his home town fail, he returns to England, with his naïve young lover Sophia at his side. His attempts at a living here also fail, so a meeting with Daniel Defoe is arranged, but Defoe's sense of a Christian morality is easily combined with commercial gain, and sees him planning to erase both Selkirk's unusual spiritual sense and his national origins in his retelling of Selkirk's story:

> ALEX: (*with difficulty*) I found that, though they listened [the people of his home town], they were not listening to me – but to something in themselves. Speaking to them damaged what I'd found.
> DEFOE: Oh, I only want facts, Mr Selkirk. I want to pin my adventures against facts. (*burst of enthusiasm*) I'm fascinated by the lives of those who live by their wits – for I live that way myself. Englishmen are marvellously strong and sensible in adversity. I have always found that to be so.
> ALEX: I am a Scotchman, sir.
> DEFOE: (*ignoring this*) I have decided to write an adventure – but a moral tale – a Pilgrim's Progress. (p. 135)
> [...]
> DEFOE: A Moral Tale cannot be founded on a quarrel, Mr Selkirk. But it can very well be founded on a shipwreck.
> ALEX: I was right to quarrel with Stradling! God showed me I was right. Not once – but several times!
> DEFOE: Divine Intervention delivered you to the safety of the island, and divine intervention released you later from it.
> ALEX: *Released* me!
> DEFOE: And rewarded your faith and endurance with a fortune! Eight hundred pounds! Do you realise that at this moment, Mr. Selkirk, you are a richer man than I!
> ALEX: To hell with rescue! Reward? I've lost my reward – forever. Don't you understand? I would forfeit seven fortunes to live – to find – (*tries very hard to control himself*) How will you end this moral "adventure"?
> DEFOE: How would you have it end?

> *No answer.*
> It must have a moral ending. And the people will prefer it to be a happy one also. (p. 138)

The final tragedy, though, is not perhaps that of Selkirk, carried back to sea and a final fate amidst all his turmoil, but of Sophia, a young woman abandoned far from home in country of which she knows little. Glover's play is quite unlike Brown's, yet in this denouement, it is quite similar.

*

Peter Arnott's *White Rose* (1985) was one third of a festival season that is often said to have saved the Traverse Theatre from, at the very least, some severe austerities, after leaks from the Scottish Arts Council in 1984 indicated that the theatre might be the next victim of Thatcherite cuts in arts budgets. In response, perhaps as a last throw of the dice, Artistic Director Peter Lichtenfels and his Associate Director Jenny Killick commissioned Arnott's play alongside Jo Clifford's *Losing Venice* and Chris Hannan's *Elizabeth Gordon Quinn* as a hat trick of radical, socially critical plays, all of which employed historical metaphors to lacerating effect against the cultural and economic status quo of 1980s Britain. The legendary success of the three plays with both critics and audiences is still seen in some quarters as providing a much-needed miracle for a flagging, perhaps fated, new writing theatre. This author has produced a longer commentary on this season in earlier work.[4]

It is notable that Arnott's play is the only one of this three that was not published soon after the productions went up and has had to wait until now to appear in print. This in no way reflects the quality of the piece, but might perhaps indicate that, having pushed the funding bodies so far, it might seem foolhardy actually to publish a play about a Soviet military fighter ace, given the hysterical anti-communism stoked by western leaders then on both sides of the Atlantic.

White Rose tells the story of Lilya Litvak, known by those around her as Lily, who, in her brief career, shot down a succession of Nazi aircraft. Arnott slightly truncates the facts around the real Litvak, but remains close in spirit, which better enables him to create a memorable character.

---

4 Steve Cramer, 'The Traverse, 1985–97: Arnott, Clifford, Hannan, Harrower, Greig and Greenhorn', in Ian Brown (ed.), *The Edinburgh Companion to Scottish Drama* (Edinburgh University Press, 2011), pp. 165–76.

Yet in many respects the real central character is her friend Ina, who remains conscious of the dynamics of both class and gender, while Lily, given the privilege of piloting (this job was allocated to women in the Soviet Union by 1942 – the RAF would follow this lead, in 1992) begins to lose sight of both. Ina remains a committed socialist, perhaps because of this, rather than in spite of it, never joining the Communist Party of the Soviet Union. Her understanding of the dynamics of inequality extends to her observation about the self-confidence of Lily in advancing her case to be a pilot.

> INA: Confidence. That's what my grandmother said the great ladies had in the old days. She said you could always tell a real lady by her quiet confidence. Of course they were fucking quiet. They had nothing to do all day. It was my granny did the work. A princess had nothing to distract her from getting on with being a princess. But do you remember how at Engels . . . how calm and purposeful everyone was . . . even me? When it was just the women. How surprised everyone was there was so little bitching going on. The instructors just got in the way. It was just us . . . just us being together with a purpose we shared. (p. 172)

But as Lily is elevated to the status of pilot, and Ina remains a ground-staff mechanic, the two grow apart. Arnott explores the politics of the elites here, as those admitted to a higher echelon become increasingly blind to the problems of those left behind. After Ina has a confrontation with a sexist pilot, who refuses to allow her to touch his aircraft, Lily will not help.

> LILY: The men . . . will take time to adjust.
> INA: Oh yes. Let's all be reasonable about it. It's fine for you. They've adjusted to you flying all right.
> LILY: You know how long that took. You know the time I had.
> INA: I know that I stood up for you. I supported you. But you will still not choose to stand for me against one of your precious bloody pilots. Because you're a pilot. And it is too much of me to ask you to show me some support . . . too much to expect a little solidarity.
> LILY: I'm a pilot first, Ina. They all know that. I'm not married, I've got no children, so it doesn't make any difference.

> INA: You're such a fool sometimes, Lily. You think you know when you're well off. But you don't know that you're insulted. When they insult me. And you pretend to yourself it isn't there.
>
> LILY: What isn't there?
>
> INA: You don't hear the things they say. The things I hear when I finish work and they're all drunk. And you didn't see the disgust in that little boy's eyes when he thought of my hands on his engine. You've forgotten what it's like. To hate yourself. The way men can make you hate yourself. (p. 176–77)

Ultimately the play picks upon a sense that the elites of a society inevitably become wilfully ignorant of the suffering of others, a feeling that only seems to increase as our journey into neoliberalism continues, and the elites become even more distant in terms of their economic power. Be this through the sexism of an objectifying propaganda film director, who is interested in filming Lily not because of her skills as a pilot, but because of her looks ('She is lovely. She'll photograph very well. She's not at all severe looking.' p. 164), or the Luftwaffe pilot who refuses to believe he has been shot down by a woman ('You're Lily Litvak? Oh, thank God! I thought you were just some woman.' p. 187), Lily feels above the fray.

So too, while both Lily and her lover Alexei are cynical about the ultimate aims of the Soviet bureaucracy, they remain, like an upper class anywhere, oblivious to the real problems faced by ordinary people.

> INA: It's easy up there in the sky. It is! Why do you think those boys have such a wonderful time up there? Why do they act like royalty down here? Like they do? Because it's easy for all of you. Oh, ask any of you why you're doing it and you'll spout some pre-digested crap about the motherland. Ask you what you'll do after the war, and you'll dribble out some shit you've got memorised about reconstruction and the forward march of socialism . . . because you just see the world from up there . . . where it looks like a map . . . with clear directions and targets of opportunity . . . well it's not like that for most of us, it's a mess . . . (p. 201)

Be it in Scotland or the former Soviet Union, Arnott's play explores to great effect the gap between the planners and those for whom they plan.

INTRODUCTION

*

Jo Clifford's *Playing with Fire* (1987) sets itself at the greatest distance from its own time of all the plays in this volume, yet it brings alive most vividly the conditions under which lower-income earners were compelled to live. It seems appropriate that its first performance at the Traverse coincided with an election night that saw the Thatcher Government returned with a majority of 102 seats, a result greeted by most of Scotland with despair. If this sense of loss is reflected in the play, it is sustained by the complex mix of fantasy, philosophical speculation and humorous moral fable which has been noted as a feature of Clifford's work.[5]

The piece centres on Justina and Fernando, an impoverished couple who work at alchemy from a fifteenth-century crypt in a Paris cemetery. Even in their situation of poverty there is hope. For all the misfortune they face and their everyday bickering, there is between them a deep affection, which gives rise, as love often does in Clifford's work, to a sense of quiet optimism.

> JUSTINA: The seeds are everywhere. In every plant, every pot, and every stone. In everything that makes the world. And in every person too. Each and every one. Full of seeds. The possibilities of change.
> FERNANDO: I wish it were true.
> JUSTINA: It is true. I know it is. The world is dark. A dark and bitter place. Everything is locked within impurity and filth. Like a prisoner locked inside a jail. And there's our hope. There's always a door. Even if it is locked. A doorway to endless possibilities. Every prisoner can be set free.
> And we are looking for the key. The philosopher's stone. That will end all want. Meet every need. Cure the sick. Make the old young. Turn evil into good.
> Bring freedom to the world. (p. 212)

After an explosion damages their little charnel house home, Fernando departs to buy bread and Justina is deceived into releasing the Devil,

---

[5] Sarah C. Rutherford, 'Fantasists and Philosophers', in Randall Stevenson and Gavin Wallace (eds), *Scottish Theatre Since the Seventies* (Edinburgh University Press, 1996), pp. 112–24.

who has been incarcerated in their stove. This character has a distinctly modern feel, showing the slickness of a modern salesman of dodgy goods, who indignantly denies his cold transactional nature.

> DEVIL: Do you take me for some merchant, that buys and sells? Do you think yourself a mere commodity?
> JUSTINA: It is the way of the world. People give, and people take.
> (p. 223)

The denouement sees a distinctly modern, post-financial deregulation vision of the world espoused by the newly enriched Fernando:

> JUSTINA: Shouldn't we work?
> FERNANDO: The rich don't work. Not nowadays. No-one makes money by working. They make money from having money. They get richer for being rich already. The rich sit on high balconies and look down on the tumult below. They watch the porters coming from the market, staggering to and fro under heavy loads, and they say: the poor are poor because they don't know how to work.
> We'll do the same. We'll stay in bed all day. We'll sip exotic drinks from crystal glasses and we'll throw a coin down from time to time. The life of the intellect.
> That's the life for me. I'll become a philosopher. Or perhaps an economist. (p. 230)

It is the simplicity (a difficult effect to achieve in theatre) that makes Clifford's vision of the world so powerful in this play, where a straightforward morality fable demonstrates that the price we pay for wealth is a lack of empathy and a loss of the capacity to truly love; a message as relevant today as when this piece was composed.

*

Rona Munro's *The Way to Go Home* (1986) is the only play in this collection to be set at the time of its production, but even here, the characters' actions are inscribed with history, both political and personal, if such a distinction can be made. It begins as a humorous female 'buddy' story, but slowly progresses to something much darker, incorporating a parallel between the colonisation of nations by the military and economic power of the United States, and that of women's bodies by men. In it, Sharon a twenty-two-year-old from Craigmillar seeks out the company of Liz, a twenty-nine-year-old from Glasgow, who has long since moved to London. Sharon has arrived in Turkey courtesy of a ticket from her mother, who has been abandoned by her partner on the eve of her holiday, but has lost both her ticket home and passport, and begun to live by her wits and significant abilities as a pickpocket. Liz assumes a certain guardianship upon her, though she seems in recovery from emotional troubles of her own.

The two women find themselves diverted from the characteristic tourist destinations of Turkey as they are pursued through the country by the dangerous former CIA assassin Mackenzie, who has been jilted by Sharon. Sharon's explanation for this chase is as instructive on the gender politics of the day as it is about the desire to treat a culture of origin as another object to be consumed.

> LIZ: What did you do?
> SHARON: Too much. Na, na I did naething, naething me, I'm telling you. I was a lump of wood. Yes John, no John. You want tae eat John? Okay. Want me tae sit and wait John? Okay. Want tae fuck John? Okay. (*taps her head*) Dummy.
> LIZ: What's he after?
> SHARON: Me. Aye that's right me. It's the accent, that wee twang genuine Caledonia, that totty wee hint of urban deprivation in the way I belted back the man's food that put him in mind o' his heiland ancestors and the Clearance ships, that skirl I've had in my walk since I lost the heel off my shoe on the Bosphorus ferry that called back his dear great-granny hurpling up the brae wi' a bucket of coal on her heid. 'Sides that there's my fresh young nubile body in assorted matching shades of skin tone. Drove him mad wi' desire.
> The man's a moron I'm telling you. (pp. 270–71)

The news is especially concerning for Liz, whose earlier journey to Nicaragua leaves her with memories of Maria, whose story (told in a series of brief flashbacks) of brave resistance to the CIA-backed Contras eventually leads to a horrific death at their hands.

As the action unfolds towards a violent climax, the women are overlooked by the Eye of Fatima, a charm that is said to ward off evil spirits in both Islamic and Jewish culture, and is specifically associated with feminine power. Although the symbol predates all three Abrahamic religions, the stories associated with it tell us much about the dilemma faced by women. In the Islamic version of the story, Fatima, the daughter of the Prophet Mohammed, sees her husband entering their home with a new wife as she is preparing his dinner. She drops her spoon, but demonstrates her dedication to him by continuing to stir her boiling pot with her bare hand. In Judaic culture, the symbol is associated with Miriam, who helped her brother Moses to cross the Red Sea, but then rebelled against his authority, and was struck down with leprosy as a punishment from God. In other words, for women there is pain for both conforming to the will of the patriarchy or resisting it.

For all that, there is a certain sense of possibility, as well as some quiet instruction that the way to go home is via Scotland in the play's conclusion:

SHARON: How long since you were hame?
LIZ: Two weeks.
SHARON: (*helping* LIZ *on with socks and shoes*) No I mean right hame.
LIZ: I left Scotland five years ago.
SHARON: You want tae come back, it's getting pretty bad, you want tae see it. Listen I'm telling you, you want tae set the world on fire Niddrie's the place tae dae it.
LIZ: You laughing at me?
SHARON: (*grins*) What do you want me to dae? (p. 308)

*

If one makes the short walk from the neglected and seagull-spotted statue of Alexander Selkirk back towards the centre of Lower Largo, it takes just a few minutes to encounter the village's great tourist attraction and guest residence. Boasting fine dining in its restaurant, splendid views of the Firth of Forth and luxurious rooms above, this recently renovated hotel is called 'The Crusoe'. That Defoe's entrepreneurial, colonialist and fictional Yorkshireman continues to supplant Alexander Selkirk in the commercially instructed mind of many a tourist is enlightening. The resistance to this hegemonic discourse, where the violence and complexity of history and nation itself is traduced by a more economically viable surrogate, shows a common bond between these latter manifestations of the early New Wave and its precursors in the early 1970s.

But there are also significant differences. Perhaps the most notable and immediate occurs around gender. This is not to say that the earlier work was entirely neglectful of female characters. To cite an example, in the figure of Una, in Hector MacMillan's *The Sash* (1973), we encounter a vivid character, whose Northern Irish Catholic origins act as a trigger to the final confrontation between the sectarian bigot Bill and his more progressive son Cameron. Yet the play is the story of these two men, more than either Una or Cameron's girlfriend Georgina, however authentic these latter characters feel.

The selection of plays seen here are quite different. The centre of Brown's play is indicated by its title, as well as the much projected-upon character of the 'real' Mary, trapped within the macho political chicanery of the men around her. Ksenija Horvat identifies Sue Glover as the starting point for a new school of Scottish female dramatists in 1980 with *The Seal Wife*.[6] In *An Island in Largo* she centres the action upon a man, but the play would not work on an emotional level without its two most empathetic characters, Euphan and Sophia, each of whom lavish vast resources of love upon Selkirk, only to be abandoned in favour of his self-absorbed quest. Arnott's *White Rose* is without doubt a compelling picture of the female fighter ace and her partner Alexei, but it is quite unquestionably Ina's play. Her suffering as a woman 'on the ground', asking questions about the role of the elites in the war-torn Soviet Union, but also a contemporary society where the wealth of the few was escalating wildly above the incomes of the many, is telling. As, in our own time the neoliberal political consensus established over the period of this selection begins to decline into a series of frighteningly undemocratic oligarchies, the questions Ina asks us seem more, not less, relevant. At the heart of *Playing with Fire* is Justina, who discovers that the old saying that when poverty walks in the door, love walks out, is less true than when wealth makes the same entry. Clifford's astonishing and visceral descriptions of a growing poverty and inequality live long in the mind, yet the significant electoral date of this play's premiere marked the

---

6 Ksenija Horvat, 'Scottish Women Playwrights Against Zero Visibility', *Études écossaises*, 10 (2005), pp. 143–58, doi:10.4000/etudesecossaises.157

moment when the new, economically unjust normal began to be accepted, however despairingly. The two women at the centre of *The Way to Go Home* are less troubled by the Soviet Union than by its violent opponent in the shadowy figure of Mackenzie, after he has learned of Sharon's grandfather, a member of the Scottish communist party. His sinister technology-driven stalking of the two women (symbolised by the flashes of the photographs he takes of them in their travels and the voiced-over recordings of his commentaries upon them) is a manifestation of the same ideologically driven anti-communism that has caused massacres in Central America. Even the most conservative of audiences might be tempted to cheer for Liz and Sharon when the CIA freelancer's violence is turned against him.

I have spoken earlier of the significance of history as metaphor in these plays, and this subject is deftly broadened out by David Archibald,[7] but combined, almost inevitably, with this is the internationalism of the texts. While such troubling issues identified by the earlier dramatists as sentimentalised nationalist versions of rural environs, violent manifestations of masculinity and sectarianism are still present in this collection, there is also a sense that Scotland's desire to define itself against England is less important than defining the nation as part of a broader world. This opening out allows for parallels with other postcolonial writing. This author has written before about the almost uncanny resonances in both timing and thematic concerns between the original Scottish New Wave and the movement given the same name in his native Australia.[8] And the subsequent exploration of such larger themes as globalisation and more contemporary forms of colonialism than the British Empire was also paralleled in Australian work. The dramatists in this volume were contributors not just to international themes, but the audiences to go with them. All have been performed outside the islands of the UK, with Clifford and Munro enjoying particular success in this regard. All helped to pave the way for writers such as Zinnie Harris and David Greig who are commonly performed around the world today. It is no reflection on

---

[7] David Archibald, 'History in Contemporary Scottish Theatre', in Ian Brown (ed.), *The Edinburgh Companion to Scottish Drama* (Edinburgh University Press, 2011), pp. 85–94.

[8] Steve Cramer, 'No Wrang – Jist Different: Some resemblances between Scottish Drama of the 1970s and the Australian New Wave', *International Journal of Scottish Theatre and Screen*, 6.1 (2013).

Greig's high standing to say that these texts are one of the reasons that I was able to arrive home to Australia in 2016 and see, within a couple of days, a production of his play *The Events* at a major Adelaide theatre a few hundred metres from my hotel.

This volume contains plays to be enjoyed not as period pieces, but as work that can speak to us as clearly as they did at their times of production.

University of South Australia

MARY

by Ian Brown

First performed at the Lyceum Little Theatre, Edinburgh, 18 August 1977

Cast in order of appearance

John Knox	*James Cairncross*
Lord Henry Darnley	*David Bannerman*
Earl of Moray	*Gregor Fisher*
Maitland of Lethington	*Robert Robertson*
Earl of Lennox	*John Grieve*
Earl of Morton	*Ron Bain*
Earl of Ruthven	*Tom Cotcher*
Mary, Queen of Scots	*Miranda Bell*
Mary Hamilton	*Maureen Beattie*
Mary Seaton	*Janet Michael*
David Rizzio	*Peter Laird*
Earl of Bothwell	*David Sands*
Huntly) a Guard)	*Simon Tait*

AUTHOR'S INTRODUCTION

Ian Brown

I was weaned on lively drama, often sentimentalising Scottish history – early Robert McLellan Border-reiver plays or Sydney Goodsir Smith's 1960 pageant *Wallace* – and wrote a first version of *Mary* in romantic Scots-language blank verse during a 1967 summer job in Alloa's National Coal Board stores, among miners who spoke Scots. Alan Brown, Royal Lyceum Literary Manager, on meeting me in 1969, said it was too raunchy for the Lyceum, but had something.

Drawn by Scottish historical figures' complexity and family stories of my Carnegie mother, Andrew Carnegie's first cousin's granddaughter (he left her grannie an annuity), I then wrote *Carnegie*. Influenced by Brecht's, Weiss's and La Mama's experiments, I used various theatrical modes to reflect the Scots-US Robber Baron's ambivalence. Before a 1972 announcement Prospect Theatre Company and the Royal Lyceum would merge to form a building-based National Theatre of Scotland (spoiler alert: merger didn't happen), Prospect needed rights in a Scottish play. It would premiere *Carnegie* in the 1972 official Edinburgh Festival in Forest Road Drill Hall where *Black Watch* opened. J. B. Rankin, senior Bank of Scotland apparatchik and Festival Council member, however, hated my treatment of Carnegie, blocking that production. Premiering as a joint Lyceum–Prospect 1973 production and featuring in Pittsburgh's 1976 US Bicentennials, Carnegie-Mellon University's President said of *Carnegie*, 'The really damaging thing is: it's all true'. Working on it, I realised how elusive, multi-faceted and politically-inflected 'truth', especially 'historical truth', could be. In *Carnegie*, a union leader calls the strike-breaking philanthropist a 'three-faced bugger', arguably understating his brutal hypocrisies.

Bill Bryden arrived at the Lyceum in 1971 as Associate Director, inviting me in 1973 to allow his remarkable company, including actors like Fulton Mackay, Eileen McCallum, Roddy McMillan, Clare Richards and Paul Young, to perform *Mary*'s first version in one of Mary's favourite castles: Craigmillar. When I recently told Douglas Maxwell I'd refused this offer, he looked astonished, responding, 'You turned down the chance to work with Fulton Mackay?' But, after drafting *Carnegie*, I'd left the first version behind, starting a deconstructed '*Mary/Mary*', exploring theatre's potential to express her possible varieties. Not to mention her nobles' Mafia-like varieties of manipulation, alliance, corruption, betrayal, powerplay – and sexism. Cordelia Oliver talked of a 'kaleidoscope, all shifts and surprising arrangements – high and low comedy cross cut with bawdy satire and a strong sense of the factual reality which surely underlay the myth [... Brown] is adept at meaningful alienation through jump-cut reference'.[1] In its various theatrical ways, my play foresees the view of historian Catriona Macdonald: 'Mary, more so than any other Scottish monarch, lived and has been remembered at the interface of multiple ways of knowing: she does not exist beyond this.'[2] My play seeks to recognise the humanity of the being at the centre of those multiple ways and how those ways, as we see them play out in *Mary*, become, as Mary says in her final line, 'this pain'.

Bill promised that, if I let him present the first version at Craigmillar, the Lyceum would later present the version I really wanted. My agent, Peggy Ramsay, deeply – and cynically – knowledgeable of theatre's ways, advised me, 'Whatever they say now, darling, they'll only put on one version'. So, I held out.

When Hector MacMillan's mentor, Stephen MacDonald, succeeded Clive Perry as Lyceum Artistic Director in 1976, he at once said he wanted to direct *Mary*. Fifty per cent of Stephen's three Lyceum years comprised new plays.[3] I'm proud *Mary* was one. And some of Bill's wonderful company were in its cast.

---

1   Cordelia Oliver, 'Mary', *Guardian*, 20 August 1977.
2   Catriona M. M. Macdonald, 'A tracked and hunted creature', in Steven J. Reid, *The Afterlife of Mary, Queen of Scots* (Edinburgh University Press, 2024), p. 195.
3   Ian Brown, 'The New Writing Policies of Clive Perry and Stephen MacDonald at the Royal Lyceum Theatre, 1966–79', *International Journal of Scottish Theatre and Screen*, 2.2 (2001).

Cast

EARL OF MORAY: Mary's half-brother, later regent

MAITLAND OF LETHINGTON: a diplomat and politician

EARL OF LENNOX: a Catholic noble, later regent

EARL OF MORTON: a Protestant noble, later regent

EARL OF RUTHVEN: a Protestant noble

JOHN KNOX: a church-leader

DAVID RIZZIO: an Italian musician

LORD HENRY DARNLEY: Lennox's son, Mary's second husband

EARL OF BOTHWELL: a Protestant noble, later Mary's third husband

GUARDS etc.

MARY: Queen of Scots

MARY HAMILTON: her lady of the chamber

MAID (MARY SEATON): her personal maid

MARY

PART ONE

Scene 1

JOHN KNOX *strides forward.*

KNOX: Let us pray. Bow yer heids. Come on, A'm no here tae waste ma time. Fir whit youse're aboot tae see, may the Lord mak youse truly gratefu.

DARNLEY *dressed as* MARY *enters.*

DARNLEY: I'm going to be Mary, Queen of Scots. Really. Well, for the time being. Now, some people have said I'm a gay queen. And some people have said I'm a romantic queen. And some people have even said I'm the great Catholic[1] martyr. All I can say is that I was born in 1542. My father died six days later, which was almost immediate and most inconsiderate, and my mother sent me to France when I was only six years old. I never saw her again. Old trout. I was betrothed at the age of one to Edward,[2] the son of Henry VIII of England,[3] and then, at the age of six, to the Dauphin[4] of France. My reputation as a precocious and demon lover derived from this double and premature engagement. As a matter of fact it all rather put me off the idea of sex. Well, anyway, I returned to Scotland in 1561, married Henry Darnley in 1565; he died in 1567, and I married Jamie Bothwell in the same year. And the next year I left for England. Oh yes, and I had a little baby boy in 1566. A lot easier than having those rough men. I suppose Scotland was busy, you know how it is. But do you know, I spent less time in Scotland than in any other country I visited. I died, that is to say, Mary died, in 1587. Frankly, it was a bit of a relief.

KNOX: Ye're a whore, Mary Stewart.

DARNLEY: And you're a bore, Mr. Knox. Such a fierce man.
KNOX: Let's get on wi it.

   MARY *pinches* KNOX *as they go out.*
KNOX: Slut.

   They leave.

Scene 2

MORAY *and* MAITLAND *enter.*

MORAY: Bit A dinnae see why ye're sae hard on the lass, Maitland.

MAITLAND: A'm no hard, bit A think she's gaun tae cause trouble fir the land.

MORAY: She seems gey ready tae be helpfu.

MAITLAND: Moray, ye ken as weel as A dae that she's a sowel wi her ain mind.

MORAY: She's no usin it an that's aw that matters.

MAITLAND: How long will it be till she does?

MORAY: A doot she'll never use her mind. She jist wants her own way.

MAITLAND: Some sowel might gie her an idea. A mean, A'm a good servant o the Queen, Moray, bit A serve fir the sake o the peace an weel-bein o the land, not tae help chaos an destruction. If she does find her ain mind, or whit someone tells her is her ain mind, trouble'll flow flood-like fae it.

   GUARD *wheels on an upright box, curtained at the front, and leaves it towards one side of the stage.*

MORAY: Troubles we've aw had. It maun be settled. Lennox'll help, even if he is a Catholic. We maun settle the land tae peace an prosperity. Withoot troublin the queen, so long as she helps. It's Morton an Ruthven that worry me. They're awfy strong Protestants.[5]

MAITLAND: It's Ruthven's the wild yin.

MORAY: Aye.

   LENNOX *enters.*

LENNOX: So we're here tae sit on judgement on Huntly?[6]

MAITLAND: We're here tae deal oot justice.

LENNOX: Och, smile, Maitland! Armageddon isnae due till the morn's morn. A got telt at the kirk.

MAITLAND: This is serious business, Lennox. A man's tae be tried fir his life. Ye maun act wi decency.

LENNOX: Och, Maitland, if ye werenae held thegither by reid tape roond yer parchment chaps, ye'd fa tae bits.

MAITLAND: Whit hauds ye thegither, Lennox? Scabs?

LENNOX: A'm no scabby!

MAITLAND: If they piled yer whores the yin on tap o thither ye'd hae a fine pillar tae dose yer pintle. Ye've worn oot yer brains through yer breeks.

MAITLAND *walks away.*

LENNOX: Whit's intae him?

MORAY: He's jist worried aboot gettin this trial finished. Dinnae push him, Lennox. He does a fine job.

LENNOX: A was only haein a wee joke, Moray. Thon Maitland. He's too dry, him. Ye're a gey fine administrator an ye dinnae hae a dry tongue.

MORAY: Neither hae ye, though. Drinkin again last nicht, were ye?

LENNOX: Weel, ye ken hoo it is. There's a lot o money gone intae makin this belly a mine.

MORAY: Aye. A can see that.

MORTON *and* RUTHVEN *enter.*

MORTON: Aye.

MORAY: Morton.

MORTON: Whit a job.

MAITLAND: It maun be done.

MORTON: Fancy it though.

MORAY: It's a bit ridiculous.

MAITLAND: Huntly rebelled against the queen's majesty. Thon's no ridiculous. He maun be tried fir his life.

MORTON (*pulls back curtain on box to reveal dead body*): But he's deid awready. At least, he looks it tae me.

MAITLAND: It doesnae matter. The law's the law. If he's guilty, he maun be sentenced to death.

MORAY: Aye, bit ye'll admit it's a wee bit superfluous.

MAITLAND: Even if he is deid . . .

RUTHVEN: What d'ye mean 'if'? He looks gey deid tae me. A'm kind o surprised she didnae join wi Huntly though.

MAITLAND: Ye'd hae liked that fine, wouldn't ye?

RUTHVEN: Why?

MAITLAND: Ye'd hae had a fine war an killed some papes.

LENNOX: That's enough o that language. Papes, indeed.

MORTON: Catholics, Lennox, folliers o the Pope in Rome, ken? Like yersel?

LENNOX: A ken whit papes are.

MORTON: Well, that's a relief then. Jist the same she could hae joined wi Huntly here. Killed Moray an Ruthven an me an made the land pape. Jist needit a bit o blood.

MORAY: Maybe she wants peace.

RUTHVEN: Peace ma erse.

LENNOX: A'll hae a piece o that any time.

RUTHVEN: Ye're a dirty bugger, Lennox

MORTON: We're here fir tae condemn Huntly tae death fir treason, if we find him guilty. That's aw. A mean, A think he's beat us tae it, bit never pay heed. And we'll see yet hoo far she'll go fir peace, Moray.

RUTHVEN: She'll no.

LENNOX (*prods the body*): Still when we condemn him, he'll no answer back. Speakin as an auld judge, that's a great advantage in an accused.

MAITLAND: It's an auld law. Livin ir deid, they maun be brocht tae trial an tae justice.

LENNOX (*shakes the hand of the corpse*): Hello there, Huntly, hoo's it gaun, son? Aw richt? A hope he's cosy enough in there.

RUTHVEN: When's the queen coming?

LENNOX: No till she gets a man.

RUTHVEN: Ye're a dribblin gowk, Lennox.

LENNOX (*to others*): A'm a canny man, bit thon yin aye gets my goat.

MORTON: Watch yer tongue, Ruthven. Will the trial tak long, Maitland?

RUTHVEN *is fiddling with the body.*

MAITLAND: There's nae defence bein put up.

MORAY: Will ye leave the pair sowel alane?

RUTHVEN: He doesnae mind. Thon's a braw belt.

LENNOX: He's a braw sowel. If he wasnae deid.

MORTON: Thon's a handicap richt enough.

RUTHVEN: It's no a handicap fir Lennox, an he's a half-deid pape.

MORAY: Ruthven.

MORTON: Shut up.

LENNOX: Fancy diein o a burst gut wi eatin ower muckle afore the battle.

RUTHVEN: It's a fine thing when indigestion's mair fatal than insurrection.

MORAY: Aye, weel. Seein my lord Huntly's body has been preservit an brocht afore us, it is oor duty tae answer tae oor minds on the chairge that he committed treason, bearin in mind the evidence we hae aw seen an any new-found here. An tae treat him wi some respect. It's no awbody that commits treason. An it's no jist onybody that's tried efter he's deid.

MARY *enters with* MARY HAMILTON *and a* MAID.

MORAY: Dignity, ma lords.

MARY *mounts the throne. The* NOBLES *bow.*

MARY: My lords, let us proceed with this distasteful business.

MAITLAND: The chairge is that my lord Huntly has committed maist heinous an foul treason in that he did, wi ithers kent an unkent, lead a rebellion against the peace o Mary Stuart, Queen o Scots, an o her sovereign land, an fir the Catholic cause.

MORAY: How does ma lord Huntly plead?

They all look at the corpse. Silence. They look away.

RUTHVEN (*from behind the box*): Not guilty.

They all stare. RUTHVEN *appears.*

MARY: My lord Ruthven.

MORTON: Ye'll get mair trouble than ye want jist the noo.

RUTHVEN: It was a joke.

MORTON: Joke, ye silly bugger. He apologises, yer grace.

MORAY: Get on with it, Maitland.

MAITLAND: Ma lord Huntly, hae ye ony defence? Dae ye deny the chairges? Hae ye onythin tae say in mitigation? Dae ye accept the judgment o yer peers?

LENNOX: He's awfy quiet. Sic a nice-lookin corpse.

MORAY: Is that aw, Maitland?

MAITLAND: Ye hae the richt, ma lord Huntly, tae mak a final speech appealin fir mercy.

MORAY: A suppose we hae tae assume silent admission o guilt.

MAITLAND: A hae tae ask ye lords assemblit here in cooncil, dae ye in yer herts an minds find the Earl o Huntly here arraigned guilty o treason as libelled?

NOBLES: Aye.

MAITLAND: An is that the verdict o ye aw?

MORAY: Aye.

MAITLAND: Then the Lord God hae mercy on his sowel. The verdict is guilty, yer grace.

MARY: Then his body will be treated with the way for traitors.

MAITLAND: That's no quite the richt way tae say it, yer grace.

MARY: Have I done wrong, Maitland?

MAITLAND: It doesnae maitter, yer grace.

MARY: My lords, only this further wish I to say on this sad affair. My lord Huntly desired that I shall join with him in a plot against the Protestant lords of this country even before I am come here again. (*Looks at* MORAY. *He reassures her.*) He advised me to overthrow my nobles and cause blood to be shed. This I have refused to consider. He strove to capture my very person, which is proof I gave him nae encouragement. He rebelled on his own account. Let this event and the trial of today be proof of my good intent. I desire only peace for your land. I desire accommodation between those of the new church and those of the old. We may live together for the good of our country. I have in my conduct shown good faith both to Protestant and Catholic.

MORAY: Yer grace, we would want ye to ken that we think ye've acted wisely and weel.

MARY: Remove the body.

LENNOX: A'll see tae it. Pair Huntly.

The GUARDS *remove the body,* LENNOX *following.*

LENNOX: He'll never be the same again. (*Leaves*)

MARY: The audience is ended.

LORDS: Yer grace.

MORTON: Fir aw she says, she's still a pape. Even if she does want peace. We'll need tae watch.

RUTHVEN: Peace? It's peace wi the wolf.

MORTON *and* RUTHVEN *leave.*

MARY: Well, James? How did I manage my task which I had?

MORAY: Ye acted yer part very weel, Mary.

MARY: I'm glad you approve.

MORAY: Ye're a good lass.

MARY: A distasteful scene.

MAITLAND: It's the law. Ye're daein weel, yer grace.

MARY: There is too much blood new on the stones.

MORAY: A said that to ye yesterday, Mary.

MARY: I see it is true, James.

MORAY: Aye, ye're a gid lass, Mary.

MAITLAND: A doot there's mair trouble aboot religion tae came, though.

MORAY: Nae doot, bit we'll tak it an mak a settlement.

MAITLAND: Weel, ye ken the nobles willnae gie their lands tae the new kirk o John Knox. Even though thae lands belongit tae Rome, an were gied tae be held in trust, they willnae return them.

MORAY: The new kirk wants money tae build schools an that.

MARY: To read their Bibles and teach heresy.

MORAY: Heresy is everywhere. Show me an idea an A'll find ye a sowel tae cry it heresy in five minutes.

MARY: But heresy is heresy.

MORAY: Whit's mair important is this new kirk is upstart an ower share it's richt. They believe each man has an equal access tae God.

MAITLAND: Thon's no the trouble. It's when they act as if it was true.

MORAY: Weel, this isnae a democracy, thank God. We'll mak some peace even atween Lennox an Ruthven. Yer Grace. (*Makes to leave*)

MARY: Did I do well, James?

MORAY: Well? Oh aye, a braw job, lass.

MORAY *and* MAITLAND *leave.*

MARY: See, there they go, leaving us here, as if we mattered not.

MARY H.: Oh well, my lady. They like to think they have weighty matters to deal with.

MARY: Well, I shall not be annoyed by them. I am the queen and they must come to me if they want to do anything in this land of theirs.

MARY H.: Yes, your grace.

MARY: Is it warm outside?

MARY H.: Not too cold, your grace.

MAID: A little breeze.

MARY: Well now, that is to be expected though, is it not?

MARY H.: (*laughs*) Were you thinking of going out?

MARY: To take my horse and to ride forth in the park. That would be good. What think you, Marie?

MARY H.: It's a fine day for it.

MARY: To shake off my back the cares of the court. Did you look at that dead man?

MARY H.: It was hard to miss him.

MARY: What a ceremony. What a justice.

MARY H.: It's a ritual, madame.

MARY: I know it is necessary, but it is also bizarre.

MARY H.: There's a lot of life necessary, but also bizarre.

MARY: Marie, I must have friends around me, those I can talk to. I am uprooted. I have no real roots. Francis[7] was not yet my full husband. Then he died and they did not want me in France as the Dowager Queen. They simply have sent me away. I was not close to those I thought it might be I was close to. I have thought there was my home and they did not want me more.

MARY H.: It is hard, your grace.

MARY: You know this land, Marie. Will you be by me and help me?

MARY H.: A will, your grace. A will.

MARY: That is good. Let us ride forth.

They leave.

Scene 3

KNOX *as* LOU G. RADE, RUTHVEN *as his* AIDE, MAID *as* WRITER, *and* MORTON *as* DIRECTOR *sweep down from the back of the auditorium. They are followed by a* SECRETARY *taking notes.* LOU G. *talks into a dictaphone.*[8] *He never stops walking. The* AIDE *always follows him.*

LOU G.: *(takes cigar from his mouth)* Right, I got it. I gotta great idea. Mary, Queen of Scots.

Pregnant pause.

Just think of it.

AIDE: Fantastic, Lou G.

LOU G.: My name ain't Lou G. Rade[9] for zilch.

DIRECTOR: Amazing.

WRITER: Mary Queen of Scots. Jesus Christ.

LOU G.: You don't like it, we can always get another writer.

WRITER: Mary, Queen of Scots.

AIDE: List of writers, LG?

LOU G.: This is a strictly commercial story of human passion, love, lust, and frailty. A Highland Star is Born[10] – Roots[11] in Kilts.

AIDE: Fantastic.

LOU G.: What would you say to tall romantic, red-haired, short-sighted Vanessa Redgrave[12] as the tall romantic red-haired . . . was she short-sighted?

WRITER: No.

LOU G.: That can be arranged . . . as the tall romantic red-haired, short-sighted, lovelorn highland queen. Whaddya say?

DIRECTOR: I wouldn't say anything.

LOU G.: Knew it would take your breath away. We'll need some Scotch actors. Find out the names of some.

AIDE: At once.

Talks into pocket radio.

LOU G.: Plot ideas?

WRITER: Just getting them. Just thinking.

LOU G.: Don't take too long. Thinking costs time. Okay. I see I got the creative juices flowing. I wanna romantic tragic serious film, aimed at the audience, right? Not anti-Scottish, but there's the English market to consider. Hey, why don't Elizabeth[13] and Mary have a meeting?

WRITER: Schiller[14] did that already.

LOU G.: Schiller, you mean Schlesinger?[15]

DIRECTOR: No, Schiller.

LOU G.: Schiller, Schmiller, they meet twice, we can beat that bum. And don't forget, bagpipes for the American audience.

DIRECTOR: My God.

LOU G.: You do it or you don't do it?

DIRECTOR: I do it.

LOU G.: Good boy.

They leave.

Scene 4

MAITLAND *and* MORAY *enter.*

MORAY: You've telt Knox tae come?

MAITLAND: He'll be here.

MORAY: Aye.

MAITLAND *works at his desk.*

MORAY: Bloody fool.

MAITLAND: He believes in whit he's saying.

MORAY: Belief is nae excuse. A man can believe whit he likes, bit when he acts on his beliefs he has tae answer fir them. An the fact he believes is o nae accoont. The act is whit coonts.

MAITLAND: An whit fowk think on the act.

MORAY: Weel, A ken whit A think on Knox's acts.

MAITLAND: He'll be here soon.

MORAY: Aye. Weel A'll gie him a word or twa . . . when he's bidit a bit.

MORAY leaves. MAITLAND goes on with his work.

KNOX comes in, sees MAITLAND and stands. MAITLAND works on.

KNOX coughs. MAITLAND looks up.

MAITLAND: Oh, aye, Mr. Knox, it's yersel.

KNOX: Aye, Maitland.

MAITLAND: Aye.

MAITLAND works on.

KNOX: I thought Moray was here. He was tae see me.

MAITLAND: He'll be here by the by.

KNOX: Punctual is he?

MAITLAND: The way ye're talking, Mr. Knox. Nae use. It's nae way tae win yer case. Ye maun be less absolute.

KNOX (*slightly anglicised accent*): I'm here to see Moray, not to be lectured by you. They cry you Michael Wylie. And Machiavelli[16] was a papist twisted mouth whoring politician with no sense of godliness or truth.

MAITLAND: He would miss a good Scots upbringing, him bein a pair Tally. Ye nearly missed yin yersel tae, bein awa sae lang in England.

KNOX: I believe in the virtue of God's righteous kirk.

MAITLAND: So dae we aw, John, so dae we aw. Bit whiles it's gid tae temper rectitude wi policy.

KNOX: Policy is a devil's word.

MAITLAND: A doot the deil's whit we dinnae like.

KNOX: I dinnae like sin and I dinnae like politic compromise, cry it what you like.

MAITLAND: Aye weel, we baith serve ma maisters, Knox.

KNOX: You're an ill-minded lost gomerel, Maitland. Dinnae pucker your face the like of that. An honest man loves the truth.

MAITLAND: Nae doot. His ain truth.

KNOX: Politician. What does my lord of Moray want with me here?

MAITLAND: A dinnae ken. Bit A doot he'll tell ye hissel.

KNOX *walks around.*

KNOX: I cannae wait.

MAITLAND: Aye.

MORAY *enters.*

MORAY: Mr. Knox, it's grand tae see ye.

KNOX: Aye, my lord, and what is it you want to say?

MORAY: Jist this, Mr. Knox. Preach yer word. Bit affairs o state an the queen's marriage arenae ony concern o yers at aw.

KNOX: I must preach the right in all things, my lord Moray. I can be ruled by nane in that. I must . . .

MORAY: Mr. Knox. Ye can say whit ye like, sae lang as A like. Mind wha's in power an mind yer principles as best ye can.

MORAY *leaves.*

KNOX: He's gone.

MAITLAND: Aye. He's gone. Best mind whit he says. It's the realities o politics.

KNOX: I was just going to say –

MAITLAND: He wasnae listenin, Mr. Knox. He wasnae listenin.

They leave.

Scene 5

MARY *and* RIZZIO *enter. They are at ease.*

MARY: I do not understand always this country so well, David. I wish I could see the high bright sun again. This is a cold country and a grey city with the rain that drizzles on its grey streets.

RIZZIO: It has a stern church and many brothels.

MARY: I do not understand the women so well either.

RIZZIO: They say they are passionate sometimes. And they sit in their churches, listening to the thunderings of hell from their dark angels in their high pulpits. So high those pulpits, so erect.

MARY: *(laughs)* David Rizzio, you are a wicked man.

DAVID: Wicked? Me, your grace?

MARY: Wicked. You men.

RIZZIO: Tell me what you did today.

MARY: I went riding on the hill. It was good. I saw birds, flocks of wild birds. I should have had my hawk with me. Beautiful birds. They rose high when I approached like a wave of greeting and the pale sun lay glistening in the water. Sometimes, in the morning, David, I think this green wet land may even be alive.

RIZZIO: You bring life to it.

MARY: *(laughs)* Oh but this town. Moray tells me I do not understand it. That it is smug and respectable. I think sometimes it may not be true, but then again I am proved wrong. I saw a women in the street today so self-assured, caring for nothing but her own self, her skirts tucked high to miss the mud and filth of the street, her body hidden in a bodice the fashion of last year, and when a beggar asked alms, she drew in her breath, scandalised.

RIZZIO: What happened?

MARY: The beggar called her something I did not understand.

RIZZIO: The great thing about airs and graces is that they protect one from feeling.

MARY: I laugh, David, but their vices are their strengths. From self-satisfaction springs corruption, cruelty, and callousness, and, if you tell them of these, their complacency makes them impervious to criticism, and, if you tell them of complacency, they tell you you do not understand. They have a wonderful innocence of what they do not wish to know.

MARY HAMILTON *enters.*

MARY: Marie, is my new dress arrived?

MARY H.: No, madam.

MARY: *(laughs)* You see, David. And if I take them to task, no, do not laugh, listen. If I take them to task, the dressmaker blames the clothmaker and the clothmaker the silkworm. And how can you punish a silkworm?

MARY H.: I told them to be quick.

RIZZIO: But this is Edinburgh.

They laugh.

MARY: Because this is Edinburgh, I must go naked? What would my nobles say?

MARY H.: They'd be astonished. And you'd be cold.

MARY: You are a joy to me, Mary.

MARY H.: I would always lend you one of my dresses.

MARY: And I would change my shape to fit it.

RIZZIO: Those nobles. All they want is you unsexed, unmarried. To be virgin would be best.

MARY: David!

RIZZIO: Then they can promise you in marriage to whoever they wish to ally with for the moment.

MARY: Yes.

MARY H.: Shall we go to the country?

RIZZIO: If the nobles allow you, and the mist.

MARY H.: David!

MARY: Leave him, Marie. I do not mind today. I feel at rest. (*laughs*) But the trees take so long to grow their leaves here. And the hills, heather! No flowers, only a strange bush that scratches your legs. Itch! Itch!

RIZZIO: It is not France.

MARY: That is very true. My country!

> MARY H. *picks up some sewing and works on it.* RIZZIO *picks on a lute.*

MARY: Don't do that.

> RIZZIO *stops.*

MARY: I left it when I was six and expected never to see it again, never. I have forgotten it. It is no longer in my bones. It was to be a province of France.

MARY H.: Madam, it is not good to worry about these things. It is bad to miss your parents, to be brought up by others not your own, but now you have friends and a land. You have us.

MARY: Those who brought me up! Those not my own! They are mine. They are what I had in place of parents. I do not want this lonely land.

MARY H.: Madam.

MARY: I do not want you.

RIZZIO *plays on his lute.*

MARY H.: Madam.

MARY: Marie, I am sorry. Forgive me my temper. I do care for you, Marie, I do.

RIZZIO: We should go hunting again.

MARY: Yes.

MARY H.: Oh yes, madam, that would be good.

    MAITLAND *enters.*

MAITLAND: Yer grace.

MARY: I do not want to talk to you.

MAITLAND: Ye hae an audience wi Knox.

RIZZIO: Knox.

MARY: I thought it was later. Tell him to go away.

MAITLAND: It cannae be. He maun be met.

MARY H.: Allow me, madam. (*Tidies* MARY's *dress*)

    RIZZIO *plays on his lute a little more.*

MARY: Now?

MAITLAND: Ye ken we hae talked o this. We hae telt ye fine whit best tae say.

MARY: Yes, my lord.

MAITLAND: Aye. (*Looks at* RIZZIO) Aye.

MARY: David, you had better leave for now.

    RIZZIO *goes.*

MARY: Why may I not have my friends, Lethington?

MAITLAND: You may hae aw the friends you want in private.

    MARY H. *finishes tidying* MARY's *dress.*

MARY: Thank you, Marie.

MAITLAND: Dae A let him in?

MARY: You may.

    MAITLAND *goes out.*

MARY: Stay by me, Marie.

MARY H.: He talks a lot, madam. He's a great man they say.

MAITLAND *and* KNOX *enter.*

MARY: Thank you, Lethington.

KNOX: Aye, go, man. You're not needed.

MAITLAND *goes.*

KNOX: What do you want to speak to me for?

MARY: I wished to speak to you concerning some matters which have happened.

KNOX: I'm not used to wasting my time in wandering round the main matter. I dinnae need humoured.

MARY: Mr. Knox, your preaching is becoming intolerable. You interfere with my private matters, and incite my people to not like me.

KNOX: There's none find the truth mair intolerable than they that lie.

MARY: Why are you so proud, Mr. Knox? Why will you not listen?

KNOX: I've only the pride of my faith, and the humility of my heart guarantees that.

MARY: Why so fierce?

KNOX: You're the woman at the head of the land, and that's not a woman's place, and you're a papist.

MARY: We must have peace.

KNOX: Then put away they that are liars and followers of Antichrist. I found the truth in your faither-in-law's galleys. I felt the whip on my shoulders. The blood down my back. I felt the tiredness in my arms so tight, so drained of life the sinews were only knots of wood, no life there, no feeling. I suffered for truth and I saw death. Do you know what that means?

MARY: I have seen heretics die. At home in France.

KNOX: My co-religionists.

MARY: As my co-religionists have died in this land. Death is rarely beautiful, but often necessary. We must settle.

KNOX: I sat on the sea and I felt this callous here, and here, on my hands, hardening, hardening. Working, I knew that all this pain was only for God, only for the righteous, only for the truth. It had to be. Whatever you faither-in-law or your mither did to me was nothing for in me was the truth.

MARY: I do not want to hear all this, Mr. Knox. Perversity is only interesting up to a point, then it is tedious.

KNOX: Truth is not perversity, never tedious.

MARY: I wish us to find an agreement.

KNOX: Moray put you up to this, Moray and Lethington.

MARY: You may chastise me as you think fit and to keep me in correct ways and to hear my confession, and, in return, you must not preach in public of my affairs, not attack my household.

KNOX: I must preach the word of God. The Lord's way must be done. I will have none other.

MARY: The Lord's way with girls, Mr. Knox. Sixteen years and younger.

KNOX: My relations are godly.

MARY: A scandal, Mr. Knox. Your relations are a scandal in the face of God. Children, I have heard. They have told me.

KNOX: My enemies say many things.

MARY: Is it true?

KNOX: I preach the truth.

MARY: Your truth. Your truth. Not the truth of a true God. You must no longer preach against my marriage whenever it will come. I and my council shall decide. We will decide. You must not call together your church without you consult the power civil. Only the queen may call together her subjects. My council has decided.

KNOX: There is one greater than all.

MARY: I have tried, I have tried to find an accommodation and you will have none. Is it my fault?

KNOX: I must do the will of the Lord.

MARY: Go, Knox, go. You are evil. You have such certainty you have truth. You are wicked. Go. Go. Go.

KNOX *leaves*.

MARY H.: Madam. Ma lady. Here. Yer grace.

MARY: I have tried. I have tried. I am his queen. He does not listen. I can say nothing to him. Mary, I will be revenged. I will be revenged.

MARY H.: Madam, calm yourself. Calm yourself.

MARY: I have tried to make peace with the advice of Moray. I have tried. And this is what has happened. I do not understand. I have tried. I will be revenged.

MARY H. *helps* MARY *out*.

Scene 6

MAID *as* MARY *sits at the front of the stage*.

MAID: I sit here by the fire, little me, little Mary, waiting for the carriage to come and take me to the ball, and my wicked sisters have taken away my invitation, sold the carriage, torn up my dress and cancelled the ball. No balls for me, they said. What shall I do?

MORAY *as* KNOX *appears through a trap*.

MORAY: Hello, Mary, I am your good fairy Knox at the window. I have heard you crying. I am a good fairy and I like to help.

MAID: I am so unhappy, Fairy Knox. I am alone and sad and I wanted to meet a handsome prince.

MORAY: Handsome princes are not that easy to come by, beautiful maid.

MAID: I'm not a maid.

MORAY: Then it might be easier.

MAID: Can you find me one then?

MORAY: Let me look in my little book of handsome princes and I will see. Prince Siegfried; no, he's for the Palace, Leith.[17] Student Prince; no, he's for the Palace, Kelty.[18] Finger Prince; no, he's for the Palace Distillery. I know. I know. I know.

MAID: Oh, fairy Knox. Good fairy Knox. Kind fairy Knox. Could it be?

MORAY *flashes wand and through trap appears* BOTHWELL *dressed as* DARNLEY.

MORAY: Prince Charming Darnley, played by Mr. Jamie Bothwell.

MAID: Oh, he's beautiful.

MORAY: He is sweet, isn't he?

MAID: How can I ever thank you enough, fairy?

MORAY: Don't try. It's all part of a day's work.

Silence.

MAID: Does he speak?

MORAY: Only in the romantic moonlight. (*pause*) Moonlight. (*no change*) Moonlight!

Moonlight appears. MAID *and* BOTHWELL *freeze.*

MORAY: Little does she know that I am in reality the wicked fairy. Knock at the door and it shall be slammed in your face. Heh. Heh. Heh.

Exit in a diabolic flash.

Moonlight.

MAID: I love the moonlight.

BOTHWELL: It's so terribly, terribly fragile.

MAID: Yes, Henry.

BOTHWELL: Yes.

MAID: A beautiful night.

BOTHWELL: Mary, I don't know how to say this.

MAID: What, Henry?

BOTHWELL: It's so dashed difficult, Mary. I'm not used to saying things. Oh, Mary, Mary, I love you.

MAID: Oh, Henry, Henry, this is so sudden.

BOTHWELL: Yes, I suppose it is.

MAID: Sometimes things that are sudden are very beautiful.

BOTHWELL: The moonlight is terribly, terribly pretty, like your eyes, Mary.

MAID: Oh, Henry, am I dreaming?

BOTHWELL: I don't think so, Mary.

MAID: Henry. Henry, you're so handsome. It's a fairy tale come true.

BOTHWELL: Dare I hope you could feel perhaps a little for me, Mary?

MAID (*looks away*): Oh, Henry, how could you ask such a question?

BOTHWELL: I know I'm only an earl's son with a royal granny and a claim to the English throne, but even with the distance between our relative social positions, I hoped . . .

MAID: Oh, Henry, silly Henry. I do, I do love you. (*tinkling laugh*) I have loved you secretly since I met you. You're so manly.

BOTHWELL: Shall we elope?

MAID: Oh, Henry, you're so masterful.

BOTHWELL: Oh, Mary.

MAID: Oh, Henry. (*rubs the back of his thigh*)

BOTHWELL: Nothing can approach the perfection of this night.

MAID: Mm.

BOTHWELL: It is perfect.

MAID: Mm.

BOTHWELL: The honeysuckle on the breeze.

MAID: Mm.

BOTHWELL: The perfume of your hair.

   MAID *bites his ear.*

BOTHWELL: Oh, why did you bite my ear, Mary?

MAID: Oh, Henry.

   They leave.

Scene 7

Three golf balls roll on to the stage, one after another. MORTON, RUTHVEN, *and* MAITLAND *enter. They are playing golf.*

MORTON: Tae mairry Darnley. Whaur's ma baw?

RUTHVEN: It's trouble, Maitland.

MORTON: Tae mairry a maist certain pape.

MAITLAND: It certainly wasnae very tactfu. There's yer baw. Is this mine?

RUTHVEN: Ye're a cuddie, Maitland. A bloody cuddie. Aye it is. A Catholic mairriage. It's a question o religion.

MAITLAND: A ken it's a question o religion.

MORTON: Whit's mair tae the point, Ruthven, it's a question o power.

   RUTHVEN *lines up his putt.*

MAITLAND: Aye. A dinnae ken hoo A came wi youse boys on this game. Concentrate.

RUTHVEN (*beginning his address*): See, we could depose them.

MAITLAND: Hey, depose the queen?!

RUTHVEN: Dinnae disturb ma putt, will ye no?

MORTON: Cannae putt yet. Moray's still in the rough.

RUTHVEN: It's the road tae Rome.

MORTON: No. It's the rough.

MAITLAND: Och, it's jist a mairriage. Darnley's a young fool. We'll manage him.

RUTHVEN: And Lennox?

MORTON: Fir Christ sake, Moray! Will ye look at him? It's gaun tae rain an he's oot there prunin the whins fir hisself. He should play wi a sickle, no a club.

RUTHVEN: She never took the advice o her cooncil. Tae choose thon Darnley!

MORTON: The cooncil? It's Moray an his bloody settlement. Moray's kept us quiet an fir whit? He wants a balance o power, an she's nae use at thon. Look whit she's daein! She cannae understand the need fir peace, ir at least hoo tae achieve it. She wants her ain way, an noo Moray, A dinnae think he kens hoo tae settle this game o gowf the noo, let alane settle the land.

MAITLAND: It's no . . .

Ball bounces on. RUTHVEN *traps it.*

MORTON: Pit it by the hole ir we'll be here tae Michaelmas.[19] Here he comes. Why no try gowf, Moray?

MORAY (*enters*): Bloody whins.

MAITLAND: It's no jist she's silly.

MORTON: Then whit is it?

MAITLAND: It's love.

MORTON: Love. Love? She's the queen o this land an she wants tae mairry fir love on tae a pape?

RUTHVEN: Thon's no love. Thon's insanity. Can we no get her certified? Wha's tae putt?

MORAY: We'll see, Ruthven. It jist wasnae aw that tactfu.

MORTON: Ruthven's putt. We shouldnae hae let her back. We should hae had a richt protestant state an made ye the king, Moray. Ye wouldnae mairry Darnley.

MORAY: Darnley wouldnae hae me. Onywey, A've mair taste.

RUTHVEN: A'm tryin tae putt.

MORTON: He's a lady's boy.

RUTHVEN: Ssh. (*Putts out*)

MORAY: Very good.

MORTON: A richt sprig. Tut, tut.

RUTHVEN: Doesnae matter. England'll no like a papist mairriage.

   MAITLAND *putts out.*

MORTON: No bad, Maitland, fir ye.

   MORTON *putts and misses.*

MORTON: Oh Christ.

MAITLAND: It's yer grip. It needs practice.

MORTON: There's naethin wrang wi my grip. A had a hole in six the ither day.

RUTHVEN: She'll mak him king.

   MORTON *putts out.*

MAITLAND: At lang last.

MORTON: Aye, an they've baith made a claim tae England's throne. We need the money we aw get fae Elizabeth tae keep the land safe fir the true religion.

MORAY: Knox keeps the land safe fir the true religion. We keep the land safe fir oorsels.

RUTHVEN (*whistles and looks round*): Money? Fae Elizabeth? Wha gets that?

MORAY: Ye werenae even born innocent, Ruthven.

   MORAY *makes to putt.* LENNOX *enters, carrying clubs.*

LENNOX: Ma lords.

MORAY (*straightens up*): Is that no enough tae mak ye gie up the gowf?

MAITLAND: Aye, Lennox. Whit are ye here for?

LENNOX: Practice. That's aw.

MAITLAND: Aye.

   Silence. They all look at LENNOX.

LENNOX: Aye, A cannae control the affections o the young.

MORTON *laughs.* MORAY *smiles.*

RUTHVEN: Lennox, ye're standin there like a bag o tripe an no a pund o it hingin the richt way.

LENNOX: A jist want tae play ma game. A dinnae want tae quarrel. A cannae control him.

MORAY: Yer ain son.

LENNOX: He's aye been the same, a nutter. She jist fell fir him. See, let me practice. A've an awfy heidache an it's gaun tae rain soon. An A've jist lost my baws. Can onyyin gie me a spare yin?

RUTHVEN: Ye pape politician.

LENNOX: A've worked fir the settlement. A dinnae want sufferin. Jist gie's a baw an A'll play on my ain, quiet-like.

MAITLAND: Quiet-like ye've nae chance o. It doesnae maitter if ye didnae work fir this mairriage. Ye cannae play on yer ain. Ye'll need tae shelter fae the rain sometime.

RUTHVEN: A trust ye nane, Lennox.

MORTON: See ye on the next tee, Moray.

MORTON *and* RUTHVEN *leave.*

MORAY: The twins o the true faith. (*putts out*)

LENNOX: Aye. A couldnae stop it. She is the queen.

MORAY: Yer ain son as king. Did ye want tae stop it?

LENNOX: A ken things change. A ken the days fir yin o us tae grasp the power fae the ithers is done. A'm no Huntly wantin tae be deid. It'll be aw richt, though. The cooncil hauds power.

MORAY: The cooncil has held thegither the balance o power jist because it has seen nae man fit tae ride the queen an tak her the yin way or the tither. A dinnae ken whit weight yer ain son has, Lennox, bit a doot it's ower muckle tae balance.

MAITLAND: Lennox, it isnae very wise.

LENNOX: Weel, we'll see. We can maybe haud the balance yet. Keep oor lands. They're jist ying fowk.

MORAY: Aye.

MAITLAND *and* MORAY *start to go.*

LENNOX: Hae ye got that spare baw?

MORAY: Aye. (*throws him one*)

MAITLAND *and* MORAY *leave*. LENNOX *addresses the ball and plays off.*

MORAY (*offstage*): Ow! Silly bugger, Lennox!

LENNOX: Oh, Jesus, Mary an Joseph. They did fine when they banned this game.

Leaves.

Scene 8

MARY *is sitting up in bed.* DARNLEY *is wearing a robe and is pacing up and down, drinking.*

MARY: Henry, what is wrong.

DARNLEY: Wrong?

MARY: Why are you so unsettled? We danced well tonight. It was fine.

DARNLEY: You danced well.

MARY: Smile a little, Henry. You change your moods so.

DARNLEY: Yes.

MARY: Henry, come to bed, my love.

DARNLEY: I'll come when I'm ready.

MARY *lies back.* DARNLEY *drinks.*

MARY: Henry.

DARNLEY: Can't you leave me alone? I am not tired.

MARY *draws the sheets around her and sits up.*

MARY: Why are you so hard to me?

DARNLEY *is silent.*

MARY: I have heard of the things you have done.

DARNLEY: What?

MARY: I have heard you have been with other women.

DARNLEY: Have you?

MARY: My women.

DARNLEY: If you know about it, it's probably over.

MARY: Henry.

DARNLEY: Mary.

MARY: What is wrong so suddenly?

DARNLEY: You think you're the power in the land, yet you had to send Moray away before you could marry me. And you really think he will return to meet you half-way? You should give me the power I should have. I have been your husband for four months. I have the right to be crowned. I am king.

MARY: King.

DARNLEY: King Henry.

MARY: You had your name called king put in a window at Falkland Palace.[20] You are a king of glass.

DARNLEY *sits*.

MARY: Henry, you have been with other women within a week of our marriage.

DARNLEY: They were women.

MARY: Am I not a woman?

DARNLEY: You're nothing. No use. You don't excite me. I might as well lie alone. I might as well masturbate. You don't kiss. You administer a lip.

MARY: You have shown me no tenderness, only demands. I want to learn. I want to know.

DARNLEY: Do you? There's a moment with a woman, a moment when she gives herself. Totally, Mary. She is yours and you hers, the way she moves and breathes says I want you and I know you want me. That is giving. That is trust. But you? You're so tied up, you don't live. You don't know.

MARY: I want to know.

DARNLEY: You don't. You can't want to know. It's in you. One either does, Mary, or in your case one doesn't. You're nothing.

MARY: I thought I loved you.

DARNLEY: You don't know how to love. Look at you. You're hiding your body just now. Look.

MARY: What help have I had? Help me, Henry. I am alone.

DARNLEY *is silent*.

MARY: Henry, I am to have our baby.

DARNLEY: No. Not mine.

MARY: It is your baby, Henry. I have slept with no . . .

DARNLEY: I don't want to know.

MARY: But it is so.

DARNLEY: It is not mine. Not ours.

MARY (*shows herself to* DARNLEY, *but not to the audience*): I want you to hold me.

   DARNLEY *finishes his drink and goes in silence.* MARY *leaves.*

Scene 9

MAITLAND *and* MORTON *enter. They have been eating and each is gnawing a drumstick from a goose.* MORTON *also carries a goblet of wine.*

MAITLAND: It's a grand goose.

MORTON: Aye.

MAITLAND: The queen has a good cook.

MORTON: Thon's aboot aw she has that's good.

MAITLAND: D'you never cease, Morton?

MORTON: A jist agreed. It's a grand goose.

MAITLAND: Aye.

MORTON: Aye.

   LENNOX *enters. He is carrying a bottle of wine. He sees* MORTON *and makes to leave.* MORTON *sees him.*

MORTON: There ye are.

LENNOX: No, Morton, ye dinnae need tae say onything. A ken it.

MORTON: Weel, ken it.

LENNOX: A'm no wantin war atween us twa.

MORTON: Then mak share there's nane.

LENNOX (*coming on*): Ma son's a wild yin, so he is. A didnae entirely want him tae mairry her. Bit A certainly didnae want them tae claim the English throne too an stir up Elizabeth.

MORTON: Weel, that's whit they're daeing.

LENNOX (*pours* MORTON *some wine*): It's braw wine, Morton.

MORTON: Aye.

LENNOX: An braw goose.

MORTON: Bonny goose.

LENNOX: Weel, bit Darnley hasnae brocht me ony power.

MORTON: Rizzio's been gied power.

LENNOX: Bit A'm no Rizzio's faither.

MORTON: Secretary o State fir French Affairs. It's a shame. Rizzio!

LENNOX: A ken we need peace wi England. A ken it's awfy gey near. Jist doon the road there, really, England is. See, Maitland, A didnae like ye yince, bit A see ye're jist daein yer best fir the land. Ye cannae help yersel, can ye? Ye're a good laddie. (LENNOX *is getting drunk*)

MORTON: Weel, efter the claim on the English throne, A cannae haud fowk like Ruthven firever. Especially seein she's exiled Moray. Ye'd think she'd ken better.

MAITLAND: She doesnae seem tae.

MORTON: No. (*finishes his bone and looks round to dispose of it*)

LENNOX: Och, he's a gid laddie.

MORTON: Aye. (*throws bone over his shoulder and offstage*) Here, Rover.

There is the sound of a dog snarling. BOTHWELL *enters, kicking back at the dog.*

BOTHWELL: Bloody dugs. Why'd ye no watch whaur ye put yer bones, Morton?

MORTON: Lovely weather noo ye're back, Bothwell, d'ye no think?

BOTHWELL: Aye. Is there ony wine, Lennox?

LENNOX *gives him his bottle.* BOTHWELL *tips it up. It is empty.* LENNOX *reaches inside his doublet, produces another, bites off the cork and gives* BOTHWELL *a drink.*

LENNOX: Dinnae tell onyyin noo, Bothwell. Tween oursels, OK?

BOTHWELL: Aye. (*drinks*)

MORTON: Hoo are ye daein, Bothwell?

BOTHWELL (*ignoring* MORTON): Lethington.

BOTHWELL *and* LETHINGTON *talk at side.*

MORTON: Share o hissel, thon yin.

LENNOX: He's the queen's friend.

MORTON: An Darnley's?

LENNOX: Mair wine?

MORTON: Aye. Tell me, though, Lennox. Tell me, d'ye trust him?

LENNOX (*loudly*): Bothwell?

MORTON: No.

> BOTHWELL *looks over.*

MORTON: Jesus Christ.

> BOTHWELL *looks back.*

LENNOX: Oh, aye. A believe in him.

MORTON: Bothwell.

LENNOX: A thocht ye said Jesus.

MORTON: Jesus.

LENNOX: Aye, that's whit ye said.

MORTON: A mean Bothwell.

LENNOX: Bothwell?

> BOTHWELL *looks over to them.*

MORTON: Aye. Bothwell.

LENNOX: Why the hell were ye talkin about Jesus, then? (*sees* BOTHWELL) Hullo, Bothwell. Nice day.

> BOTHWELL *looks back.*

MORTON: Dae ye?

LENNOX: Whit?

MORTON: Trust Bothwell?

LENNOX (*loudly*): He's aw right. (*drinks more*)

> BOTHWELL *looks round.*

MORTON: Keep yer voice doon.

LENNOX: A dinnae bother too much. A'm yer friend, ye ken that, Morton.

MORTON: See, it's like this. A'm no prejudiced. A mean, A'm no Moray, no yin a thae politicians, bit A'm still fir peace. It's jist we cannae hae Catholics.

LENNOX: Bit A'm a Catholic. A'm a gid Catholic. A mean, when A wis in England wi Henry the Eighth, A wis a Protestant, bit noo A'm a Catholic.

MORTON: So ye are, bit A'm no biassed. Tae let ye ken, A'm no Ruthven. See, he's biassed. A wouldnae tell jist onyyin else, Lennox, bit he is. Ye've got tae tell the truth, hae ye no? Onywey, A say live an let live so long as the Protestants are the boss.

LENNOX: A'm saying, A'm a good Catholic. There's those that arenae, bit A'm are.

MORTON: Ye're no bad, Lennox. A grand man.

LENNOX: Morton, Morton, ye're a fine grand sowel. So ye are.

RUTHVEN *enters.*

RUTHVEN: Aye. A see the pope's brither-in-law's back.

MORTON: Ruthven!

RUTHVEN: Mairried Catholic Huntly's Catholic dochter? Thocht he wis a Protestant. Is it the money ir the power he's after?

MORTON: Ruthven! This isnae the time ir the place.

BOTHWELL: A've nae doot we'll find the time an the place, Ruthven.

LENNOX *falls over.*

MAITLAND: The queen's gid faither.

MORTON: He's jist a wee bit owercame. Maybe it's the heat.

BOTHWELL: Let's get him oot.

MAITLAND *and* BOTHWELL *drag* LENNOX *off.* MORTON *holds back* RUTHVEN.

MORTON: We maun haud oor peace wi Lennox. We maun side wi Darnley tae kill Rizzio.

RUTHVEN: Side wi thon peely-wally papist?

MORTON: Yin at a time. Wi Darnley we hae Lennox an we kill us a foreign pape. If Darnley helps us, she'll blame him. Yin at a time.

RUTHVEN: Bit tae side wi him! A'd rather hae Bothwell.

MORTON: Bit Bothwell willnae hae us. He's the hard yin.

They leave.

Scene 10

MARY HAMILTON *enters and busies herself laying out jewellery.* MARY *enters, wearing a dress with a high bosom.*

MARY: There you are, Marie. Are ye feeling better?

MARY H.: Yes, yer grace. Thank you.

MARY: It is sad to feel sick when a fine evening at dance is to come.

    MARY *looks at jewellery.*

MARY H.: A'm better, grace.

MARY: Where are my pearls?

MARY H.: In the chest, madam. A will get them. (*goes offstage*)

    MARY *looks after her, sighs and looks at jewellery.* MARY HAMILTON *returns with the pearls.* MARY *takes them.*

MARY: Marie.

MARY H.: Your grace.

MARY: Do they suit? (*holds them against herself*)

MARY H.: Yes, your grace.

MARY: My baby begins to kick.

MARY H.: That's wonderful, your grace. It will be a boy.

MARY (*holds out the pearls*): Try them on.

MARY H.: Me?

MARY: Yes. Go on. They are attractive, are they not?

    MARY H. *holds the pearls and looks at them.*

MARY H.: How does it feel, madam? The babe?

MARY: Like a fluttering of the heart. Like new things to come. Like excitement.

MARY H.: It will be a true and royal baby.

MARY: Yes.

MARY H.: An heir for the kingdom. It will be a good thing.

MARY: Good for the kingdom, they all say so. They say I have done well. They say I have the power and the kingdom, my own foreign friends and my enemies exiled. I know one thing alone is lacking.

MARY H.: But now you carry it under your heart, madam. To cradle and grow to birth.

MARY H. *starts to put on the pearls.*

MARY: And what do you carry under your heart, Marie? To cradle? To grow?

MARY H. *stops putting on the pearls.*

MARY H.: Grace?

MARY: My pearls, please, Marie.

MARY H. *returns the pearls.*

MARY H.: Grace.

MARY *puts them on herself.* MARY HAMILTON *tries to help, but* MARY *won't let her.*

MARY: I need not your assistance. (*fastens pearls*) Marie, it is difficult to resist a beautiful man. I know. But you have ought to resisted him. You have ought in all honour and all friendship. You have ought to resisted his attention with all your strength.

MARY H.: A tried.

MARY: He is my husband, Marie. You have acted with my husband. How could you?

MARY H.: Your grace.

MARY: With my husband is bad, but to do after you have known how he has been to me, that is wicked. I thought you to be my true friend, Marie. I do not care for his lust, it is commonplace, but that my friend has acted so in unkindness, it is too much.

MARY H.: Grace.

MARY: I cannot bear it.

MARY H.: Your grace.

MARY: I do not want to hear. You have acted so, have listened to my troubles and gone to the bed of the man who has made those troubles.

MARY H.: He forced me.

MARY: The forces of lust are in your own body. In yours.

MARY H.: Madam, A tried to resist.

MARY: It is the sorrow of the weak that they are blamed for the exactions of the strong. I have loved you as a sister, as a friend. I will not stand it.

MARY H.: My baby.

MARY: Your baby. You must die. Your baby must die. It is nothing. Guards. Guards.

MARY H.: Your grace. Be merciful.

GUARDS *enter.*

MARY: Your acts were treason, grand treason, grand treason to my body and my lonely heart, Marie. To me. Take this woman away. She is to die. Marie, you will say to none who is the father of your ... To none.

MARY H.: Oh, Mary.

MARY: After all these years. I cannot bear the sight of you. (MARY *turns her back and the guards take out* MARY HAMILTON) After all these years.

MARY *holds her belly and walks out. She does not cry.*

Scene 11

KNOX *as* COMIC 1 *enters.*

KNOX: And now ladies and gentlemen, a little dramatic recitation from my friend and yours. Yes, madam, this is the cultural bit, the bit you've all been waiting for, the bit you can have a kip in, the bit between your teeth, the tackety bit, a little cultural recititation from my friend and yours, me. You didn't know I wrote poetry, did you? Well, I don't. I write verse. Every morning, from bed to verse. And so ...

LENNOX *as* COMIC 2 *enters.*

LENNOX: I say, I say, I say.

KNOX: Excuse me, excuse me, excuse me.

LENNOX: Whitfir, whitfir, whitfir?

KNOX: I'm trying to give these ladies and gentlemen, these good people, a touch of the great literary tradition for the lady in the back row, thank you madam. An extraordinary, contemporary, literary perspective on the historical historicity of Scotia.

LENNOX: Scotia who?

KNOX: Scotia breed fae the Jewish baker.

LENNOX: I do the gags, pal.

KNOX: What gags?

LENNOX: Never mind what gags; my contract says I do the gags.

KNOX: Never mind what your contract says. What does your audience say?

LENNOX: I say, I say, I say.

KNOX: As I was saying before I was so rudely interrupted. The lay of the last minstrel.

LENNOX: Or Mary Queen of Scots.

KNOX: Mary Queen of Scots, a sonnet by me.

LENNOX: A what?

KNOX: A sonnet about Mary, Queen of Scots.

LENNOX: A bonnet?

KNOX: A sonnet. Fourteen lines of iambic[21] pentameter, rhyming *abba, abba, cdecde*, containing a change of thought after the first octave.

LENNOX: Oh.

KNOX: So piss off. Sorry about this, ladies and gentlemen, get off.

LENNOX *half goes, but stays fascinated.*

KNOX: As I was saying, before I was etcetera . . . (*strikes pose*)
"Mary, Queen of Scots", a sonnet by me.
O fair and tragic, magic, lovelorn queen
I wot . . .

LENNOX: You what?

KNOX: I wot that dark and dismal troubled mind . . .

LENNOX: I say, I say, I say.

KNOX: What is it now?

LENNOX: My wife's gone to the Hebrides.[22]

KNOX: Staffa?[23]

LENNOX: Uist[24] to.

KNOX: I do not wish to know that. Kindly leave the stage. And now, ladies and gentlemen, from the charming contemporary literary heritage of Scotland's Muse.

LENNOX: I say, I say, I say.

KNOX: I am treating these gentle people to a wee tottie taste of the gloriositties of Scotland's literatury masterpisses; a rolling braeside from the wee bit hill and glen of the great Jock Hairy literary historicalary . . .

LENNOX: There's nae need for that, you know.

KNOX: What?

LENNOX: That.

KNOX (*bemused, shakes head*): Where was I? Oh yes . . . (*strikes pose*)
   Though life itself is filled with joy pristine . . .

LENNOX: I kent her.

KNOX: Who?

LENNOX: Joy Pristine, the tragic lead in a thousand dramas to touch the cockles of your heart in the front row of the Regal.[25]

KNOX: Are you serious?

LENNOX: Dead serious. Look. (*strikes pose*)
   Mary had a little lamb
   His name was Henry Darnley
   She took him as her husband
   For he was so big and manly.
   But he played her false with other dames
   And would not beg her pardon
   So she took him down to Kirk o' Fields
   And spread him round the garden.

Thank-you, thank-you, thank-you. Don't applaud, throw money.

KNOX: I was delivering my sonnet.

LENNOX: I do not wish to know that. Kindly leave the stage, the Scotsman, and two pints of milk, please. How's that for delivery?

KNOX (*strikes pose*): O fair and tragic . . .

LENNOX: I say, I say, I say.

KNOX: What is it now?

LENNOX: What do ganders say in winter?

KNOX: I do not know. Tell me, what do ganders say in winter?

LENNOX: Geese a kiss.

KNOX: No. No! Bit A'll gie ye a sang.

BOTH *sing*: There's a wee highland hame
   Whaur a mither sits alane
   Waiting fir her laddie tae return fae far away
   She kens A'll no forget her
   In her hame amang the heather

Waiting fir her lad wha's sae far far away
Aye she sits all alane
In her grannie's hieland hame
Just waiting fir her laddie to return fae far away.

They leave on the trot, return for quick bow, and exeunt.[26]

Scene 12

RIZZIO *comes on. He brings on a joint table and stools. He returns and brings on a tray with wine and some fruit. He brings on his lute and tunes it. He is relaxed and abstracted.*

RIZZIO (*sings to same tune as* COMICS' *song*):

Vorremmo due posti insieme
Maria va molto bene
Ci si puo andare a piedi domani?[27]

MARY (*offstage*): David.

RIZZIO: Oh, sheet. Si.[28]

MARY *enters. She is largely pregnant.*

MARY: Pour for me some wine, David.

RIZZIO *does so.* MARY *sits.*

MARY: I get so tired. So tired. This little baby kicks me so.

RIZZIO: Si. E difficile.[29]

MARY: I'm glad there is you one may talk to. You are a good friend.

RIZZIO: E bene. (*gives her wine*) Sono poco stanco anche.[30]

MARY: Stanco, poverino?[31] Why are you tired?

RIZZIO: I am worried.

MARY: Why are you worried?

RIZZIO: Darnley, he makes threats.

MARY: He has no brain.

RIZZIO: We are not involved in an intellectual disputation.

MARY: Si. E grave. (*laughs*) Do not be so solemn, David.

RIZZIO: I am tired of this town.

MARY: We have made our own world in it.

RIZZIO: It is not France.

MARY: No. It is not the beautiful France. To think that I was to be a French princess and a French king's wife, and a French king's mother. Then Francis died. And I have come here to be a politician and learn to rule. Elizabeth was taught to be politic. I was taught to be a princess in a glittering court.

RIZZIO: And now you have taken power.

MARY: I have had to send away Moray who was wise, and for what? Darnley who is nothing. That is my power, my politics. I am only glad there is you.

RIZZIO: But I am a friend, not a politician. And you have made me one. The Pope asked me to observe, not to participate. It is not so discreet.

MARY: I must have those I can trust near me. I have known so few I could trust. That is all.

RIZZIO: The lords do not like it. They do not like me.

MARY: I like you, David. I need you to be there. To keep my secret thoughts safe.

RIZZIO: But my life is not so safe either.

MARY: I need you. I have no-one. I am once widow and I have a baby to a man I hate. You must be my friend. Else I am alone.

RIZZIO: Darnley has said we are lovers.

MARY: He is a fool.

RIZZIO: He will kill me.

MARY: He will not dare.

RIZZIO: He can find power elsewhere. Morton and Ruthven will help him to hurt you.

MARY: He will not dare, David.

RIZZIO: Perhaps.

MARY: You must not worry. To be civilised in a country barbarous is not safe. That is all. Va bene.

RIZZIO: Si. Un po' de vino?

MARY: Si. (*gives him her glass*)

RIZZIO *goes to the wine and returns with* MARY's *glass filled. She smiles.* DARNLEY *bursts in followed by* MASKED MEN.

DARNLEY: Whore! (*gestures at* RIZZIO) Him!

RIZZIO *hides behind* MARY's *skirts.*

RIZZIO: I have done nothing.

DARNLEY: Adulteress.

MARY: Go, Darnley. Leave.

DARNLEY: It's too late. Him. Him!

The MEN *go for* RIZZIO *who is holding* MARY's *skirts.*

MARY: Leave this room at once. Leave at once.

RIZZIO: For nothing. All for nothing.

The MEN *drag him out. As he is dragged out he drags* MARY's *skirt with him. She is left standing in her underwear and the top part of her dress. Her false belly falls to the stage.*

MARY: Oh, I've dropped my bundle.

DARNLEY: Your grace . . .

RIZZIO *screams from offstage.*

MARY (*starts*): God. What's that?

DARNLEY: Oh God. Yes. Eh. He's dead, Mary.

MARY: For God's sake.

DARNLEY: Come on. Whore.

MARY: Rizzio has done nothing.

DARNLEY: Is that baby his?

MARY (*picks up bundle*): I don't think so. I hope not.

They leave.

END OF PART ONE

PART TWO

Scene 13

LENNOX *enters. He is dressed in a white painter's overalls, stained with red.*

LENNOX: So youse think unemployment's bad, dae ye? Weel, A'm here tae tell youse it's never been worse in ma trade. Ye see A'm whit ye'd cry an Artistic Embellisher an History Enlivenin Operative. Oh aye, A hear youse askin each other an whit the hell's that? Weel A'll tell ye. Noo youse've heard o a furniture stainer, richt? – an youse've heard o an abstainer – O.K? – weel, A'm a bloodstainer. Richt enough A stain blood. Ah weel, it's maybe no jist real blood. Naw, it's mair whit ye might cry paint. Bit it's reid paint ye ken, reid, jist like blood! Aw now, A'm no daft. Ye see fir years A used tae go tae a certain royal palace no sae far fae here fir tae freshen up a certain bloodstain on a certain flair jist ootside a certain apartment whaur a certain queen had her certain private bevvies. A'm very sorry A cannae tell youse which wan seein A've signed the Official Secrets Act an that. Onywey, aw they tourists wis very taken wi this stain, an they'd come in their thoosands fae miles aroon jist fir tae gawp at the bloodstain on the flair there, whaur some pair Tally cried Rizzio fell bleedin perfuseley fae a number o wounds on his bum. Are ye findin this awfy movin, though? Weel, A'm gaun tae let youse intae a wee secret. Ye see that isnae the real flair that Rizzio fell on. Naw. They pu'd up the real flair hunners o years ago an changed the hail shebang! Oh! Bang goes ma official secrets vow! A'm awfy sorry, yer Majesty!

Onyhow, the tourists wantit their blood, an it was ma job tae see that they got their official genuine, certified blood; an if A may say so masel, freends, A was a braw bloodstainer. Oh yes, A mind fine the day the Prince o Wales – ye ken, him that was Edward the Whitsit – paid us a visit. He took me tae one side an said tae me, "Jimmy", he says, "Jimmy", mind ye, ma name's Sandy, bit A didnae like tae argie-bargie wi him, him bein a royal prince an aw that. "But Jimmy," he says, "You do a lovely line in bloodstains."

An A said, "Weel, ta very much, yer Worship, an aw that." An he said "Yes indeed, Jimmy. Here take this." an he handit me a tanner. Weel, A mean, ye cannae argue wi them can ye?

Oh aye, A wiz a somebody wance! That is until the day this big official gowk – see he had a big gold badge sayin "Official Gowk" – he comes up tae me an says, "Look here, my man. That is not a genuine bloodstain on the flair there." Weel, A could hae telt him that masel, seein as how A'd paintit the bloody thing! "That's not a genuine bloodstain," says he, "Let's replace it with a brass plaque. It'll be much more tasteful." More tastefu! A brass plaque! It's blood the people want. They'll ayewis want blood. Youse'll see. Officialdom will realise the error o their ways one o these days an they'll come beggin me fir tae come back again. Oh aye, Sandy the Bloodstainer Royal, that's whit they'll cry me – A mean, A ask ye, a brass plaque! Wha's gaun tae believe that Rizzio fell doon there on that spot an drained awaw the last drap o his life's BRASS!

Scene 14

MORAY *and* MAITLAND *enter.* MORAY *has a falcon on his arm and a cigarette in his mouth.*

MORAY (*sees audience*): Christ. (*stubs out cigarette*)

KNOX *comes on, picks up stubbed cigarette and puts it in a tin.*

KNOX (*sees audience*): Christ. (*leaves*)

MORAY: Fir God's sake, Maitland. Rizzio's death brings dishonour tae the queen. It's tae say her man thinks she was bein rogered by a servant. In the evening in the queen's rooms.

MAITLAND: A've seen wiser men an wiser deeds. It wasnae fu o tact.

MORAY: Tact? Tact isnae the word fir it, neither the killers nir the pair o them. (*looks round sky for quarry*) Nae wee quarry yet.

MAITLAND: Darnley's becomin an embarrassment.

MORAY: He was never onythin else.

MAITLAND: Aye, that's fine, Moray, an ye're back in the queen's favour while she needs ye.

MORAY: A'll no be wanderin again. (*walks to back of stage*) A dinnae ken. The huntin's pair the noo.

MAITLAND: Try fir a settlement again.

MORAY: A'd prefer a rabbit. This bird's heavy.

MAITLAND: A dinnae see whit the appeal o hawkin is.

MORAY: The quiet.

MAITLAND: We can use the son.

MORAY: Pair wee get.

MAITLAND: He's no a get.

MORAY: She hasnae got it in her tae mak a get.

MAITLAND: She's yer sister.

MORAY: She's my half-sister, an when A see whit she gets up tae when A'm no here, A doot she's a half-wit tae.

BOTHWELL *enters, with a falcon.*

BOTHWELL: Aye when there's private talks tae be, there ye see Lethington.

MAITLAND: It's ma job.

BOTHWELL: Tak nae offence, ye canny man. A'm here tae hawk.

LENNOX *enters opposite, falcon on arm.*

LENNOX: A'm here fir tae hawk.

BOTHWELL: See this bird. It's not a sparrie.

LENNOX: Yer bird looks like it's paralysed.

MORAY: Christ, Lennox, we cam here tae hunt an hae a quiet friendly conversation. No tae squabble.

LENNOX: A brocht my bird. Whit are ye girnin aboot? This is the best haggard A hae. A grand hawk. A reared it masel. Is there ony quarry?

BOTHWELL *looks at* MORAY. MORAY *nods.*

BOTHWELL: Darnley.

LENNOX: Darnley? Here, that's my son.

BOTHWELL: Maist would keep that quiet, Lennox.

MORAY: Darnley's the topic, no Lennox.

BOTHWELL: Darnley an Ruthven an Morton aw killed Rizzio. The queen has exiled Ruthven an Morton, bit she's made friends wi Darnley. Darnley's alane.

MORAY: A cannae disagree, Bothwell. Thon's braw jesses[32] on yer bird.

BOTHWELL (*rings the bells*): Aye, the wife's a dab hand.

LENNOX: It's no jist richt.

MORAY: When was Darnley jist richt fir onythin bit weemin? An he wasnae even carefu aboot whaur he went wi them.

BOTHWELL: He's lassy-daft, skirt-happy.

MAITLAND: Hence his illness. Genital is it no?

MORAY: It maun be cut aff.

LENNOX: No! Onythin bit that!

MORAY: See. There. (*Pulls hood off his hawk. Its wings spring up. He removes the jesses and swings up his arm.*) Go, ma proud beauty. (*The hawk swings up on a wire into the flies.*)[33] *All watch it soar.*) No cut "it" aff. Cut "him" aff. He maun be removit fae the place o scandal.

MAITLAND: The Queen's name's bad an it maun be purged. Darnley dirties it.

LENNOX: A ken.

MAITLAND: A ken ye ken. He maun die.

LENNOX: A ken ye ken A ken. Bit he's ma son.

MORAY: A ken ye ken he kens ye ken, bit whit power does Darnley bring ye, Lennox? He micht as weel be deid fir that. See, she's seen a doo.

LENNOX: A'll no hae it.

BOTHWELL: Ye'll hae it, Lennox. She's stoopin. Braw.

MORAY: Aye. A bait.

BOTHWELL: She's cairrying.

MORAY: She'll roost near. A'll lure her. She's weel-trainit.

LENNOX: Ye want tae kill ma son an aw ye can dae is talk aboot hawkin.

MORAY: Weel, ma bird's jist taen quarry. Whit d'ye expect?

LENNOX: A'll see the man that does it deid.

BOTHWELL: What use is Darnley? He's nae use tae ye.

MAITLAND: We cannae divorce fir the sake o the bairn.

LENNOX: Look, he's got the . . . He has a social disease. Let him die in peace o't.

MORAY: Aye, there's that tae it.

LENNOX: Keep him quiet. Let him lie in Glesca till he dies.

BOTHWELL: An hoors an is a shame tae the queen. While he lives poxy, he's a shame tae the land.

MORAY: We want peace, Bothwell, no blood.

BOTHWELL: We've had blood. Darnley killed Rizzio.

MORAY: Rizzio's naething.

BOTHWELL: He was Secretary o State fir French Affairs, a high office, ma lord. An he was the queen's servant.

MORAY: An ye're the queen's servant. We aw are. Whit stirs ye is he was also fir France an France is fir yer pairty.

BOTHWELL: A hae my pairty, Moray, an A hae my power noo, an ye hae yer place only while A want ye there. Morton an Ruthven are gone.

MORAY: Aye. We'll see whit like yer strength is. Ye cam back fae exile, even efter they tried auld Huntly. So did A in my time. So may Morton an Ruthven.

LENNOX: Quarry. See. Quarry. D'ye want it, Bothwell?

BOTHWELL: A'll hae my time. Ye try fir it, Lennox.

LENNOX: Braw bird. Ma ain hand trained her. (*Takes off hood from his hawk and her wings spring up. He raises his arm.*) Go, ma proud beauty. (*The hawk falls over and swings upside-down from his wrist. The* LORDS *have been looking up to see her soar. They realise she has not soared.*)

MORAY: Yer best bird.

LENNOX: Bloody doo.

MAITLAND: A doot its mither was scared by a bat.

LENNOX (*tears the hawk from his wrist and flings it offstage*): Doesnae ken its trail fae its jesses. (*A dead pigeon is thrown back onstage*)

BOTHWELL (*picks up pigeon and gives it to* LENNOX *without showing any sign of surprise*): Knox is preachin. Wha let him?

MAITLAND: He's gaun awfy wild.

MORAY: An so is Darnley. Lennox, see tae him an tak thon bloody hen oot o here.

LENNOX: At least ma hawk didnae fly awaw intae the trees. (*leaves*)

BOTHWELL: Darnley maun be brocht tae Edinburgh.

MORAY: Why?

BOTHWELL: He's safer here.

MORAY: Oh aye?

BOTHWELL: Moray, there can be nae agreement atween us twa. Ye want yer auld power. It cannae be. Knox maun be stopped.

MORAY: Are ye huntin or shoutin? He kens religion is religion an power is power an power has naethin tae dae wi him.

BOTHWELL: He's rousin the fowk.

MORAY: He's lettin fowk cry oot aboot the death o Rizzio an the exile o the Protestant lords, an work awaw their anger.

BOTHWELL: An attack the queen an Catholics.

MORAY: A diversionary fire.

BOTHWELL: The man that starts the fire maun ken whaur it'll finish its burning.

MORAY: A ken.

BOTHWELL: Ye bastard, A doot ye dae.

MORAY: A'm a royal bastard.

BOTHWELL: A've nae mair tae say tae ye, Moray. A'll hunt elsewhaur. (*leaves*)

MAITLAND: A stormy time.

MORAY: If Bothwell does harm Darnley, then we're rid o them baith. A hope he does kill the cratur.

MAITLAND: Ye certainly didnae drive the idea fae his mind.

MORAY: A wasnae tryin te. Let's find my hawk an my quarry.

MAITLAND: High stakes, Moray.

MORAY: Peace.

A skinned rabbit falls from the flies. MORAY *picks it up and looks at it. He looks up. He shrugs his shoulders. They leave.*

Scene 15

DARNLEY *is lying in a bed. His face is covered.* MARY *comes in slowly.*

MARY (*offstage*): Thank you, Margaret. You need not wait. (*enters*) I can't stay. One of my maids is having a wedding supper tonight. I am sorry. It is tonight only.

DARNLEY: You never stay.

MARY: Do not sit up, Henry. It is necessary to rest.

DARNLEY: Damn this pox.

MARY: I do not feel well. My side is sore.

DARNLEY: You'll be all right.

Silence.

Why did you bring me here from Glasgow?

MARY: I thought it would be good to have you near. To have the boy near you.

DARNLEY: James.[34]

MARY: James. Your mouth looks bad tonight.

DARNLEY: It's the mercury. It blackens my gums. Makes my breath smell.

MARY: Yes.

DARNLEY: Do you want to see? (*Takes off the mask. His face is poxy.*)

MARY: Henry.

DARNLEY (*replaces mask*): You see.

MARY: Once you had sweet breath.

DARNLEY: You should have made me King. Who told you to bring me to Edinburgh?

MARY: Moray, Lethington and Bothwell thought . . .

DARNLEY: Bothwell. Moray. Oh God.

MARY: They are kind.

DARNLEY: Two of a kind. Why are you not kind to me?

MARY: I did not give you the pox.

DARNLEY: You wouldn't know how.

MARY: Oh.

DARNLEY: What's wrong?

MARY: My side. It's all right.

DARNLEY: Yes. I'm sore all over.

MARY: Yes, Henry.

DARNLEY: I wish there was someone to talk to. Anyone. You're not very interesting. Don't go.

MARY: I'm not going.

DARNLEY: I like you to visit me.

MARY: Henry, my side is very sore and my doctors do not know what it is.

DARNLEY: I can't do anything.

MARY: I want to talk about it. It worries me.

DARNLEY: It's nothing.

MARY: I want to talk.

DARNLEY: It's nothing. Mary! Please don't go.

MARY: I must. I promised to be back. I will see you tomorrow. I am sorry.

DARNLEY: You're leaving me just like the rest.

MARY: I hope you feel better tomorrow.

DARNLEY: You don't care. No-one does.

MARY: I must go, Henry. There is fruit and some wine. (*goes to leave*)

DARNLEY (*as she leaves*): Bitch.

> DARNLEY *remains lying. There is silence. A sudden noise is heard. He moves offstage. The stage blows up.*

Scene 16

KNOX *enters.*

KNOX: Dearly beloved. We are gathered here together in the sight of the Lord God Almighty the day, and I will not hide it from you that my heart is sair. I will share with you my many sorrows for you and this braw land, that you might ken the weight that harrows my soul and my mind. It is well-kent that in this town has come an agent of antichrist, who has kept in the privacy of her ain chamber secret and foul rituals. I have laboured sair in my heart, and in my mind, and in my soul to see what is the way of the Lord God in this matter, for I will damn none withoot due and godly consideration of what yet might be. Yet it is well-kent and attested to by men of honesty and probity that this creature has had to her favourites those that are not the favourites of good, honest and godly people. She has brought to us the smell of the pit and of death. And the final abomination, dearly beloved, she has come to, we have seen before us. This woman can cause none but ill. I see in her face, I see on her hands, I see in her heart, blood. Nothing but blood.

Her husband is deid by methods we ken nothing of, but we may suspect. Her conversations with those who do not love our kirk, we may suspect.

We can ken nothing about her dealings with regard to the late terrible death of her husband, but we maun ken that from her can spring no good.

There is in the land a new spirit, a new life from the new true kirk of the Lord God. She is of the kirk of antichrist. She brings nothing but sorrow. Dearly beloved, I have struggled long and pondered in my heart before having said what I have said. But I will not hide from you my heart is sair and you must ken the reason. There is in this woman no peace. She is a woman of blood. The Lord's truth must be upheld. I say this and say it from my heart. We can no mair bear the insults of the unjust. This cesspit of sin stinking to the heavens till the very sun is darkened must be seized and its stench given cease. Amen. The blessing of the Lord God of Israel, Father, Son and Haly Ghaist, be with you now and forever mair. As it was in the beginning is now and ever shall be, forever mair, world without end. Amen.

Leaves.

Scene 17

Someone is moving about. A light shines and we see MARY *in bed. A* MAID *is carrying the light.*

MARY *screams.*

MAID: Yer grace.

MARY: Take away that light

MAID: There are lords tae see ye, yer grace.

MARY: I will see none.

MAID: Yer grace, they hae bidit fir days tae see ye.

MARY: I will see none. Are you all against me? I am Queen.

MAID: Yer grace.

MARY (*lies back*): Bring me food.

MAID: Aye, yer grace.

MARY groans. The MAID enters with a tray.

MARY: Where was that food? Why was it brought so quickly?

MAID: Seein that ye eat sae rarely we keep food by fir ye.

MARY: I do not want it. Take it away.

MAID: Bit yer grace . . .

MARY: Take it away.

MAID: Yer grace.

MARY: What is it?

MAID: Some bread an meat.

MARY: Bring it here. Oh, this pain.

MAID gives MARY food.

MAID: It's good.

MARY takes a little.

MARY: Who is outside?

MAID: Ma lord Bothwell an Maister Maitland o Lethington.

MARY: Oh.

MARY eats. The MAID goes to a window.

MARY: Do not touch that window. I cannot bear light.

MAID: Bit madam. A only meant tae let in some air.

MARY: I need no air. Get out. Leave me alone. Leave me. Have I not suffered enough?

MAID leaves. MARY eats slowly.

MARY: Food is bad. Why did they do this?

MAITLAND enters quietly.

MAITLAND: Yer grace.

MARY: Who let you in? Go.

MAITLAND: A must talk wi ye, yer grace.

MARY: No.

MAITLAND: Ye hae lain fir weeks, yer grace, refusin tae see the light. The state maun run on.

MARY: You men have paid no attention to my mind in the running of my land. You have acted against me.

MAITLAND: There can be nae peace while Morton an Ruthven are abroad in England wi an interest in stirrin trouble at hame.

MARY: They did not need to break the poor body. He was so sick. His sores wept.

MAITLAND: It wasnae nobles in exile that had tae dae wi yer man's death. Bit Bothwell was acquittit. He had an airmy o three hunner men, bit nae maitter, he was acquittit.

MARY: I did not wish Henry to be killed.

MAITLAND: In yer hert, madam.

MARY: My heart. I am not allowed to feel with my heart here. My heart feels nothing.

MAITLAND: Bit ye are queen an maun act as queen.

MARY: He was not yet twenty-one, Lethington. I am only twenty-four and I have lost two husbands already. I have no family, but his child who I am not allowed to see.

MAITLAND: Sovereigns hae nae life bit as sovereign. If they try tae live their ain life, they may hae it taen fae them. It has happened often enough in England. It even happened yince in Scotland, tae James the Third,[35] yer ain . . .

MARY: They killed Darnley.

MAITLAND: It doesnae muckle maitter wha killed him. There a few wantit that. He's deid. Ye're alive. The land doesnae die fir the loss o yin like thon.

MARY: And I have a pain in my side.

MAITLAND: Ye hide here in the dark an see nane o yer advisers. Time'll come, yer grace, when they willnae want tae see ye. There's nae rule wioot guilt. Ye maunnae care. If ye lead noo, ye'll avoid the comin fight.

MARY: Go, Maitland. You have no right to speak to your queen.

MAITLAND: A'm quiet, yer grace. A serve ye truthfully, an A haud my tongue. Bit noo, A maun speak. There's forces noo released that we cannae stop, only maybe steer. Ye maun decide.

MARY: I want my maid.

MAITLAND *goes. The* MAID *enters.*

MARY: Take away the light.

Darkness again.

Scene 18

MARY HAMILTON *as* MARY *enters followed by* RUTHVEN *as* BOTHWELL.

MARY H.: False, deceitful, perjured profligate. Why held you me against my will? You have some wicked motive. I see it in your eye.

RUTHVEN: Eh?

MARY H.: Go, artful crocodile. Never will I submit to your vile attentions, nay, even should death be my reward.

RUTHVEN: It serves no end so entreating in this matter. I must be resolute.

MARY H.: Quite, quite resolute?

RUTHVEN: By Heaven, in matters of this kind I must be relentless.

MARY H.: My Lord of Bothwell, how harsh you are! How horrid your aspect! Know you not I am your queen?

RUTHVEN: My queen I know you to be. But your queendom is in mortgage to your heart and your heart in mortgage to mine.

MARY H.: Dare you claim my love?

RUTHVEN: I dare. I dare.

MARY H.: Release me, release me at once from this scalding passion thrusting its way through every last tissue of my poor woman's body. Release me, I say.

RUTHVEN: I heard you the first time.

MARY H.: You and your army met me at Cramond[36] and took me by surprise.

RUTHVEN: I found you not unwilling to be led away.

MARY H.: It is a vile thing you say. It is a vile thing you do. Think of my child. Think of my kingdom. Think of my reputation, unsullied and pure. You have brought me I know not where to do I know not what.

RUTHVEN: To my castle of Dunbar.[37]

MARY H.: To your castle of Dunbar. And do you intend I know not what?

RUTHVEN: I'm sure I don't know what you mean.

MARY H.: Oh, come my lord. You must have had women in your power ere now?

RUTHVEN: Certainly there's the wife.

MARY H.: Your wife?

RUTHVEN: Yes.

MARY H.: I thought you were divorced?

RUTHVEN: What gave you that idea?

MARY H.: Think you I would be here, kidnapped or no, thought I not you were free?

RUTHVEN: We're going to get divorced.

MARY H.: I've heard that one before.

RUTHVEN: But we are.

MARY H.: Have you told her?

RUTHVEN: Well, not quite.

MARY H.: Christendom knows that I am imprisoned by one of my wildest and most lawless nobles and that he is set to oblige me to marry him, and to have his will of me. And now he tells me he hasn't got round to informing his wife of her changed circumstance!

RUTHVEN: Would you tell her?

MARY H.: Me?

RUTHVEN: Yes.

MARY H.: How?

RUTHVEN: I don't know. You could improvise.

MARY H.: Send her to me.

RUTHVEN: Jean! I'll just get her. (*hurries out*)

    MAID *enters as* JEAN, LADY BOTHWELL.

MAID: What is it now?

MARY H.: O cruel, wicked woman, why do you hold your ex-husband in thrall against his wishes?

MAID: He's not . . .

MARY H.: Heaven be praised, by me he will be released from his bondage to your sinister charms.

MAID: Just a minute.

MARY H.: I have wealth, boundless wealth, and I must use it to crush you who have so ensnared my love.

MAID: But . . .

MARY H.: You will be scorned, loathed, despised by all.

MAID: I think there must be some mistake.

MARY H.: No mistake except in thinking you could elude the fearful clutch of justice. Your husband has captured me to have his way with me. Unfortunately he omitted to divorce you first.

MAID: Now I see.

MARY H.: Your fate is inexorable. Bungle or no bungle, I am his and he mine and you must give way and play your part.

MAID: Such tyranny is not to be borne.

MARY H.: Borne it must be and in patience. Your husband is a great man and I am a great queen and in such a case as ours our will will brook no despite. You must divorce him.

MAID: It is more than can be. I cannot bear it. I cannot bear it. Yet bear it I must. My heart is breaking. Oh, I will divorce him!

MARY H.: Good.

MAID: I swoon, I swoon.

MARY H.: There now. This way, dear. (*helps* MAID *off*)

Scene 19

RUTHVEN, MORTON *and* MORAY *enter. They carry bows.*

MORAY: It's serious though.

RUTHVEN: Bothwell should never hae been trusted.

MORAY: Aye.

RUTHVEN: Papish traitors. They've run aff thegither.

MORAY: A didnae think it was apart. We've got tae work oot whit tae dae.

Draws his bow and looses arrow.

MORTON: Good, Moray. Next time ye'll hit the target. We hae the son.

MORAY: Aye.

MORTON: Knox can say whit he likes?

MORAY: Aye. Aye. He has the freedom he had efter Darnley's unfortunate accident. Ye'll get aw the trouble ye want, Morton.

MORTON: It's nae trouble; it's victory.

RUTHVEN: We should drive aw the papes oot. Darnley an Mary couldnae be trusted, an noo look at Bothwell. An he's supposed tae be Protestant.

MORAY: He abducted her in Cramond.

MORTON: He's no choosy. (*looses arrow*)

RUTHVEN: The luck she has, A doot he isnae.

MORAY: The bairn's whaur the power is noo. She's finished. Tae go wi Bothwell! A was never share if he did kill her man, bit it kinda seemed likely, an noo she's gone wi him! That was a braw shot, though, Morton.

MORTON: Awbody thinks they can bang at her door. Aye, at least it hit the butt, eh? An they trample on the land tae get tae her.

RUTHVEN: An when they get there whit dae they find, a peely-wally sowel wi foxy hair?

MORAY: Like ma faither.

MORTON: Yer faither was a king. Hoo could he get yersel an her?

MORAY: Same as maist. Different mither.

RUTHVEN: Bit listen, ye worked at us. Ye got us tae see we could aw win if we settled. Ye talked some sense. No like her. Ir Bothwell. Bit ye cannae trust extremists.

MORAY: Ruthven, see, A trust ye. Shake my hand. (*twists his arm*) When the prize is power, every man wants peace till he sees the chance o an advantage. Ye A trust because ye dinnae see how tae get mair power the noo. Gie ye the chance an . . . (*lets him go*)

RUTHVEN: There's faith an honour.

MORTON: If a state is tae be ruled in peace the yin thing ye maun never hae is honour, only an eye tae keepin control.

RUTHVEN: Aye, ye're turnin politician, Morton. (*looses arrow*)

   LENNOX *enters clutching arrow to breast.*

RUTHVEN: Fir Christ sake.

LENNOX: A'm fadin fast, ma lords. (*takes arrow off*)

RUTHVEN: Stupid bugger.

LENNOX: Jist a wee joke.

MORTON: Christ, it taks the fun oot o archery, though.

MORAY: Has Lethington come yet?

RUTHVEN: Talkin here is nae use. Gie me a horse an an airmy an A'll find Bothwell.

MORTON: We maun hae sense.

RUTHVEN: Time was ye preferred action tae sense. (*leaves*)

LENNOX: A shouldnae hae scared him.

MORAY: Och. he's anither. Gie him his heid an he'll loss it.

MORTON: No jist yet.

LENNOX: The queen's been taen under guard by Bothwell. A doot it micht be rape.

MORTON: Rape?

MORAY: It doesnae matter if it is. She's spent. She's no richt in the heid, A doot. She was aye easy forcit by fine words an fancy promises.

LENNOX: She can never see her son again.

MORAY: A gid Protestant teacher fir him.

LENNOX: Protestant?

MORAY: George Buchanan.[38] We maun destroy the queen's name.

MORTON: Destroy it? She's done it fir us.

MORAY: France'll no like us shamin her, bit they didnae like Darnley, an they fir share willnae like Bothwell. Aye get yer ain knife in first. Buchanan'll write history fir us.

LENNOX: Moray, why could we no hae had yersel fir king?

MORAY: Thon's the wey o't.

MORTON: Let's get against her.

   MAITLAND *enters*.

MAITLAND: A've warned the civil authorities.

MORTON: Fine, Maitland.

MORAY: Morton, we'll need aw ready in very few days. Ye can dae it?

MORTON: Aye.

MORAY: Lennox, ye'll come tae punish Bothwell?

LENNOX: A see whaur my duty lies.

MAITLAND: Ma lords.

    MORTON *and* LENNOX *leave.*

MORAY: Wha'd hae thocht tae see they twa haudin hands?

MAITLAND: As an agent fir the Pope, she's a grand mussulman. She's unified the land. Fir a couple o weeks.

MORAY: Aye. Mary's deid.

    They leave.

Scene 20

MARY *enters, in riding clothes. She is pacing up and down. There is a sound in the corridor, she listens, then goes on pacing up and down.*

    BOTHWELL *enters. He is carrying part of his armour and wears the rest.* MARY *turns to him. He looks at her.*

MARY: Are the lords near?

BOTHWELL: Near enough.

MARY: Why will they not leave me in peace? Is it too much to want?

    BOTHWELL *starts to put on his armour.*

MARY: Why?

BOTHWELL: A cannae decide whether ye're daft ir stupit. A bit o baith, A think.

    MARY *turns away.*

BOTHWELL: Ye maun ken, A was loyal tae yer mither, tae the governance o the country. Then A abducted ye. Then ye mairried me. Can ye no begin tae guess why they dinnae like ye?

MARY: Why did you marry me?

BOTHWELL: Mary, ye're nae miracle in bed, bit ye're queen an A want ye. Whit ye are is powerless, bit whit ye mean is power.

MARY: Is that all? (*winces and clutches her side*)

BOTHWELL (*stands up*): Men mak up whit ye are in their ain mind cause ye gie naething. There's a few think tae roger a queen is better than tae lie wi fifty kitchen maids. Weel, A ken better.

Bit still A had my picture o ye in ma mind. That's why A killed Darnley, partly. Only the first in a lang queue, fir yersel an fir him.

MARY: I would not believe you killed him.

BOTHWELL: Ye're my wife an if we win, A'll be king an ye'll dae as ye're telt, ma lady. An if we loss, we're baith lost.

MARY: I have your child inside me.

BOTHWELL: Weel, it was made oot o nae joy o mine.

MARY: Why are you so cruel?

BOTHWELL: Ye should hae stayed in France, been a court beauty, untouching, untouched, untouchable. Here ye're bankrupt.

MARY: You have not been with me in my darkness for months. In all my life, two weeks of love, and you too sleep with maids!

BOTHWELL: Ye're awfy fertile though. Twa babies in twa weeks o the deed.

MARY: No-one was tender. No-one cared.

BOTHWELL: Jist so. We maun go. If we loss the day, A can die crazed o the pox fir aw A care.

They leave.

Scene 21

MAID *as* MARY *is brought in by a* GUARD *who stands behind her. She walks up and down and then sits. She cries.*

DARNLEY *as* MORAY *enters and looks at the* MAID. *She does not see him.* RIZZIO *as* MAITLAND *enters.*

RIZZIO: The time has come, your grace, to talk again.

MAID: The turbid mob in muddy Royal Mile,
    Have me called names that utter can I not.
    Filthy they be, and unfit queen to say.

RIZZIO: Go must thou, madam, where scape is there not;
    To exile can we never let thee go,
    As queen of this land.

DARNLEY: So now let it be.
    Release is none from weighty sentence hard;
    The castle of Loch Leven[39] be thy home.

MAID: That dank and dismal tower, where scarcely
  Cries swift, calls gull, or mews the muted coot,
  Whence few return or even many go,
  Where lost is hope and hope is lost again!
  Hurteth it doth my heart so used to be.

RIZZIO: Thy cousin Moray, Grace, regent maun be.
  But for thy actions causing stirrings rife,
  We yet had made peace settled through the land
  And ended had, besides, blood-boltered strife
  That brother did set against brother
  And waggle willy against the wife

DARNLEY: James, thy son, is sure our king proclaimed,
  And thou, my gracious sister, must retire
  To towered Leven's Loch, the whence if
  Thou escape, it smaller now shall be of
  Consequence than sparrow dying death
  Midst rotting eaves, or totty moose in hole.

They leave with grandeur and a sennet.[40]

Scene 22

MORTON *is working at a desk. A* GUARD *enters.*

GUARD: Maister Knox, ma lord.

MORTON: Aye.

GUARD *leaves.* KNOX *enters.*

MORTON: It's nae good comin tae me, Knox.

KNOX: You're the leader of the Protestant nobles.

MORTON: So is Moray.

KNOX: I believed you to be an honest and a godly nobleman, ready to fight for the kirk. I had believed you would continue in that ardent support.

MORTON: A dae, Knox, A dae. Dinnae doot it fir a meenit, man.

KNOX: Then I cannae understand why you seem so . . . so complaisant now.

MORTON: A'm no. Jist workin quietly an strangly fir the faith we baith serve, Maister Knox. Ye're a hasty man fir the kirk, an A admire it in ye, bit the state maun hasten slowly.

KNOX: Moray says the kirk is the creature of the state.

MORTON: We are the state, Knox. Us. The nobles. Aye were an aye will be. They that hae the lands an the moneys. Moray was aye yer lord an weel ye ken it. Bit we look favourably on yer kirk.

KNOX: The Lord's kirk.

MORTON: The Lord's kirk. Jist so. Believe that. Time will show.

KNOX: A havenae much time left me.

MORTON: Man, man, the Lord's will will be done. Is that no certain?

KNOX: Aye.

MORTON: We will work an pray thegither.

KNOX goes. MORTON takes out a paper, reads it, shakes his head.

RUTHVEN enters.

MORTON: Ruthven.

RUTHVEN: Aye.

MORTON reads on.

RUTHVEN: The kirk isnae pleased wi the cooncil's delay.

MORTON: Jist so, ma lord. Jist so.

RUTHVEN: Ye're turnin intae anither Lethington, Morton. Anither servant.

MORTON: A've been in exile an A've seen oor side win. A dinnae need tae breathe fire.

MORAY enters.

MORAY: Is that the report on the Hamiltons?[41]

MORTON: Aye. (*Gives* MORAY *paper*)

RUTHVEN: Hamiltons! Vipers!

MORAY: Fir Christ sake, Ruthven, is it no aboot time ye improved they auld words ye've been giein us these mony years?

RUTHVEN turns away.

MORAY: The danger is my sister. As lang as she's a prisoner every malcontent will want tae lead his revolt. The Hamiltons think they can come intae the game late an clear the table.

MORTON: Whit are we tae dae wi her?

MORAY: A dinnae ken, If she escaped, we could try her fir treason against her son.

RUTHVEN: Escape! Thon vicious hoor.

MORAY: Bit escape's nae use. We'd hae difficulty makin it real enough. An if we let the Hamiltons dae it, it would encourage them.

RUTHVEN: She could drown escaping.

MORTON: An see whit France would say.

RUTHVEN: Since when hae ye worried aboot France?

MORAY: She's also Elizabeth's cousin.

MAITLAND *enters. He is older.*

MAITLAND: Mair reports, ma lords.

RUTHVEN: Reports, reports, reports. This land is run by reports.

MORTON: It's the way tae ken whit ye're daein an goin tae dae. An why.

RUTHVEN: Ye're turnin cold, Morton.

MORTON: A ken hoo tae rule.

RUTHVEN: Ye dinnae rule.

MORTON: A work wi Moray.

MORAY: An A rule, Ruthven.

RUTHVEN: Aye. (*leaves*)

MAITLAND: A hotheid.

MORAY: A bloody fool. There's trouble tae be sorted yet, bit we've won share enough. Gie me thae reports, Maitland. Come an see me in a few meenits, gentlemen, when A've seen these. (*leaves*)

MAITLAND: Aye seekin a settlement.

MORTON: Aye a balance. Aye changin.

MAITLAND: Ye're turnin awfy shairp, Morton.

They leave.

Scene 23

LENNOX *is sitting in a chair, dressed as an old woman. He is knitting.* KNOX *enters, dressed also as an old woman.* LENNOX *puts down his knitting.*

LENNOX: Oh dearie me, is it yersel, Jeannie Knox?

KNOX: Aye, it's me, Aggie Lennox.

LENNOX: Sic a ding ye gied ma pair pulsin hert. Hirplin in there the like o an oossie puddock.

KNOX: Aye, hinnie. It's a dour lift aboon us baith an a queer eldritch nicht the nicht. The birdies an the beasties, Aggie, the birdies an the beasties is ower awfy restless. The hens're ill tae lay an the kye's kicked ower the mune. The hoonds're howlin, the hoolets hootin, and, hoots, it's gey eerie the nicht, a nicht fir bogles an whigmaleeries.

MARY HAMILTON *enters as* MARY.

MARY H.: Is everything ready, my women?

LENNOX: It's a cauld an oonchancie wey the ravens wheech roon the tooer though.

MARY H.: Yes. I think so. You have been faithful servants to me.

KNOX (*sobs into a handkerchief*): Oh, dinnae say thon, madam.

MARY H.: You have.

LENNOX: A ken, bit dinnae say it, madam. (*sobs into a handkerchief*)

KNOX: Aw, ma lady, aye, ma lady, bit ye're a braw sowel, ma lady. Ma mither, God rest her sowel, whaurever it may be, ma auld mither, wise wummin that she wis, aye said a bonny lass wis a bonny lass an ye cannae gainsay thon. She aye said it an the gipsy Tam wi the reid ee aye swore she hid the second sicht.

LENNOX: She needed it wi her cross-een.

MARY H.: Tonight's the night, ladies.

KNOX: Oh aye, the nicht. Weel, it's no a braw bricht moonlicht nicht the nicht.

LENNOX: Richt eneuch.

KNOX: Aye, ma lady. Whit nicht wid it be?

LENNOX: The nicht, Jean, the nicht.

KNOX: Och aye, Aggie. The nicht?

MARY H.: It is a long way I must go tonight to my destined destiny.

KNOX: Eh? When?

LENNOX: Muckle hoodie-facit puddin ye are. The nicht.

MARY H.: Is Willie Hamilton ready?

LENNOX: Aye, ma lady. He's ready. Reid-shanks Willie Hamilton, son a Cuddy-heidit Jamie that mairried on tae Spavin-fuitit Jessie o the drummlin linn. He's a braw laddie, so he is.

KNOX: A braw boy.

LENNOX: A braw boy.

MARY H.: Then let him enter. It is a hard thing to bear this imprisonment on a narrow tower in a deep loch. Mewed up here, I have felt nothing, nothing, I swear, but pain in my heart. But little Willie will free me.

LENNOX: Willie, will he?

KNOX: Will he?

LENNOX: Aye, Willie

MARY H.: I shall ride away through the darkness, up and down through the night, to freedom. I am ready. Let my peoples come.

LENNOX: Come on then, Willie.

MORAY *enters, dressed as* WILLIE HAMILTON, *a shambling oaf.*

LENNOX: Whit a sleekit mannie, ye are noo, carle. Aye though, toots, A'm gettin on noo, bit ye're a fine laddie.

KNOX: Sit yersel doon noo, laddie. Hoo's yer mither gettin alang noo, son?

LENNOX: He's weel brocht up, though. Nane a yer rough gomerels that cry theirsels jailors.

MORAY: Ma lady, the boats is ready an A'm at yer service, bit. (*giggles*)

MARY H.: This is most noble of you, Willie.

MORAY: Oh, aye, hen. It's ma duty like, bit.

KNOX: D'ye tell me that noo? (bustling WILLIE *to a seat*) There's a thing. Noo, afore ye gan sit yersel doon an hae a wee dram tae yersel .

LENNOX: He hisnae the time, ye daft auld besom. Hae ye goat aw ye need?

MARY H.: We must fly. Time passes and I now see hope of a new release.

LENNOX: Dinnae run afore yersel, hen, yer majesty. Time disnae wait fir onybody, bit whiles we maun wait fir time.

MORAY: Is that right?

LENNOX: When A look at ye, Willie, ye'll no be wantin tae gan oot in it jist yet. Warm yersel by the fire an gie an auld wummin the chance tae hae a look at ye.

MARY H.: My freedom beckons me from beyond the woods. I must plunge to my destiny.

KNOX: Stoap fiddlin wi the lad, Agnes.

LENNOX: Aye. Hiv ye goat everything, then? Jist check. It'll no tak a meenit.

MORAY: See, ah've goat everythin A need. Here. Hanky, money, key. Key! Ah've firgot the key.

KNOX: He's firgot the bliddy key.

LENNOX: There's nae need fir that language.

KNOX: Willie Hamilton, ye're a muckle stupit, docent, donnart, threepin gangrel.

MORAY: It's no ma fault.

LENNOX: That's whit they aw say.

MORAY: Ah never meant it, bit.

KNOX: Ye never meant it. Yer maw never meant tae hae ye. Ye great stookie.

LENNOX: Aye, bit naebody's perfect, Jeannie, jist the same.

KNOX: Aye, bit he disnae need tae mak a profession o't.

MORAY: Here it is. It fell doon ma breeks.

LENNOX: Doon yer breeks, ye say? See, ma hert. Here, A'll get it fir ye, Willie.

WILLIE: Here, whit are ye daein, bit?

KNOX: Behave yersel, Aggie. In front o the lass.

LENNOX: A'm jist tryin tae help the boy.

KNOX: At the age ye are tae.

MARY H.: We must hasten.

MORAY: Okey-dokey.

KNOX: Are ye aff, then?

MORAY: Aye, bit.

KNOX: Weel, see an enjoy yersels an hiv a gid time. An dinnae ye stay oot late. Ye're a fine laddie.

LENNOX: Are ye aw warmed up, ma laddie? It's a gey sair nicht an thwart.

KNOX: The trees are yammerin. An thon's a bad sign A'm thinkin.

MARY H.: Willie, are you ready to free me?

MORAY: A'll try ma best an that, ken.

MARY H.: Then let us plunge on to our fate.

LENNOX: Thon's the wey.

KNOX: Dae they no mak a braw pair? It gars ye greet jist tae think on't.

MARY H.: To escape from this Loch Leven again. To raise my standard. To fight again. Let me look once more on this prison that I may remember it and forget it. Let us go to my glorious fate.

MORAY: We'll row tae the land. It'll be a long ride the night.

MARY H.: Over the loch to freedom. Over the sea to sky.

LENNOX: We'll jist see ye aff, though.

KNOX: Jist tae say cheerybye an that.

WILLIE: The door's jammed.

LENNOX: A'll see tae it. It's they jilors that hisnae iled it again. (*Shoulders door open*)

MARY HAMILTON *and* MORAY *leave.*

KNOX: A bonnie pair.

LENNOX: A'd nae idea he wis sae muscular.

KNOX: A'd nae idea ye wis sae muscular.

They leave.

Scene 24

This scene switches from one side of the stage to the other. On the one side is MARY *with her* MAID *and on the other* MORTON *and* RUTHVEN *in a church.*

MARY *is sitting, sewing. Her* MAID *sits near her.*

MARY: I hear that Bothwell is dead.

MAID: Yes, madame.

MARY: Forgotten. Elizabeth has been so unkind. I would not have deposed her. I would have waited till she died to be Queen.

MAID: Yes, madame.

MARY *rises to her feet to put away sewing. She has a formidable limp. The* MAID *takes her sewing for her. She limps back to her seat.*

MARY: Bothwell. Even Bothwell's baby twins died from me. And now my son will not hear from my letters unless that I call him the King.

MAID: Dinnae think o't, madame.

MORTON *and* RUTHVEN *are standing to sing. The tune of "I to the Hills Will Lift Mine Eyes" is heard.*

RUTHVEN: Archbishops in the kirk!

MORTON: It's aye easier tae control thon way. They've had eleven years tae theirsels. Noo they've gied us the land, they can buckle under. An A'll tell ye mair. A'm cawin the Catholic Huntlys an the Catholic Hamiltons thegither wi me, an A'm makin peace.

RUTHVEN: The Hamiltons killt Moray. They shot him in Linlithgow.[42]

MORTON: Aye.

RUTHVEN: He was a martyr fir the faith.

MORTON: The best thing aboot martyrs is that they're deid.

They sit and pray.

MORTON: The Hamiltons, hooever, are alive, an they're talkin tae us.

RUTHVEN: They're papes.

MORTON: Ye're daft, Ruthven. Ye're no a rebel against the queen noo. A'm regent. We hae the boy an we hae the power. We're the rulers.

RUTHVEN: Bit they're our enemies. Amen.

MARY *sits alone. Her* MAID *is standing behind her, sleepy.*

MARY: Elizabeth, I never meet her. She never meets me. Why does she fear me to lock me this way? Poor Elizabeth. She is jealous. I have a child and a birth legitimate. I am not bastard and I am not barren. It must be the pox of her father that harms her. Do you sleep?

MAID: No, madame.

MARY: Rest yourself. (*the* MAID *leaves*) She has never met me. We are nothing to the other, nothing but something, some figure in a game. We do not know one another. I am only a person.

MORTON *and* RUTHVEN *are still at prayer.*

MORTON: Moray shot. Moray was the richt yin, Moray an his settlement. Lennox regent; Lennox died, an auld man, nae hert.

Mar Regent; Mar died, nae hert. In three years as mony regents. Maitland died by his ain hand; lost hert tae rule. A made ma ain way here. A'll talk tae the Hamiltons. A've hert fir rulin.

RUTHVEN: Ye've nae faith, nae honour.

MORTON: A workit wi Moray an made ma power. A'll hae nae warrin nobles an A'll hae a quiet kirk. Ye can work wi me if ye like. Amen.

There is the sound of clearing throats. MORTON *rises.*

RUTHVEN: Amen. (*rises to sing*) The auld queen?

MORTON: Mary? (*laughs*) A figment o the imagination. Wha cares aboot her?

RUTHVEN: It's a travesty.

MORTON: Aye, son, it's aw a travesty.

MARY *is sitting alone.*

MARY: I sit and plot now to make pass the time. I can plot now for only the death. I am alone. Always I was alone. I have failed. I have made no-one happy. No-one has made me happy. I have done nothing. Nothing. All that blood, all that hope, and all that blood from my body in births. And the Scots call me whore, the English danger, and the Catholics they already call me martyr. They call me all these things and I am no-one. Who cares about me? I could be neither public nor private. Myself. I am nothing. All my life is this pain.

A giant cardboard cut-out of MARY *descends. The* CAST *appear behind her. She sits still as they move forward, singing the* COMICS' *song:*

>   There's a wee royal hame
>   Whaur a lassie sits alane
>   A-waitin for her laddie wha's sae far far away
>   She kens he'll no forget . . . (CAST *freeze*)

MARY (*stands*): All my death this pain.

THE END

MARY – GLOSSARY

The glossary consists of some technical and less commonly used terms as well as Scots words and spellings. The gloss of Scots terms here does not include words ending in -it, the equivalent of -ed, or -in, the equivalent of -ing, when the meaning of the word can be deduced from forms shared with English, e.g. acquittit, 'acquitted', or cawin, 'cawing'.

A: I
aboon: above
aboot: about
accoont: account
aff: off
afore: before
ain: own
airmy: army
alane: alone
alang: along
anither: another
arenae: aren't
argie bargie: dispute
aroon: around
atween: between
auld: old
aw: all
awa, awaw: away
awbody: everyone
awfy: awfully (intensifier)
awready: already
aye: yes; always
ayewis: always
bairn: child
baith: both
baw: ball
beasties: beasts, animals
besom: contemptuous expression for a woman
bevvies: alcoholic drinks
bidit: stayed
bit: but (sometimes uttered to mark the end of an utterance)
bliddy: bloody
blood-boltered: matted with blood
bogle: ghost, phantom
bonnie, bonny: pretty
braeside: hillside
braw: handsome
breeks: trousers, pants
bricht: bright
brither: brother
brocht: brought
cairrying: carrying
cannae: can't
canny: shrewd, careful
carefu: careful
carle: old fellow, common man
cauld: cold
chairge: charge
chaps: chap-books, printed booklets
cheerybye: informal farewell
complaisant: obliging
cooncil: council
coonts: counts
coot: species of diving bird
couldnae: couldn't
cratur: creature
cry: call
cuddie, cuddy: donkey; stupid person
dab hand: expert
dae: do
deid: dead
deil: devil
didnae: didn't
ding: knock, strike
dinnae: don't
disnae: doesn't
docent, dozent: stupid
dochter: daughter
doesnae: doesn't
donnart: stupefied, foolish
doo: dove, pigeon
doon: down
doot: doubt; believe [nae doot: no doubt; I doot: I believe]

doth: does
dour: stern
dram: small measure of liquor
drap: drop
drummlin: troubled, gloomy
dug: dog
ee, een: eye, eyes
efter: after
eldritch: uncanny
elsewhaur: elsewhere
eneuch: enough
ere: before
erse: arse; ma erse: expressing scornful disbelief
fa: fall
facit: faced; hoodie-facit: crow-faced
fae: from
faither: father
firever: forever
flair: floor
folliers: followers
fowk: folk, people
freends: friends
fu: full
fuitit: footed
gan: go
gangrel: tramp, vagabond
gar: make
gaun: going; gone
gawp: gape, stare
gey: very
ghaist: ghost
gid: good
gie, giein, gied: give, giving, gave
girn: grumble, express discontent
glen: valley
glesca: glasgow
gloriositities: mispronounced 'gloriosities' with the final syllables expressed as 'titties', suggesting 'breasts'
goat: got
gomerel: fool, stupid person
gowf: golf
gowk: scarecrow; stupid person
gratefu: grateful
greet: weep; welcome
hae: have
hail: whole
haly: holy
hame: home
hasnae: hasn't
haud: hold
havenae: haven't
heid: head; cuddy-heidit: donkey-headed, i.e. stupid
heidache: headache
helpfu: helpful
hert: heart
hieland: highland
hingin: hanging
hinnie: honey, sweetheart
hirplin: limping
hisnae: hasn't
hissel, hisself: himself
historicalary: mispronunciation of 'historically'
hiv: have
hoo: how
hoodie: hooded crow
hoodie-facit: crow-faced
hooever: however
hoolet: owl
hoond: hound
hoor: whore
hoots: stereotypical Scottish exclamation
hotheid: hothead
hunner: hundred
iled: oiled
intae: into
ir: or
isnae: isn't
ither: other
jilors: jailors
jist: just
ken, kent: know, knew
kilt: part of Highland dress, a tartan skirt reaching from the waist to the knee
kirk: church
kye: cattle
lang: long
lass, lassie, lassy: girl; young woman
lift: sky
linn: pool; cascade of water
literatury: mispronunciation of 'literary'
loch: lake
ma: my
mair: more
mairriage: marriage
mairry: marry

maist: most
maister: master
matter: matter
mak: make
mannie: diminutive of 'man'
masel: myself
masterpisses: mispronunciation of 'masterpieces'
maun, maunnae: must, mustn't
maw: familiar expression for 'mother'
meenit: minute
mew: confine, cage (falconry)
Michael Wylie: anglicised pronunciation of 'Machiavelli'
micht: might
mind: remember; pay attention to
mither: mother
mony: many
moonlicht: moonlight
muckle: large; large amount
mune: moon
mussulman: muslim
nae: no
naebody: nobody
naethin, naething: nothing
nane: none
naw: no
nicht: night
nir: nor
noo: now
okey-dokey: all right
ony: any
onybody: anybody
onyhow: anyhow
onythin, onything: anything
onywey: anyway
onyyin: anyone
oonchancie: unchancy; unlucky, ill-omened
oor: our
oorsels: ourselves
oossie: dusty, fluffy
oot: out
ootside: outside
oursels: ourselves
ower: over; too
owercame: overcame
pair: poor
pairty: party
pal: friend, chum
pape, papist, papish: Catholic
peely-wally: thin, stunted
perfuseley: mispronunciation of 'profusely'
pintle: penis
pu: pull
puddin: stupid or clumsy person
puddock: frog
pund: pound
recititation: mispronunciation of 'recitation'
richt: right
roger: have sex with
roon, roond: round
sae: so
sair: sore
sandy: diminutive of 'alexander'
sang: song
scape: escape
Schmiller: dismissive play on the name 'Schiller'
shairp: sharp
shank: leg
shebang: business
sheet: Italian pronunciation of 'shit'
shouldnae: shouldn't
sic: such
sicht: sight; second sicht: the ability to prophesy
sleekit: smooth, sly
sowel: soul
sparrie: sparrow
spavin-fuitit: afflicted by a bone disease that affects the legs of horses
stoap: stop
stookie: stucco figure; stupid person
strangly: strongly
stupit: stupid
ta: thanks
tackety bit: hobnailed boot
tactfu: tactful
tae: to
tak, taen: take, taken
Tally: Italian
Tam: Tom
tanner: sixpence
tap: top
tastefu: tasteful
te: to
telt: told
thae: those
thegither: together

theirsels: themselves
thocht: thought
thon: that
thoosands: thousands
threepin: argumentative
tooer: tower
tottie, totty: tiny
twa: two
tween: between
unkent: unknown
wan: one
wance: once
wasnae: wasn't
wee: small
weel: well
weemin: women
werenae: weren't
wey: way
wha: who
whaddya: what do you
whaur: where
whaurever: wherever
wheech: swoop
whigmaleeries: fantastic contraptions
whiles: sometimes
whins: gorse bushes
whit: what
whitfir: what for
whitsit: 'whatever it is'
wi: with
wid: would
willnae: won't
wioot, withoot: without
wis, wiz: was
wot: know
wouldnae: wouldn't
wrang: wrong
wummin: woman
yammerin: whining
ye: you
yer, yers: your, yours
yersel, yerself, yersels: yourself, yourselves
yin: one
yince: once
ying: young
youse: you (plural)
zilch: nothing

MARY – NOTES

1. Adherent of the Roman Catholic church, the oldest established branch of Christianity in western Europe, which is governed by an ecclesiastical hierarchy led by the Pope
2. Prince of Wales, Edward Tudor (1537–1553), son of Henry VIII by Jane Seymour. He reigned as Edward VI of England from 1547 until his death, aged fifteen.
3. Henry Tudor (1491–1547), King of England from 1509. He was Mary's great-uncle, his elder sister, Margaret Tudor, having married Mary's grandfather, James IV of Scotland, in 1513.
4. Title given to the eldest son of the King of France, from 1349 to 1830.
5. Adherent to a branch of Christianity that began in the sixteenth century with a movement to reform the Catholic church of perceived abuses, and became a major cause of social, religious and political conflict in Europe.
6. George Gordon, 4th Earl of Huntly (1514–1562). Member of a noble Scottish family, whose Protestantism was qualified by religious conservatism. Initially supportive of Mary, Queen of Scots, he later withdrew his support and denied her entrance to Inverness Castle in 1562. She subsequently outlawed him. and he died after being captured by James Stewart, 1st Earl of Moray, half-brother to Mary.
7. Francis II (1544–1560), King of France and Scotland from 1559 to his early death a year later. Mary married him in 1558 when he was still Dauphin, or heir to the throne.
8. A recording device.
9. Caricature of Lew Grade (1906–1998), a flamboyant, cigar-smoking, Russian-born, British media impresario, who specialised in developing British television series for the American market.
10. *A Star is Born* – American dramatic film released in 1937, and remade as a musical in 1954, 1976 and 2018.
11. Award-winning American television miniseries about an African-American family over several generations, first broadcast in 1977.
12. English actress (b. 1937) who starred in the 1971 film *Mary, Queen of Scots*.

13 Queen Elizabeth I (1533–1603), monarch of England from 1558 until her death. When Mary, her first cousin once removed, fled from Scotland to England in 1568, Elizabeth held her prisoner, fearing that she would lead a Catholic rebellion against her rule. Elizabeth eventually ordered the execution of her rival in 1587, when Mary was beheaded.
14 Friedrich Schiller, Protestant German playwright (1759–1805), author of *Maria Stuart* (1800), a verse drama about Mary's last days.
15 John Schlesinger, television actor and celebrated film and theatre director (1926–2003).
16 Niccolò Machiavelli (1469–1527), a Florentine diplomat and author of the political treatise *The Prince* (*Il Principe*), written c. 1513 but not published until the 1530s. The treatise quickly gained notoriety as an amoral account of ruthless political strategy. The name 'Michael Wylie' is a play on his surname
17 A port town in Scotland, located near Edinburgh. It was an important centre for trade and commerce during Mary of Guise's time.
18 A coal-mining village in Fife. The Palace, Kelty, is a fictional village theatre.
19 A Christian festival, occurring on 29 September.
20 A royal palace in Fife, frequently visited by Mary.
21 A metrical unit consisting of an unstressed syllable followed by a stressed one.
22 A group of islands off Scotland's north-west coast, including Uist and Staffa.
23 Island in the Hebrides (sounds like 'stuff her').
24 Group of Hebridean islands; 'Uist to' sounds like 'used to'.
25 Common name given to a cinema.
26 Exeunt (stage direction): to leave the stage.
27 Italian: 'We'd like two places together / Mary is doing very well / If you can walk there tomorrow?'
28 Italian: 'Yes.'
29 Italian: 'Yes, it's difficult.'
30 Italian: 'It's okay. I'm a wee bit tired as well.'
31 Italian: 'Tired, you poor thing?'
32 Short straps of leather or silk used in falconry to secure a hawk's legs.
33 Flies (stage direction): the fly system, an overhead system of ropes, pulleys, and weights within a theatre that enables a stage crew to 'fly' (hoist) stage machinery and people out of sight of the audience.

34 Mary's son, the future James VI of Scotland and I of England (1566–1625).
35 Mary's great-grandfather, James III of Scotland (1451–1488), killed at the Battle of Sauchieburn; some chroniclers and historians allege that he was murdered while fleeing the conflict.
36 A village north-west of Edinburgh.
37 A coastal town, thirty miles east of Edinburgh, site of a strongly fortified castle.
38 Scottish scholar and poet, George Buchanan (1506–1582) composed a Latin poem to celebrate Mary's marriage to the dauphin in 1558, but his attitude to her soured, and, after the murder of Darnley, he helped prepare the case that led to her execution. Buchanan became tutor to Mary's son, the future James VI and I.
39 A freshwater lake in Kinross; Lochleven Castle was the site of Mary's imprisonment from 1567–1568, when she was forced to abdicate and flee to England.
40 Sennet (stage direction) set of notes on the trumpet or cornet, to accompany the ceremonial entrance or exit of a group of actors.
41 The Hamiltons were a powerful family of Scottish Catholic nobles, whose members supported Mary before and after her escape to England.
42 A town situated around twenty miles west of Edinburgh; site of a royal palace which was Mary's birthplace.

AN ISLAND IN LARGO

by Sue Glover

*First performed at The Byre Theatre, St Andrews,
1 October 1981*

Cast

Alexander Selkirk	*Alec Heggie*
Maggie Bell Selcraig)	*Jeni Giffen*
Frances Candis)	
Euphan Selcraig	*Rose McBain*
Sophia Bruce	*Wilma Duncan*
Jock Selcraig)	*Alan Watters*
Captain Stradling)	
Daniel Defoe)	
Admiralty Official)	
John Selcraig)	*Garry Stewart*
Captain Woodes-Rogers)	
Hunter)	
Frank Hall)	

AUTHOR'S INTRODUCTION

Sue Glover

I never walk along Largo beach without thinking about, or imagining, Selkirk. What kind of restless loon would try to prolong a castaway existence? Buy a pack of goats, acquire a pack of cats, and dance with the animals up on the 'Rise'? Considering how fiercely the Kirk came down on anyone (Selkirk was severely and publicly chastised for getting a barber to cut his hair one Sabbath), he was flirting dangerously with trouble. The Kirk had long, unfriendly arms, and enormous power.

I'd told Adrian Reynolds, Director of the Byre Theatre in St Andrews, that one day (i.e. 'not now') I wanted to 'do' Selkirk. But he was immediately smitten with the idea and gave me a commission.

Selkirk is the real deal – a writer's deal, I mean: a character to sink your teeth into, and chew over: loudly vocal; aggressive, argumentative; impossible to live with – or even near; disruptive in the home; in the family business. So that everyone, except possibly his mother, was delighted when he was off to sea again. On board ship the same kind of behaviour ensued, though possibly with a strong, and intelligent Captain he might have been more reasonable. But no, he's not mad. Well, maybe a bit unhinged – but sane enough to jump a ship when he knows it's going to sink. Sane enough to keep himself sane when he's alone on the island; to hide when he sees a French ship coming into the bay, and stay hidden till the ship is well on its way.

Plays can't get moving till there's at least one strong voice – and not before the character has developed the voice at least slightly. Monologue or dialogue: it is the words that give the blood to the play. It's the words that set the scene, place and time, as well as giving information about the character(s), and shape of the play.

This play (my second – much more difficult than the first to write) needs no scenery. A rock, small earth or rocky dais for Selkirk to declaim from, talk to God, etc. is the only thing needed – and his small bag of tools and utensils. Anything more seems quite superfluous to me, and would probably look pantomimish. None of my plays need much in the way of a set, and won't benefit from one.

This play never saw Edinburgh, Glasgow, Traverse or Tron. The Byre Theatre was, during the late 1970s and 1980s, described (by someone who worked there) as the Bermuda Triangle of Scottish theatre. Cruel, but something in it. Whenever it seemed as if the Bermuda cloud was lifting, it settled again, a bit lower.

The play was turned down flat by a theatre in the West, soon after the Byre production. The theatre said Selkirk made a very unsuitable working-class hero. Still don't know what to make of that.

Cast

ALEXANDER SELKIRK

EUPHAN MACKIE SELCRAIG

SOPHIA BRUCE

MAGGIE BELL SELCRAIG

FRANCES CANDIS

JOHN SELCRAIG

JOCK SELCRAIG

CAPTAIN STRADLING

HUNTER

DANIEL DEFOE

CAPTAIN WOODES-ROGERS

FRANK HALL

MAN (Admiralty official/reader of minister)

One set which although minimal, must be defined (loosely, fluidly) into three areas. A: island area represents in turn, the island, the bower/cave in Largo, and ALEXANDER's general 'isolation' throughout the play. The rest of the stage is divided into two other areas, representing: B: Largo house, Bristol house (DEFOE), Public house (CANDIS) and C: perhaps JOCK's orchard, certainly Dumbarnie Links, and all SOPHIA's scenes except Act II scene 5.

AN ISLAND IN LARGO

Act I

Scene 1

Island. ALEXANDER's *sea-chest and effects.*
   ALEXANDER *has fallen asleep against, or by the open sea-chest.*
ALEX: (*muttering in sleep*) I must not sleep . . . No . . . I must not close my eyes . . . I must not sleep . . . (*half-wakes*) No – no – no! (*Shakes or punches himself awake*) Don't sleep! Don't sleep! (*Straightens up a bit, but still on the ground by the chest.*) I must not sleep while there is light on the horizon. They will come back! Stradling must repent – and turn his ship and sail back here for me. He must! . . . I have nothing . . . (*Notices contents of chest; despair, panic:*) Axe, knife, kettle, bowls, powder, firelock,[1] bullets, bedding, bible – nothing! No salt, no flour, no nails, no – nothing! (*He is clutching the Bible, almost viciously.*) God curse you, Stradling! God curse you, Captain Thomas Stradling! God send you and your ship to the bottom of the seas. As I dreamed he would. (*Looks to the horizon again.*) . . . Unless you sail back here to fetch me? (*Pleading, pitifully*) Stradling? . . . I must keep watch on the horizon. Watch and pray! (*By rote, unbelieving, chanting, and panicking*) Our Father / Which art in heaven / hallowed be thy name / Thy kingdom come / Thy will be done on earth / as it is in heaven / Give us this day our daily bread / and forgive us our trespasses / As we forgive them that trespass against us / Deliver us – . . . Deliver me! . . . Oh, God! . . . (*Trying to calm down, to find the meaning in the words, more slowly, his eyes lowered on the Bible this time:*) Our Father, which art in heaven, hallowed be thy name, thy kingdom come, thy will be done on earth as it is in heaven, give us this day – . . . A ship! Our Father! Send me

a sail – and let it be English! Send Stradling back for me. (*Fury*) Make him repent! . . . I will grow mad in this place – I fear for my soul – O, God, in heaven, save me from myself, save me from self-destruction . . . (*Shakes the Bible.*) What is the use of this! – What is the use! I must not bend my head in prayer. I must watch the sea. I must watch the water all day, every day. Til darkness falls. And dare not sleep, even then – for fear I miss sight of a sail with the first light . . . Our Father, which art in heaven – let me see once more my mother's face. And the sweet salt waters of Largo[2] Bay – Our Father! . . . (*shouting, desperate, pacing*)

Lights fading on ALEX *and island.*

Which art in heaven! Hallowed be thy name! Thy kingdom come!

Scene 2

Lights up gradually on family. Largo house.

The voices of the family at morning prayers.

JOCK's *voice leading the prayers, dominating.*

JOCK, EUPHAN, JOHN, MAGGIE: (*flat dutiful chant*) . . . Thy will be done on earth as it is in heaven. Give us this day our daily bread. And forgive us our trespasses as we forgive them that trespass against us. Lead us not into temptation. But deliver us from evil. For thine is the kingdom. The power and the glory. For ever and ever. Amen.

JOCK: And where is Alexander?

EUPHAN: Something must have happened to keep him late.

JOHN: Again?

EUPHAN: (*giving* JOHN's *arm an angry shove*) That's enough. That's not fair on the lad.

JOCK: Where is he? Euphan? John? – do you know where he went?

MAGGIE: That's the second time this week he's missed prayers.

ALEXANDER *crosses to Largo house.*

ALEX: I'm here.

EUPHAN: Sandy, son!

JOCK: Where have you been?

EUPHAN: I'm sure the lad couldn't help being late.

JOCK: Late! He wasn't late, Euphan, he wasn't there!

ALEX: I'm here now.

EUPHAN: Well, but you started prayers a mite early this morning, Jock.

JOCK: We were not early! We have prayers when the family's up and dressed – and before we breakfast. Our day's work is bound, like a Bible, with morning and evening prayer.

EUPHAN: Don't go on at the lad so!

JOCK: (*to* ALEX) You're drenched! You stink of the sea!

EUPHAN: Well, let him go to the fire and get dry.

JOCK: Where have you been?

ALEX: Out in Mackie's boat.

JOCK: Since this morning?

ALEX: Since last night.

JOCK: (*to* EUPHAN) You knew about this!

EUPHAN: (*who did*) No – no – how would I know?

JOHN: Of course you knew.

MAGGIE: I knew.

EUPHAN: (*gives* JOHN *another shove*) Leave him alone, can't you? Picking on your brother like that. Go and eat, the both or you.

JOHN *and* MAGGIE *leave*.

(*to* JOCK) The lad must be hungry – let him breakfast now, before the others eat it all.

ALEX: It was a full moon. Father –

JOCK: How in the name of God can you learn the tanning trade by day if you spend your nights guddling round the Forth?

EUPHAN: Jock, the lad must dry his clothes and eat something.

JOCK: Eat! He does well enough without sleep – let him do without vittles[3] – he can go straight to the tanning shed.

EUPHAN: He'll do no such thing – if he goes without vittles so will I – and so will you.

JOCK: He'll go straight to the tanning shed and put in a day's work.

ALEX: Father – I'm no tanner.[4] I'm no tanner, and no shoemaker. And I don't want to be.

EUPHAN: (*low*) Oh, mercy!

JOCK: It's a trade. It's kept my family alive – and prosperous – it's keeping your brother John and his family now.

EUPHAN: Sandy was only thinking –

JOCK: Sandy thinks he can do better?

ALEX: I want to go to sea.

EUPHAN: (*trying to forestall argument*) Now – come and eat, come and breakfast – no good comes of bargling this way on an empty stomach.

JOCK: (*to* ALEX) You took your time –

EUPHAN: Jock! – Save your breath. Save your breath to cool your porridge!

JOCK: You took your time – deciding to be a fisherman.

ALEX: I don't want to be a tanner – or a fisherman.

JOCK: Want! What has want to do with it? Are there not enough folk in want in this parish? Will you join them? Will you live on my charity, and your brother John's?

ALEX: I'm not taking charity. I'm not taking Largo anymore, either. I'm going to sea. Not "guddling in the Forth". But the sea! The ocean! Father – there are galleys out there in the Forth – I saw them last night – ready for the Americas. They're sailing for the Isthmus of Darien.[5] For Fortune. For Scotland. God – I wish I was going with them.

JOCK: Don't blaspheme in this house.

ALEX: Why is it the only man who can blaspheme in this house is the one who takes the prayers?

JOCK: (*to* EUPHAN) You see what he's like – your Benjamin? It'd be almost as well if he went.

EUPHAN: Then let him go!

Pause. The other two stunned. EUPHAN *tearful.*

JOCK: What did you say?

ALEX: (*comes over to her, takes her by the arm*) Mother?

EUPHAN: Go and get your clothes dry, son, and put some porridge in you. Go on, now.

ALEX *suddenly kisses her, then leaves.*

JOCK: What's this! What are you trying to do? He's barely sixteen. And he's no sense, no sense in him at all. You don't want him to go!

EUPHAN: No.

JOCK: It should be me urging him to go – not you. He's thrown his mouth at me ever since he had it open.

EUPHAN: You never seemed to care about him, that's why.

JOCK: You never let me.

EUPHAN: A sickly wee babe. None of you thought he'd live. And just see him now – the finest lad in Largo!

JOCK: He must surely think he is – for you're never done telling him so!

EUPHAN: He's different from the others.

JOCK: Sandy's treated different, that's all. Sandy's spoiled. You ruin him. The others all had notions – until we knocked it out of them.

EUPHAN: You have three sons at the tanning and shoemaking, and three sons more at the fishing. Can't you let the seventh be what he wants?

JOCK: Being seventh means nothing!

EUPHAN: The seventh son of a seventh son –

JOCK: Nothing!

EUPHAN: – of an unbroken line of sons!

JOCK: (*fury*) There's nothing holy about the number seven.

EUPHAN: *And* born on a Sunday.

JOCK: He doesn't know the meaning of the Sabbath.

EUPHAN: (*still apparently unaware of his interruptions*) The luck of the Sabbath. And the gift!

JOCK: Oh, Euphan!

EUPHAN: He has a sight and sense that we have not! Well, the fisherfolk believe in him if you do not – they pay need to second sight –

JOCK: Once – or maybe twice – he's said a storm was brewing. Once he told Mackie he shouldn't go out to fish, and, yes, one of the boats was lost. Rab Wilson's was lost. But any fool could have foretold it!

EUPHAN: Well – they didn't! Only Sandy! . . . And they all say it's lucky to have him on board.

JOCK: Because he knows how to navigate, Oh, ay, he's handy with a boat, I'll give him that.

EUPHAN: Then let him go to sea! Let go! If every father thought as you –

JOCK: I'd let him go! But for you! What would you do? How would Euphan Mackie be without her seventh son?

EUPHAN: (*absolute confidence*) But he'll be back. With silver. And lace. With the luck of the Sabbath. He'll make his fortune and come back safe.

JOCK: You believe too much. Too easily. (*Suddenly very angry – with* ALEX.) His dreams told him that, did they? Dreams! Even the honest name Selcraig isn't good enough for him now. On, no, it's Alexander Selkirk he cries himself now. Makes us all a laughing stock.

EUPHAN: Selkirk's a grand-sounding name. It has a fine ring to it.

JOCK: Selcraig seemed a good enough name for you once. And an honest tanner seemed a good enough kind of a man.

EUPHAN: I'm talking about my son!

JOCK: Ay – your son! Since he could talk – and even before – he's darkened this house, divided it.

EUPHAN: He's always been a loving son to me. He's a very loving son, in his way. You couldn't stand the sight of him, the sight of his cradle even . . . Maybe it was a daughter you wanted for the seventh.

JOCK: It was you I wanted. You were a mother six times over, and still my loving friend til you bore Alexander.

EUPHAN: I'm sure I always am your wife and friend.

JOCK: You were my loving friend – til Alexander was born . . . (*awkward pause*) . . . But like he said – it's not wee fishing boats bobbing about in the Forth – it's galleons he's after, with cannons, sailing to the edge of the world.

EUPHAN: It's what he's always wanted. He'll never settle for less. Best give him your blessing and let him go.

JOCK: If you want to learn to pray – go to sea. That's what your brother Mackie says – and he should know . . . "If you want to learn to pray, go to sea" . . .

Lights fade on house.

Scene 3

Lights up on island.

A pot of some kind on a cooking fire. Two wooden or pewter bowls.

ALEX: I was listening to my mother calling on the shore. I could hear her – as clear as if these sands were Largo sands. 'Sandy, eh, Sandy son?' . . . Hers is the only voice that I can faithfully remember. The very tone of it! I wanted – I longed to hear, imagine I heard – it again. (*Anger*) But the noise got in my way! Seals and sealions mass together down there on the shore as if they had no other place on earth to live. Bawling, whelping, mating, screaming! . . . They remind me of us – seamen roaring and whoring through London or Lima[6] or any other port of call . . . The noise! It maddened me! I took my axe and waded in amongst them, hacking and slashing. Screaming at them; like them . . . Stradling! – It was Stradling's name I screamed with every blow. They should have turned on me and killed me. I saw a sailor once bitten to the bone by a seal. He died later of the wounds. Good-tempered Hopkins, well-beloved by the whole ship's company, who'd read prayers for us once a day ever since we passed the Equinox. Dead from a single seal! And here the brutes were in such crowds – why couldn't they see me? It was as if I wasn't there! I killed several and must have hurt many more. Yet the rest of them hardly seemed to notice . . . Why didn't they kill me! I stopped only when my voice cracked, and wouldn't scream. And the axe slipped in my hands because it was so sticky and thick with blood. I went to wash myself in the sea . . . I knew I was mad. Or had been mad. I took my axe and washed it very carefully and saw it glint beneath the water and thought: this is my only axe, I must take care of it, if I'm going to live. If I am going to live on this island, my life depends on this axe.

I crawled up here amongst the trees. And curled up like an animal, disgraced, disgusting. I woke next day to sunlight, and humming birds, and the sweet perfume of piemento[7] wood . . .

This is a kind of prayer . . . God . . . I will make my home amongst these trees. These last two days I have turned carpenter. (*Kind of a laugh*) With my precious axe . . . I've built one hut for myself and one for my supplies. Tomorrow I will turn tanner – like my good brother John. For I must line the huts with goatskins before the winter months . . . If I am going to live here.

These last two days I have not searched, nor even thought of searching, for a ship. I have not thought of how to leave. I've been too busy thinking of how to stay. And work has made my hungry – as well as happy . . . or at least busy – too hungry for a mere handful of wild plums, or raw herbs. So here I have prepared boiled cabbage palm, and goat stew. Flavoured with piemento nuts . . . (*very awkward*) . . . Lord:

He ladles out food into a bowl.

I have it in my mind to offer you . . . But Mr Magill, the minister at Largo, would be fair affronted at the notion of an offering! . . . Papism![8] . . . But this is my land, and I must be my own minister.

Takes the bowl of food, solemnly places it in a fitting spot.

. . . And I must thank you for my food . . . And my sanity . . . And if the rats eat it – which they will! – perhaps they'll bother me less tonight. For they're a worse plague here than they ever were on board the *Cinque Ports*[9] . . . they gnaw my feet while I sleep. *Your* rats, Father . . . (*Steps back from offering, awkward still at such communication – and still with the rats on his mind.*) . . . If the rats should eat it . . . or the cats! . . . There must be at least one hundred cats on the island – no – many more than that! You give me rats to plague me – but there are cats for comfort! Their ancestors were ships' cats, after all – they might become less wild. If they come to me for food . . . If the cats should eat this! And come for more . . . And keep the rats at bay! (*Laughing, more confident.*) This is a kind of prayer, Father. (*Devout again. Holds up food offering.*) Our Father! Which art in heaven! Bless these vittles, my house, my island, my soul . . . In the name of God, Amen.

The lights have been gradually fading on island.

Scene 4

Lights up on house in Largo.

MAGGIE *is howking a heavy pail of water into the house.*

MAGGIE: In the name of God! What have you been doing to Andrew? . . . He's away up to the tanning shed howling for John, and left me to fetch in the water . . . Sandy? . . . He says you beat him! Your own brother!

ALEX: I never beat him.

MAGGIE: He says you did.

ALEX: I was showing him a few holds, that's all. Self-defence, that's all. Just a bit of fun.

MAGGIE: Fun? We've had more than enough of your fun. There's too much work to do. They're very busy in the shed, the men . . . (*sharp*) Could you not lend them a hand?

ALEX: I'm no tanner.

MAGGIE: Oh, I forgot! Mariners are too perjink to skin leather and cobble shoes. Used to a more dainty kind of a life! You'll be telling me next that you've slaves skivvying for you on board like your mother and I slave for you here.

ALEX: Ay, we had slaves on board. And women slaves, too.

MAGGIE: No doubt! I've no doubt what kind of women they were. I've no wish to hear about them!

ALEX: Ah, but you have, Maggie Bell. You don't wish to *ask* – but you're longing to hear. There's nothing like a woman of thirty years and more – or a man for that matter – married and tied – for speering the ways of the wide, wicked, free world.

MAGGIE: Free! Oh, I'm sure you all are – *very* free!

ALEX: We had a woman slave give birth on board, once.

MAGGIE: Brought to bed with a bairn! In front of a shipful of sailors!

ALEX: We treated her very well. We gave her a cabin to herself. And a jug of thick Peruvian wine . . . (*laughs*) And told her not to do it again.

MAGGIE: A black woman?

ALEX: Yes, a negress. A seamstress and laundress.

MAGGIE: The poor wee heathen bairn!

ALEX: It was a bonny black bairn – with red hair.

MAGGIE: They're bonny, then, the black women?

ALEX: All women are bonny, when they're young.

MAGGIE *livid – but speechless.*

Of course, your Spanish women, in the Americas, they're ladies, high born. Dripping with gold. You can see their gold chains and coins and anklets shimmering through their dress. For in that heat they wear cloth woven so thin, it's near transparent.

MAGGIE: And the black women – what do they wear?

ALEX: Nothing, very much. So you see, Largo is a dull kind of a place, by comparison.

MAGGIE: Is that so? And what brings you back here, then?

Pause.

ALEX: I don't know.

MAGGIE: You've plenty tall stories, and wild tales. But what about the lace and silver you promised Euphan you'd bring her back? What about your famous fortune?

ALEX: Don't you fret – I made my fortune.

MAGGIE: And lost it, did you?

ALEX: Spent it.

MAGGIE: All of it!

ALEX: Most of it spent before we even got to London.

MAGGIE: What have you got then – that you're so much better – and so much better off! – than the rest of us?

ALEX *rises, doesn't answer.*

Where's the sense in winning a fortune and losing it again?

ALEX: (*he's at the pail of water*) It makes a lot of sense, if that's what you want.

MAGGIE: But is that what you want?

ALEX: (*he's about to drink from the pail with a dipping cup*) It was good while it lasted. The sea's still there – the sea – and the Spanish galleons. It's in my blood now . . . Navigation – that's an excitement of its own. An extra sense – almost as if depth and reef and shoreline were things to smell and taste. (*Drinks – splutters – spits out.*) God Almighty! Seawater!

MAGGIE *roars with laughter.*

MAGGIE: You were saying you'd a taste for the sea!

ALEX: You witch! You did that on purpose!

MAGGIE: Not me – it was Andrew that fetched that water – not me!

ALEX: You set that up, Maggie Bell!

ALEX *gets hold of* MAGGIE *to shake her. She's still laughing at the whole business, he's definitely not.*

MAGGIE: Let go – leave me be – let go!

ALEX: But you won't set me up again.

JOHN *enters – stops a moment to take in what is going on.*

JOHN: (*roaring*) Sandy!

ALEX *pushes* MAGGIE *roughly in* JOHN's *direction.* MAGGIE *very indignant, but still amused, teasing.*

MAGGIE: He was going to drink the brine. Andrew's filled the pail with brine. (*To* ALEX) You great lazy loon – fetch the water in for yourself next time!

ALEX *lunges towards her.*

JOHN: Leave her!

ALEX: You evil besom!

MAGGIE: It was only a bit of Andrew's fun. I thought you liked a bit of fun!

ALEX *lunges at* MAGGIE *again –* JOHN *intervenes again.*

JOHN: Leave her alone! Damn you! Do you want to fight the whole family? First you beat up Andrew, then my own wife.

MAGGIE: He's a taste for the sea – he was just saying –

ALEX *threatens* MAGGIE *again.*

JOHN: Sandy! I'll not tell you again – leave her alone.

ALEX: You leave *me* alone – all of you. I've had enough – leave off nagging, and baiting. Tell that bitch of yours to leave me alone as well.

JOHN: You deserve a bloody good thrashing.

ALEX: Just try it – go on! Try! (*He gives a wild kind of laugh.*)

MAGGIE: You tell him, John – go on, you teach him.

ALEX: I'll kill you. (*Pause . . .*) You think I wouldn't? My pistol's up the stair.

Suddenly ALEX *tries to dart past them in the direction of the stair.* JOHN *tackles him, brings him down, they're wrestling on the ground,* MAGGIE *trying to grab an arm or leg of* ALEX's *when she can.*

MAGGIE: Oh, God ... Oh, help! ... (*becoming more fearful – louder*) Murder – Help – Murder!

She's helping JOHN *keep* ALEX *down, pinned to the ground.* JOCK *enters.*

JOCK: What in hell is going on here? – Sandy! – I might have known.

MAGGIE: Keep him down! Here – Father, sit on him – he's going for his pistol to shoot us all.

ALEX *is still struggling. Eventually the two men are sitting on him.* MAGGIE *bends down to shout in his face.*

MAGGIE: You false loon – will you murder your brother *and* your father?

ALEX: (*to* MAGGIE – *with difficulty*) I'll murder you.

EUPHAN *enters.*

EUPHAN: You've the whole village gawping at the door, with their ears a-waggling – did you know? (*Sees the heap of bodies. Her very presence causes them all to slacken, become more foolish than fierce.*) In the name of heaven, what are you doing down there? (*very sharp*) John! Will you never learn to leave your brother alone?

Pause. Something like a laugh from the still smothered ALEX.

Jock! That's your own son you're sitting on! Get up!

ALEX *gives a heave. The two other men topple off him, but remain down on the floor beside him.*

EUPHAN: (*very angry*) Get up! Jock Selcraig, get up! What do you think you're doing?

JOCK: (*starts slowly to get up. Furious. Frustrated.*) I don't know what I'm doing ... All I know is ... All I know is – we had six years of quiet while Alexander was at sea ... six years. (*He regards all of them bitterly.*) I was beginning to get used to it!

He is leaving. To MAGGIE *as he passes her:*

I was getting fond of quiet. (*Muttering as he goes*) ... peace and quiet! ...

MAGGIE *is nursing her head ostentatiously.* ALEX *has started to giggle hysterically, still lying on the floor.*

EUPHAN: You're supposed to be grown men! Get up! Both of you! It's no laughing matter! Grown men!

MAGGIE: It was Sandy's fault. He hit me on the head. My head hurts.

EUPHAN: I'm not surprised it hurts. You'll do yourself a mischief, screaming like that – I could hear you at the top of the brae!

MAGGIE: It was Sandy! He was going to shoot us with his pistol!

EUPHAN: Hold your tongue. D'you want to set the whole village gawping and clacking? Get up, John, get up!

As JOHN is about to get up, ALEX pulls or trips him down on the ground again beside him.

MAGGIE: (*snivelling*) I'm going to tell the elders! My head hurts sore! I'm going to tell Mr Magill and John Guthrie and the others. (*She's exiting, turns for a parting shot.*) Sandy tried to kill us!

EUPHAN: (*to* JOHN) Now see what you've done! You'll have the whole family compeared before the pulpit! Again! (*She goes out after* MAGGIE.) Maggie Bell – come back. Right this minute – Maggie!

ALEX and JOHN still on the floor. ALEX all this time has lain, listening, giggling now and then, but not bothering to watch the proceedings, or even sit up.

JOHN: See what *I've* done! Did you hear that? See what *I've* done! It's all *my* fault!

ALEX gives another giggle. JOHN *nudges at him roughly with his foot.*

You're the very devil, Sandy. The very devil! D'you know that?

ALEX: D'you call that a fight? Man – you want to fight a Spaniard!

JOHN: Try telling Maggie that!

ALEX: You took something on when you married her!

JOHN: Try telling the Kirk Session it wasn't a real fight!

ALEX: Oh – Mr Magill!

JOHN: You can laugh. The last time *you* were supposed to appear before the pulpit you ran away to sea – and stayed away for six years!

ALEX: We could do it again!

JOHN: *We*!

ALEX: Yes. Right now, if you like. There's nothing to stop you.

JOHN: I'm married. I've bairns to look after. And a business. And Father.

ALEX: We've five brothers! Not to mention Maggie Bell – she could look after anything on her own.

JOHN: I swear to God, Sandy, the sea's addled your brains. You're more of a loon now than you ever were before. You're twenty-five. When are you going to settle?

ALEX: Going to what?

JOHN: You know what I mean . . . What did you come for?

ALEX: I wish to God I knew.

JOHN: It's a long way from London, you must have had a reason. Perhaps you had a notion to get wed . . . Don't you want children to live after you?

ALEX: No. Your brats can live after me, yours and Maggie's. And all the other Selkirk brats.

JOHN: *Selcraig. We* haven't changed our names.

ALEX: Why did you marry Maggie?

JOHN: Why shouldn't I?

A laugh from ALEXANDER.

Why not?

ALEX: And you call me daft! I ran away to sea for a few years, because I always wanted to, because I'd thought of nothing else. But you! – you maroon yourself for ever and ay in the one house with the one wife . . . because you think: why not!

JOHN: You leave Maggie out of this. We manage fine when you're not here. We all of us get on fine when you're not here.

ALEX: Then why are you trying to get me to stay? What're you needling me for – you and Maggie and Father – I'm better offer than any of you – I'm stronger than you, I've more energy, I've lost more money than you've ever made, I think faster, feel more –

JOHN: Feel! – you feel nothing. You feel for yourself, maybe, but not for others. You've been home several months – you've never noticed yet that Father's sick.

ALEX: Sick! He's not sick! He's a few years older, that's all.

JOHN: Some folk grow old very sudden, and very quick. He's tired. Too tired for the rage he used to have. It's him you get your temper from. He used to rage like you.

ALEX: I'm not like father.

JOHN: The old wives say he was a wilder loon even than you.

ALEX: I've never heard that.

JOHN: You were never home to hear it.

ALEX: All he ever does is thump the Bible. And work.

JOHN: Well. He's changed.

ALEX: (*still disbelieving*) What changed him?

JOHN: Us. The seven of us. Mother. Work . . . Not that he works much nowadays. Mother thinks he's with us in the tanning-shed – but more often than not he's in his orchard.

ALEX: Orchard?

JOHN: Behind the house – he's planted the garden out with fruit trees – have you not even noticed them?

ALEX: Not specially.

JOHN: He's there for hours – crooning over his trees. Meditating, he calls it. He's tired of us all. And melancholy.

ALEX: You mean he's tired of me! His melancholy will lift wonderfully when he hears his youngest son's gone back to sea.

JOHN: You're going, then?

ALEX: (*laughs at the thinly disguised relief*) That's the best thing for all of us –

JOHN: No – no – I didn't mean –

ALEX: I'll wait til the spring – there'll be no ships sailing til the spring. But then – I'm off . . . Don't you wish you were coming with me?

JOHN: Me? I'm John Selcraig, tanner, of Largo.

Lights are fading on Largo house area.

I don't need to change my name. I don't want to change my life.

ALEX: (*quietly*) And I am Alexander Selkirk, mariner.

He crosses to island area. Lights up on island area.

Scene 5

Island.

ALEX: (*louder*) I am Alexander Selkirk, mariner, cast away. And God gave me this island. (*Pause.*) The Lord giveth . . . And the Lord taketh away – very nearly! Very nearly! . . . You could have warned me, Father. I'm your servant and your friend. You could have sent them somewhere else! Or sent an English ship! Or none at all! Did you have to hound me with Spaniards? They were here before I knew it: their ship in the bay, their boat launched. They were beached; they were plunging through the water, shouting – shooting! I can run faster now than any man, faster than my own goats – at least you gave me that. But why? O, God! – why torment me with the sight of men and make them enemies? . . . I climbed a stout piemento tree and hid, my heart pounding, stinking with fear – so how did they not smell me? Two of them searched the ground right beneath me – I could see their bare shoulders, burnt by the sun. I prayed to you they wouldn't look up. One of them had his pistol ready. The other pissed against the very tree I hid in. He shouted something while he pissed, and laughed. They walked back together, slowly, to the beach . . . Their shoulders glistened in the sun . . .

My sweat turned to tears. In my dreams I've embraced my saviours on the shore, been treated with wonder. I've cooked them a great banquet of goat stew and gone aboard a hero . . . All day I hid from them – but close – Hungry for every sight and sound of them. They killed my goats, and felled my trees, and chased my cats. Then the sound of oars and voices carrying over water, as they rowed back to the ship . . . At night, the lights from their galleon shone, like sirens, across the bay. And in the morning they were gone.

I scavenged the beach like some foul seagull, but they'd left nothing. Only dead fires, and goat carcasses. Not even a nail! If they had only left me something wonderful and precious – a sack of flour – a jar of salt! But after I had used it all I would have had to learn to do without again.

. . . If they'd been French . . . I might have let myself be taken prisoner . . . I think I might have. If they had been English . . . (*pause*) . . . If they had been English, I'd be on board now with a hundred souls to talk to.

. . . I can run faster now than any man, faster than my own goats. I can outwit a shipload of Spaniards. I have the moon to talk to, and my God. And my cats. I have no dreams. I wake content. I feel nothing – save the Spaniards – hate nothing – save the memory of

Stradling. I would rather stay here than sail again with Stradling. Rather live here than die with Stradling. (*Savouring this.*) Stradling is dead. Stradling must be already dead.

Scene 6

On board ship.

HUNTER: Captain Charles Pickering is dead. God rest him.

ALEX: (*stepping down to ship area*) God rest his soul.

HUNTER: And Captain Stradling says –

ALEX: Who? (*A strangled shout of disgust.*)

HUNTER: Stradling – Captain Thomas Stradling now. (*He spits contemptuously.*)

ALEX: God blast him! My God, we're all damned now.

HUNTER: He says Pickering is to be buried tomorrow. Not out here at sea – but on the island of Granda. With full honours.

ALEX: That's the very least he can do for a man that's twenty times the seaman Stradling is.

HUNTER: So say we all. He was a fair man, Pickering. Well – fair enough. The men are edgy. Some of them talk of staying on La Granda after the burial. But that's just burial talk – bravado.

ALEX: Bravado never made more sense. Stradling will wreck us all. The man can't tell a brace from a bow-line. I'd sooner be captained by the ship's carpenter.

HUNTER: Or by yourself?

ALEX: Why not? I'm more fit for it than Stradling – or anyone else on board.

HUNTER: Ah, but you aren't enough a gentleman.. You need a nose for wines and wigs and fancy waistcoats. You need to know how to talk without blinding and cursing when you get back on shore!

ALEX: That's what you need – is it! – to win a commission and a ship!

HUNTER: We must weather him out – if he be the devil himself.

ALEX: Why should we?

HUNTER: There's too much at stake – that's why. We're only on the threshold of the hunt. No killings yet. If we cause trouble now we'll be defrauded of our wages and our plunder share – or at the least flayed and pickled on the mast.

ALEX: We'll be pickled any way. We'll pickle in the sea if Stradling sails this ship.

HUNTER: You drank too much hipsy last night.

ALEX: Last night – while Pickering lay dying in his cabin – I dreamt that this ship foundered – and every man slipped under with her.

HUNTER: That was hipsy. Foul drink, hipsy. Much better stick to rum.

ALEX: There must be something we can do.

HUNTER: Nothing.

ALEX: Short of murder!

HUNTER: D'you want to hang when we get back to Plymouth?[10] The men might be with you, Selkirk, but not the other officers. They're gentlemen, remember?

ALEX: Gentlemen! – like Stradling? The last to board the enemy in battle, the first to take bribes from the Portuguese. A gentleman who damn near starves his own cabin-boy – and has a head so stuffed with education, there's no room left in it for memorising sea-charts and sea-lore! – a head so weak it falls apart from half a glass of hipsy!

HUNTER: We'll weather him out – we have to. His other officers all carry arms now.

ALEX: Since when?

HUNTER: Since Pickering died, and Stradling gave the orders.

STRADLING: *(calling off)* Hunter!

HUNTER: We'll weather him out – Stand fast! And weather him out!

STRADLING *enters.*

STRADLING: Hunter!

STRADLING *slightly disconcerted to see* ALEX *with* HUNTER. *He and* ALEX *barely acknowledge each other.*

HUNTER: Sir?

STRADLING: Eight of the crew have taken the yawl[11] and gone ashore. *(Embarrassed.)* With their sea-chests and belongings.

ALEX *grins from ear to ear.*

Mr Barnaby is taking some men – well armed – in the longboat.

We must retrieve the yawl – and those of the deserters worth retrieving. He needs you to go with him.

HUNTER *leaves.* ALEX *is about to go with him.*

– *not* Mr Selkirk. I do not think we need Mr Selkirk to reason with unruly crew. Why do you smile?

ALEX: What could there be to smile at? On the day that Captain Pickering dies?

STRADLING: What indeed?

ALEX: Which is no doubt why some men have already jumped your ship.

STRADLING: There is always some dead wood to be found on board.

ALEX: I know exactly what you mean.

STRADLING: I'm not sure that you do – but you will, in time you will . . . I have made Mr Barnaby first mate.

ALEX: (*appalled*) Barnaby! Barnaby is steward! He pours the wine and rinses glasses.

STRADLING: He's a man of good sense and education.

ALEX: If he were qualified in the first place to be a sea officer, why would he have been serving as a steward? Particularly since he is your kinsman!

STRADLING: I have also made him agent.

ALEX: You can't do that – not without agreement from the men.

STRADLING: Mr Barnaby is well qualified to divide out accurately whatever prizes this ship takes.

STRADLING *goes.*

ALEX: Prizes! Prizes! (*Laughs grimly; crosses to island.*)

Scene 7

Island.

ALEX: What prizes would we have taken? In a ship governed by fools! – Pickering's death – and my nightmares – they destroyed all hope of prizes.

After Pickering's burial on La Granda, the ocean was empty of all other ships – no prizes! – but seemed crowded with omens.

Vast shoals of seals and porpoises, and in the sky great flocks of chequered pintados,[12] and several albatrosses. Our vessel was hemmed in, slowed down, by endless beds of slimy seaweed, and colonies of white snakes – not plants, nor animals, but lifeless jellies – like dead souls . . . Each day I watched these things, and laughed and talked about them with the others . . . But every night I saw the ship sink under and succumb to them.

A ship of death. Pickering's death had killed our hopes. I wished myself on land – even an island like La Granda, uninhabited except for eight deserters . . . And whenever I met with Hunter, he'd clap me on the shoulder and growl "weather him out – stand fast – we must weather him out, if he be the devil himself!"

Scene 8

On board ship.

STRADLING is reading from a letter he holds. He is incredulous, furious – also afraid.

STRADLING: . . . "the reasons of our troubling you at this time are: we have good reason to believe that if what fortune we make this voyage should be carried to London, we should never receive half thereof . . . that the articles we signed at Plymouth were never read in our hearing . . . How dangerous is it for poor men to trust their fortune in the hands of the rich? . . . we make bold to present you with our due rights . . . that all plunder should be appraised and divided as soon as possible after the capture; also every person to be sworn and searched . . . That Captain Stradling should give the whole cabin-plunder to be divided . . ."! (*To* ALEX, *livid*) It was you drew up this letter!

ALEX: No, sir. It was devised and signed by all the men – that's why they sign it in a circle, to show you they are of one mind.

STRADLING: This is a mutinous document!

ALEX: No, sir – it shows the men to be uneasy. They want justice, that's all. And they'll work better if –

STRADLING: Justice! I'll give them justice –

ALEX: They do not think that Mr Barnaby means justice.

STRADLING: You are the only one who fights with Mr Barnaby.

ALEX: No, sir. For my part, I think there's time enough to quarrel over plunder, when we have found some. We've done no *real* business since Captain Pickering died. Which is hardly surprising since most of the time our Captain is ignorant of where we are! – and lies off the island of Juan Fernandez,[13] swearing all the while that we are in the wrong place, off the wrong island – and proceeds to sail south – in the wrong direction!

STRADLING: Considering the weather conditions, it was a natural error.

ALEX: Considering my advice, it was an obstinate one.

STRADLING: I am not happy to take advice from a man who sails by superstition.

ALEX: I have a sound knowledge and respect for these seas, and a reputation as a navigator.

STRADLING: But you sail too close to the wind, Mr Selkirk. I should have left you on La Granda with the other, I warn you –

ALEX: Warn me! *You* warn me! (*He is moving to island.*) I don't need you to warn me!

Scene 9

Island.

ALEX: God warns me! . . . (*ever so slightly unsure of his self-justification*) Father: it was you who sent me here to Juan Fernandez. Not Stradling! It was not my anger sent me here – it was my dreams. You warned me of death and drowning in a dream. And sent a sea of blood. And Stradling wouldn't listen. The man deserved to die.

A ship is a gentle creature. She meets the seas in a give and take way. A gale on board at sea is quieter than the same wind blowing through trees or houses – *if* the seamanship is good! . . . She was a bonny ship, the *Cinque Ports*. Ninety tonnes. Sixteen guns, seventy men. Dead souls –- all pickled in the brine . . . Weather him out? – though he be the devil himself? – Oh, Hunter! – not this blind, deaf, *idiot* devil!

Scene 10

On board ship. STRADLING's *cabin.*

STRADLING *at desk or table writing in log book.* HUNTER *enters, with small bucket of rope.*

STRADLING: (*barely looking up*) What is it, Hunter?

HUNTER: We're still becalmed, Captain.

STRADLING: Yes.

HUNTER: Captain, the sea's still blood – blood red from here to the horizon.

STRADLING: The wind'll dissipate it soon.

HUNTER: There's no sign of wind, sir, no breath of it. And a silence like a grave.

STRADLING: Well, take a deeper sounding.

HUNTER: We've taken soundings regular – since dawn. A hundred and seventy fathoms of line. Look! It can't be some kind of spawn, as you say – it doesn't separate. It's the very sea that's made of blood, not something in it.

STRADLING *examines the sample.*

Mr Selkirk bade me ask you come on deck, sir.

STRADLING: Why?

HUNTER: The men grow fearful, Captain – they say . . . this is a ship of death.

STRADLING: Superstitious nonsense!

HUNTER: They remember Mr Selkirk's dreams.

STRADLING: What dreams? . . . Well? – go on, Hunter – what dreams has *Mr* Selkirk had?

HUNTER: (*reluctant*) He dreams continually that the *Cinque Ports* slips beneath the waves, sir . . . and all the men are drowned.

STRADLING: And you believe him? Ha! If he's right – that means my ship will sink – continually.

HUNTER: He's blessed with second sight, sir. His premonitions have proved right before.

STRADLING: (*furious*) Fetch Mr Selkirk here!

HUNTER *goes to retrieve a sample.*

Leave that, man, leave it!

HUNTER *goes.*

Dreams! From a bull-headed, quarrelsome Scotch bastard who navigates by second-sight! . . . and holds most of my men in the palm of his hand.

ALEX *enters.*

STRADLING: What is the meaning of this?

ALEX: I thought you ought to come on deck, sir.

STRADLING: What for? We're in flat calm.

ALEX: I've never seen a thing like this before – nor even heard of it – and I know these seas.

STRADLING: If you weren't an officer, Selkirk, I'd flog you senseless. You know I know that you're deliberately feeding the superstition of the crew.

ALEX: The men all take it as a sign of danger, sir.

STRADLING: Because you want them to.

ALEX: We are in danger, sir.

STRADLING: From some pink fish spawn? Or from your dreams?

ALEX: We are in danger from our own ship, sir. Captain: my dreams are as truthful as the colour of this sea.

STRADLING: Your dreams were manufactured to incite first fear, then mutiny.

ALEX: If you won't think of your own skin – think of your crew – and your ship!

STRADLING: Your dreams date from Captain Pickering's death.

ALEX: They do. God rest his soul, and keep him. Look at this vessel now! Two men have to man the pumps night and day. *Still* we let in so much water our provisions are destroyed. We have no spare sails, or tackle. Half our crew lie sick!

STRADLING: Half our crew are always sick.

ALEX: We would sail better and fight better if they were got well . . . and save some of them from dying . . . Captain Stradling, I have seen rats leave this ship!

STRADLING: You'll leave this ship! I'll see to that! Get out!

ALEX: Return to Juan Fernandez. Repair your ship – and your men. Or my dream becomes your nightmare.

STRADLING: Get out! . . . (*calls him back*) Selkirk!

ALEX: Sir.

STRADLING *deliberately not looking at him, busy with his snuff box.*

STRADLING: The bucket.

ALEX *doesn't move.* STRADLING *forced to turn and look at him.*

STRADLING: Remove the bucket. The spawn.

ALEX *picks up the bucket slowly, with menace, almost threatening* STRADLING *with it.* STRADLING *turns away again.*

I had already decided to make for Juan Fernandez. As soon as the wind lifts, that is.

ALEX *smiles with satisfaction, goes off.* STRADLING *busy with his snuff, and his fury. Fade.*

Scene 11

Island.

ALEX's *voice (tape) calling against background of seashore, or echoing valley; distressed:*

Sheba! . . . Sheba! Sheeeeeeeeeeeba! . . . (*etc*).

Lights up on ALEX, *defeated, dejected.*

ALEX: God: look after the soul of the most favourite, most faithful, and most beautiful of my cats. For I know now she must be dead. She would never stay away from me this long. I've searched the whole island – from Cumberland Bay to the Rocky Point, from the Monkey Key right across the woods and valleys to the Sugar Loaf Bay. I have a hundred cats more – to share my food, and keep the rats from me at night. But she was the first I called by name – Sheba! The first comfort and companion. And not from cupboard love, either! Oh, no – on her own terms, always – which were: curiosity; and intelligence; and amused affection. When I lay on my stomach and gazed at the fire-flames in the dusk, she would lie in the small of my back and purr like a she-lion . . .

At first I did not count the days she had been missing. I'm not sure now how many it is . . . She must by now be dead . . . She had beauty. She had wit. She was the first to watch me dance. I swear she laughed. So I taught her to dance with me. Oh, my other cats dance, – but Sheba was the first – and always the best . . . We danced in Scots! A good Fife[14] spring!

ALEX *starts – quite softly and slowly – to sing "Carles o Dysart", gathers speed and gaiety, starts to dance – imagining Sheba is dancing again with him:*

ALEX: Cantie Carles o Dysart[15]
Merry lads o Buckhaven[16]
Saucie Limmers o Largo
Bonnie lassies o Leven[17]
Hey, ca thro, ca thro / We have little for spending
Hey, speed on, speed on / We have less for lending.
Some have tales for telling
Some have sangs for singing
Some have pennies for spending
Some have pints for bringing
Hey ca thro, ca thro / See the moon is sporting
On the seas where we / Daily seek our fortune.
We'll have mirth and laughter
We that live by water
Leave them that come after
To spend the gear they gather.
Hey ca thro, ca thro / Maidens dinna doubt it
There's better fish in the sea / Than ever yet cam out it.

During the song ALEX *has scooped up the imaginary Sheba into his arms. He dances with her. At its close, he releases her – watches her jump to the ground.*

. . . I'm glad I didn't find her, I searched diligently – but I didn't want to find her. I would give her Christian burial for she was my Christian friend – but I couldn't bear to find her gnawed by rats, or picked clean by gulls, She was so grey and white and graceful . . . I hope you made her death quick, Father – since you saw fit to take her from me. Bury her with falling earth and rocks – or wash her away with the tide. Please God, don't let me find her . . . I *know* she's dead . . . "Ring the bell o Lundie, gin I tell a lee" . . . Sheba's dead ... (*shouting*) "Lundie Mill and Largo and Kirton and the Keirs / Pittenweem and Anster are all big leears" ...

ALEX *begins to accompany his chants with a kind of dance, a sort of hornpipe/jig of his own invention.*

Lundie Mill and Largo
The Law and the Loch
Pittenweem and Anster
Crail and Arncroach ...
... Auchendinny, Clackendinny, and Balmain,
And Pitcairnie stands alane ...
...
The lasses o the Ferry
They busk braw
The lasses o the Elie
They ding aa
The lasses o St Monans
They curse and ban
The lasses o Pittenweem
They do the same.
The lasses o Anster
They drink strong ale –
Stops dead – then very quiet, homesick:
There's green grass in Cellardyke
And crabs intil Crail.[18]

... (*pause*) ... Don't let me die alone. Don't let me die alone like Sheba. I am well content to live alone – for as long as you please – I am even happy. But don't let me fall sick and helpless to be nibbled and gnawed at by rats before I am even properly stiff ... Let me die at sea – or at home in Largo – in bed – like my good safe shoemaker brother John. John Selcraig will die a-bed. And Maggie Bell will greet at his pillow ... and lay him in a dead kist ... My cats will befriend me – keep watch over me. But they are used to being fed by my hand every day. They will forget who I am when I am dead. Bite the hand that fed them. Gnaw it to the bone, my hand, my body. I will be devoured by my friends. Please, God, don't let me die here alone, please God. Oh, God, please God, please ... God ...

Fade.

Scene 12

On board ship. STRADLING's *cabin.*

STRADLING: (*livid*) God's blood! Don't argue with me, Hunter, go and carry out my orders.

HUNTER: Captain, the carpenters say the mast is –

STRADLING: To hell with the carpenters – and the sail-maker. Tell them to break up camp and bring the sails and tackle on board. (*Calling to* ALEX.) Mr Selkirk!

ALEX *moves from island area to cabin area.*

ALEX: (*very cold*) Captain.

STRADLING: We sail tomorrow.

ALEX: (*almost laughing*) We can't do that – it's quite impossible.

STRADLING: There's a French galleon of thirty tonnes out there to the north. A prize worth taking. You've been saying yourself the men are disgruntled. They're hungry for plunder.

ALEX: Why is it that you can only make the right decision at the wrong time? We missed that same French prize a month ago because you wouldn't give hard chase.

STRADLING: We had too many sick.

ALEX: Our ship is even sicker now.

STRADLING: This prolonged idleness on shore does the men no good!

ALEX: Idleness! – There are sails still to mend – and the main mast is eaten through with worm.

STRADLING: The carpenters light fires and laze out in the woods.

ALEX: They have no decent saws to work with. Besides, they would work more willingly if they were given something sweeter than mere water to drink.

STRADLING: Why were the men brawling on the shore this afternoon?

ALEX: That was an organised contest. To amuse the wrestlers – and the gamblers, alike. It was a very welcome diversion.

STRADLING: To make the men even more ungovernable and quarrelsome! And to take attention perhaps from a secret and more sinister meeting, held elsewhere?

ALEX: It was a stout contest – the sort of diversion Captain Pickering always appreciated. You were invited to come and watch . . . Are you afraid of your own men?

STRADLING: I am suspicious. And I don't forget that once before more than forty of my crew set up mutinous camp onshore and tried to blackmail my authority.

ALEX: I wouldn't know about it, for I was not among them.

STRADLING: You were certainly behind it! I will not brook mutiny! – or near mutiny!

ALEX: If you sail tomorrow you court mutiny – and shipwreck – and death!

STRADLING: I won't be governed by some Scotchman's dreams. I'm Captain of this ship. We sail tomorrow.

ALEX: I'm damned if I will! I'm damned if I'll sail under some silly gentleman masquerading as a mariner!

STRADLING: Then you only have one course open to you! Have you not?

Pause. ALEX *taken aback.*

You will not sail with me?

ALEX: No!

STRADLING: Then you must rot here on this island . . . til you die alone. (*Shouting, off*) Hunter! – tell Higgins to lower the yawl. (*To* ALEX) Mr Selkirk is going ashore! (*He produces from under the table, or chair, a small heavy sack – throws it in front of* ALEX.) Hatchet, kettle, powder, bullets! You may take these – together with your own things. (*Very satisfied*) I must guard against mutiny. And plot carefully against mutinous plotting.

ALEX: You will be damned in hell. And your ship with you.

STRADLING: (*calling*) Hunter!

HUNTER *enters.*

Fetch Mr Selkirk's sea-chest up on deck. And tell the men we sail this evening, not tomorrow. For I must prevent our sailing-master parleying any further with my crew before we leave.

HUNTER *stunned – looks to* ALEX *– for confirmation, perhaps even for counter orders.*

ALEX: Make haste, then, Hunter! For I'd rather face starvation than a watery grave with you lot! I'll "weather it out" on land!

HUNTER *makes no move.* ALEX *leaves, turns to speak just before exit (to island).*

ALEX: You'll drown – all of you – in this ill-kept sieve you call a ship! With this poppet you call – Captain! You're food for fish. All of you.

STRADLING: (*to* HUNTER) You and Higgins are to row Mr Selkirk ashore and leave him there. Those are your orders, do you hear? Should he grovel on his knees – on his face! – you leave him there! He's made his choice and he must keep to it. I will not take him back on board – if you try to bring him back, I will leave you stranded with him – I will flog you first and brand you – and leave you with him on Juan Fernandez. I will not have him on my ship!

HUNTER: Captain?

But STRADLING *is incapable of speaking any more.* HUNTER *leaves.*

STRADLING: I am Captain of this vessel. (*Beside himself with fury*) There is no room on board here for idiot madmen! No room!

Fade.

Scene 13

Island.

ALEX's *voice (tape) singing snatch of "Carles o Dysart".*

Lights up.

ALEX *very relaxed, content. He has his shirt off and is examining it.*

ALEX: Tomorrow I shall have a holiday. A holy, holy day. I shall climb to the high ground and feast on the last of the black plums. And wander down to the Rocky Point and visit my goats – and the kids . . . I had to break their legs! I had to. If I grow sick there must be some animals slow enough for me to catch for food . . . I've seen seamen do much worse – merely for their own sport . . . I've done much worse myself before I lived here. But it hurt me, truly, to hurt my own goats. My life may depend on it – but it sickened me . . .

After I have seen them, I shall come home slowly by the Sugar Loaf Bay – along the sands all the way . . . and light my fire, and eat, and pray, and so to sleep . . .

And the next day, back to work! I must make myself a new shirt! For the winter months. This (*he's examining his shirt*) is my last piece of linen. From now on I will have to dress in goatskin. I will be a hairy man – like Esau![19] Like a bear! The Bear of Juan Fernandez.

ALEX *rises, claps his hands, birls round as if to start a kind of dance.*

The dancing, dancing –

Catches sight of something out at sea – stops dead.

(*flat, automatic*) dancing . . . bear . . . Father, don't send me dreams . . . Don't send me Spaniards! . . . There's a clot in my eye . . . there's a cloud . . . a mist patch . . . on the horizon . . . (*Looks away, willing the patch to go.*) Don't send me Stradling! . . . Don't send me anybody! (*Feels compelled to face it again.*) . . . Are they English? If they stop here to wood and water, careen[20] and tallow,[21] they're bound to find me . . . signs of me . . . my name carved on the trees, my cave on the Rocky Point, my bower . . . They are English! . . . They could give me nails and iron, and linen and salt – and sail again without me . . . Or they could take me with them . . . Lima . . . London . . . and sweet Largo Bay. Oh, God! (*hysterical*) You wait until I'm down to my last shirt! You send me a ship – an English ship – when all that I was thinking of was how to make my next shirt!

Perhaps I won't know how to talk to them – perhaps I only think I'm talking words – but growl merely like some crazed animal. Perhaps they'll treat me like some wild bear; chain me; shoot me . . .

ALEX *is conscious of, keeps glancing at, his beard, hair, clothes – trying to see them as others would.*

I used to wonder sometimes if I were not really dead – and it was just my ghost, my soul that wandered here. I only thought myself alive – but I was in fact beneath the waves with Stradling, and poor Hunter, and the rest . . . It is an English ship . . . thirty tonnes . . . perhaps three hundred men.

O, my Father which art in heaven, hallowed be thy name! You sent me an island and I embraced it. If you send me a ship . . . then surely I must embrace it . . . I will make them banquets of goat stew, and throw my arms around them on the shore. They will treat me with wonder and kindness – I will go aboard a hero! (*Starts to put on his shirt – then thinks instead to use it as a flag. Tentative, voice weak at first, with excitement and fear:*) Hear me . . . Hear me . . . (*louder*) Hear me! . . . I'm alive! I'm alive! Do you hear? . . . Look at me! Find me! I'm alive! I'm alive.

Blackout.

END OF ACT I

Act II

Scene 1

Church.

> *Among the congregation:* JOHN, MAGGIE, EUPHAN, JOCK – *and worshipping slightly apart from them,* SOPHIA.
>
> MINISTER *droning – Luke, chapter 15.*
>
> ALEX *enters – approaches edge of church area, sea-chest on his shoulder. Drops his chest with dramatic thud. Congregation glance round –* EUPHAN *and* MAGGIE *continue to stare at him.* MINISTER's *voice continues . . .*

MINISTER'S VOICEOVER: . . . But as soon as this thy son was come, which hath devoured thy living with harlots, thou hast killed for him the fatted calf . . . And he said unto him, Son, thou art ever with me and all that I have is thine.

> ALEX *joins in with* MINISTER *for next, final, verse, in triumphant tones:*

ALEX and MINISTER: . . . It was meet that we should make merry, and be glad; for this thy brother was dead, and is alive again; and was lost and is found.

> *Silence. Then some whispering amongst the congregation.*

MINISTER: Let us pray!

ALEX: *(laughs)* Don't you know me?

> ALEX *steps well out of church area, birls round to show off his finery.* EUPHAN *steps slowly towards him.*

MINISTER: *(bangs on gavel for attention – twice, determined tones)* Let us pray!

> MINISTER's *voice in prayer continues in background, monotonous.* SOPHIA *turns again to pray.*

EUPHAN: It's my son! My son – my seventh son!

VOICES, WHISPERING: . . . Sandy . . . Sandy . . . Alexander Selkirk . . .

> EUPHAN *rushes to embrace him,* MAGGIE, JOHN *and* JOCK *hesitate before moving towards him.*

EUPHAN: (*turning to others, still holding onto* ALEX) Look – don't you know him? My Sandy, my seventh born. Father, see who it is?

JOCK: Your son.

ALEX: Father.

ALEX *steps towards* JOCK, *they take each other by the shoulders, an embarrassed embrace.*

JOCK: Well, Alexander, you've won home.

ALEX: I thought I never would!

MAGGIE: *She* always said you would.

ALEX: (*turns to* JOHN, *laughing, they embrace*) John!

JOHN: You black sheep, you – black prodigal!

ALEX *still laughing, still holding* JOHN, *surveys* MAGGIE.

MAGGIE: (*still bewildered*) Welcome home . . . Alexander *Selkirk*.

MINISTER's *voice rises slightly, warningly, determined to keep the rest of the congregation at prayer.*

EUPHAN: (*in tears*) My lad! Sandy, eh, Sandy son!

JOCK: (*to* EUPHAN) The minister's not well pleased. Should we rejoin the congregation? It would be very fitting.

JOHN: We'd only cause more stir, Father.

EUPHAN: (*laughing/crying*) Och – his congregation's turned this way anyway – they're all keeking through the door!

SOPHIA *has been keeking, turns again to prayer.*

ALEX: Let's go home. Mother, I want to go home.

EUPHAN: Ay, so you shall, Sandy son, so you shall . . .

ALEX: I've tales to tell you – Mother! – you wouldn't believe – And I've silver and lace –

ALEX *and* EUPHAN *are already walking off together.*

EUPHAN: (*turning back to the others*) Oh, but is this not a special sign – born on the Sabbath, and won home on the Sabbath!

JOHN: (*laughs*) I've a feeling Mr Magill'll no see it as a special sign!

EUPHAN: (*to* ALEX) Come on, then. (*Turns again to others*) . . . John – can you not fetch your brother's kist for him?

She goes off with ALEX. JOHN *surveys sea-chest ruefully.*

MAGGIE: Will you listen to that! Fetch his kist for him indeed!

JOHN *picks up and shoulders sea-chest.*

JOCK: (*abruptly*) He can't bide with us!

MAGGIE: Father!

JOCK: No. No – we haven't the room.

JOHN: Father, what are you saying?

MAGGIE: No room? You reared seven bairns under that roof.

JOCK: There's no room for Alexander. There isn't – the space! He needs more space than we ever had. He needs – ach, no, no – he must lodge with you, John.

JOHN: All right. He can lodge with us.

MAGGIE: No!

JOHN: What is this? "Make merry and be glad, for thy brother was dead and is alive again!"

MAGGIE: Well, but have I not enough on my hands as it is?

JOCK: You have the space – now your William's about to be married and have a house of his own, you'll have extra space.

MAGGIE: We've other sons and daughters besides William.

JOCK: (*wandering a little*) What lass is William getting wed to?

JOHN: Och, Father, you haven't forgotten again! Wee Elizabeth Pearson.

JOCK: (*walking off, talking to himself*) Ay, I ken fine, The Pearsons. From Lundie Mill.

JOHN: (*knowing* JOCK *isn't listening*) No, Father, from Kirton way.

MAGGIE: (*to* JOHN) What did you go and give in to him for? You know what Sandy's like.

JOHN: That's why. Because I know what Sandy's like. And I know what Father's like. They'll argle-bargle the both of them – then *Mother* and Father will bargle too . . .

MAGGIE: So Sandy's to set the two of *us* fraying, instead?

JOHN: He is my brother – your guid-brother. It won't be for long. He'll set himself up soon enough.

MAGGIE: Set himself off, more like.

JOHN: I didn't know him! He's been gone so long, so far – I'd thought of him as – not dead . . . but dead to us. Only mother recognised him.

MAGGIE: Oh, ay, he's very grand and English looking.

JOHN: I didn't mean his clothes, I mean –

MAGGIE: (*walking off*) But he won't have changed – don't you believe it! – he's the same braggarting black sheep he always was.

Fade.

Scene 2

VOICES OVER: (*whispering, romantic*)

> Snuff and silk and sugar,
> Tortoiseshell, beeswax and balsam of Peru,[22]
> Cinnamon and marmalade of quinces;[23]
> Pitch. Tar. Tobacco. (*Glee*) Plunder!
> (*Canny*) Eight hundred pounds English!

VOICES OVER – *each voice succeeding the next very quickly, perhaps sometimes almost overlapping.*

EUPHAN: What was it like on the island, Sandy?

BOY: Uncle Alexander, tell us about the savages in America!

WOMAN: Tell us about the Spanish ladies of Guyaquil.[24]

BOY: And the buccaneers and the Spanish Galleons.

MAN: (*slow, pompous*) Mr Selkirk: what like is it in South America?

WOMAN: Is it like in the Bible?

MAN: There's a piper come from Leven, Sandy, come down to the howff and drink some ale.

WOMAN: And London, what like's London, what do the ladies wear in London?

EUPHAN: Sandy, son, eh, Sandy?

BOY: (*calling – drawing out the name*) Uncle Sandy?

> *Lights up.*
>
> MAGGIE BELL *in Largo house area – sweeping with a broom (or leaning on it, the better to shout at* ALEX).
>
> ALEX *in cave/bower/island area.*

MAGGIE: (*calling to* ALEX – *the call follows closely on the voices over, and is an extension of them*) Alexander *Selkirk!* – Just what do you think you're *doing* up there? . . . It's as well your father's sick and in bed. I don't know what he'd say at what you've done to his orchard. He worships those trees! . . . What's that – *hole*! – you've made in the craggy wall?

ALEX: A bower. A cave. A lookout.

MAGGIE: But what's it for?

ALEX: It's for me. Up here I can see across the top of the village to the water. I can watch the sea all day. Without noticing the village at all. Without the village noticing me.

MAGGIE: And my cats! Do you have to take my cats up there with you?

ALEX: Cats make quiet company.

MAGGIE: My bonny grey and white kitten that was such a good mouser. He hasn't been near the house for days.

ALEX: Especially the grey and white mouser. My Sheba. I'm teaching her to dance.

MAGGIE: Dance, is it, now? With a beast!

ALEX: God's beast.

MAGGIE: Huh – you've a queer like notion of God.

ALEX: I know what God's like.

MAGGIE: You say you want company. Cats! There's a whole village of folk for company, but you'll have none of them!

No answer.

If it's dancing you want! In a couple of weeks when our William marries you can dance til you drop. If the lassies will have you. Ha! – which I doubt! For they're feared for you now.

ALEX: Good.

Pause.

MAGGIE: (*trying*) If you'll talk to no-one else, at least go and talk to your mother. She doesn't ask for much. All she wants is for you to walk her up the brae. Her in her best shawl, and you in your lace-trimmed jacket. She'd like you to sit in Kirk beside her, and set them all a-whispering at the lace and the silver . . . (*sharp again*) Apart from the fact that you should be in Kirk anyway! . . . She dotes on you, Sandy! She never stopped believing you'd win home. Rich and wonderful. With silver and lace . . . She can't get out just now with Father ill – Go and sit with her awhile . . . Och! – Come down from there!

ALEX: I can't talk to her.

MAGGIE: (*thoroughly exasperated*) You don't have to *talk* to her. Just go and sit with her. Euphan will do the talking. You know how she is.

ALEX: She talks questions at me all the time.

MAGGIE: Well – answer them! You can surely just do that!

ALEX: NO! . . . Her questions destroy my country . . . I am sick for my country!

MAGGIE: What country? You've won hame! You're *in* your own country now. In case you hadn't noticed. You're in the Kingdom of Fife. (*A laugh*) Oh, ay – you're in God's country now!

ALEX: My own country – in my head – and my own God!

Pause.

Lights are fading on house area.

MAGGIE: (*shocked*) Why – Alexander Selkirk! – you're greeting like a bairn!

Scene 3

Lights up on JOCK.

He walks with a stick. There's a bench for him to sit on. He's come to have a seat and meditation in his garden.

JOCK: (*wailing*) My orchard! My fine fruit – my trees! What have you done to my trees?

ALEX: I've done nothing to your trees, Father. I've not touched a twig of your trees.

JOCK: What's that – hole! – in the cliff at the top of my orchard? Yon was good bield for my trees.

ALEX: It's still good bield for your trees.

JOCK: I left you my house and my orchard in my will – must you tear it all to pieces before you've even placed me in a dead kist?

ALEX: I've only moved a few rocks, a bit earth.

JOCK: A great gaping hole. God in heaven, what's it for?

ALEX: (*fury*) It's for God – in heaven!

JOCK: Blasphemer!

ALEX: Father – it's just a kind of a cave, that's all. A kind of bower. A look-out.

JOCK: Look out! And what are you to be rescued from now? Do you think your Captain Woodes Rogers will come sailing up the Firth of Forth[25] with all his mercenaries? What are you looking for?

ALEX: I'm looking for my peace of mind, This place – and the shore – they're the only places left where there's the space to think – to talk to God.

JOCK: There's the Kirk for that. And family prayers twice a day. Which you ignore.

ALEX: The Kirk's a handy place to fall asleep in, Father.

JOCK: I never sleep in Kirk! How would you know, you're never there? I may be poorly, but I don't sleep in Kirk. You'd think, after deliverance like yours, that you'd never be done thanking and praising the Lord. Who brought you back to the human condition.

ALEX: (*with a great laugh*) The what?

JOCK: You laugh like a savage! You should remember the Sabbath day and keep it holy.

ALEX: I was at the Kirk last Sabbath.

JOCK: Liar.

ALEX: I was at the Kirk before dawn broke – in the Kirkyard. For I had smelt the weather changing all night – I knew the drought was ending. When the rain started to fall, I was there, in the kirkyard. I gave thanks for the rain. The moon shone like silk through a sea of rain. I was drowning. I took off my clothes and let the rain wash me, drown me.

JOCK It's as well that's a lie.

ALEX: It's no lie.

JOCK: It's as well it was dark, then. They'll all be crying scandal. The elders will be down there taxing you with non-attendance.

ALEX: The elders are too busy – spying on the sheep! . . . You can go and get drunk as far as Leven or St Andrews, but oh, you'll be spied on, and told on – and sat upon the stool of penitence!

JOCK: They have their work to do . . . (*appalled*) Standing naked in the rain! Oh, they're bound to hear of that – they'll be here – Mr Magill himself will come and tax you with it any day now, surely.

ALEX: Magill? That black-gaitered worm? He wouldn't dare!

JOCK: What way is that to be talking of a man of God?

ALEX: God!

JOCK: And what way is that to be talking of the Lord Himself?

ALEX: Man of God! I lived with God – with *only* God. Day and night. Four and a half years. What do you think Mr Magill can tell me of God!

JOCK: Mr Magill has studied at St Andrews University!

ALEX: He has never seen the mountains of Mexico – or the Great South Seas – or been to Juan Fernandez.

JOCK: I don't see what that has to do with the Kirk at all.

ALEX: It has to do with *me*. And my God.

He has come nearer to his father. He sits beside him on the bench.

Father . . . It was easier to fight with you before than it is to talk with you now. I try to talk to you – all of you. I wanted to come home – and talk to you.

JOCK: (*accusingly*) You told us that you were a better Christian as a castaway than you ever were at home.

ALEX: It's easy to obey the ten commandments when you live alone.

JOCK: And you said you spent the greater part of every day in devotion.

ALEX: Yes. Devotion – that is to say: delight.

JOCK: You said you never broke the Sabbath.

ALEX: (*grins*) I never rightly knew which day it was.

JOCK: You told us that your upbringing in a religious household was your strength and your salvation: that you read and prayed every day.

ALEX: Yes. I did. I read because I feared to forget how. I sang psalms for fear my voice would – die! I prayed because – I had to talk to someone – not just my cats and the evil ghost of Stradling. At first my prayers were just mouthings. As my prayers at home had always been . . . God had sometimes given me dreams before, and they told me what to do and I believed in them. Because . . . other people did . . . But speaking to him – that's more difficult. God changes with the climates!

JOCK: (*very shocked*) There is only one God.

ALEX: One God? We worshipped on the top deck of our ship, and the Papists[26] down below.

JOCK: One God.

ALEX: The Turks say that also.

JOCK: (*incensed*) The Turks! The Turks have John Wilson and James Blair in lamentable slavery. Four years they've been galley slaves ... But the elders are even now collecting money for their release.

ALEX: Indeed. God surely gave me four years goodness, then.

JOCK: He gave you deliverance. You must never cease to thank him – and thank him within the Kirk.

ALEX: The Kirk is built of cold stone.

JOCK: Hold your tongue.

ALEX: And God grows cold in Largo.

JOCK: That's blasphemous talk. Dangerous talk. Don't speak like that before your mother. Don't speak like that abroad.

ALEX: What are you afraid of, Father?

JOCK: I'm afraid for you. Dwelling in a hole like a savage. I don't feel well. (*Rises*) (*calls:*) Euphan! (*To himself*) The sun's gone in. I'm chilled. I won't hear any more. (*To* EUPHAN) Auld wife!

EUPHAN *enters*.

EUPHAN: What is it now? What's wrong with you now?

JOCK: I shouldn't have got up. I'm away to my bed. Help me back to my bed.

He exits. EUPHAN *hesitates between following to help* JOCK, *and speiring* ALEX. ALEX *wins*.

EUPHAN: He's ill. And very tired. I didn't dare tell him what you'd done to his orchard! Perhaps I should have told him, I didn't know how ... He'll get used to it in time ... I suppose. Och, yes! But you mustn't upset him, Sandy!

ALEX: I didn't upset him. He upsets himself.

EUPHAN: What were you talking of?

ALEX: God.

EUPHAN: Oh ... Oh, well ... (*turns to go, turns back*) Did ... eh – did he ask you to come to the Kirk?

ALEX: (*hasn't heard her; flatly, trying to find the meaning*) Our Father / Which art in heaven / Hallowed be thy name / Thy kingdom come / Thy will be done on earth as it is in heaven –

He breaks off. Pause.

EUPHAN: Sandy?

He still doesn't hear. He is moving toward bower. Lights fade on EUPHAN.

ALEX: Our Father, which art in heaven, hallowed be thy name, thy kingdom . . . Our Father? . . . (*despair*) Oh, Father!

Scene 4

Lights up on SOPHIA.

The bower area plus what else of the stage is to be used in this scene to represent Dumbarnie Links.[27]

SOPHIA: Oh, why do you weep?

Pause.

ALEX: (*aggressive, offputting*) Because I used to be the Governor of Juan Fernandez – and now I have become a savage without a God.

SOPHIA: That's only what the bairns cry.

ALEX: And aren't you one of the bairns? You're one of the Bruce children.

SOPHIA: I am Sophia Bruce. But I'm not one of the children. I was sixteen in the summer.

ALEX: Sixteen. When I was sixteen I was planning how to run away to sea. (*He is not really talking to her, more to himself.*)

SOPHIA: Yes.

ALEX *looks at* SOPHIA *sharply.*

I've heard folk speak of it.

ALEX: No doubt. And what other speak have you heard?

SOPHIA: That you were stranded upon a wild and desolate island, and have won home rich and famous and are the talk of London town.

ALEX: And you believe them?

Pause.

SOPHIA: I do not believe it was a wild and desolate island . . . (*hesitant*) For I have sometimes seen you weep for it.

ALEX: (*not directly to her*) It was a very gentle island. No tempests, no tornadoes . . .

Pause.

SOPHIA: No wild beasts?

ALEX: No savage beasts, no venomous bird or insect. Parsley and sithes – and a herb like fever-few, with a scent sweeter than balm . . . Wild goats and cats and dogs left behind by ships from long ago. Little quick birds that hummed like dragon flies. And birds like blackbirds but with breasts as crimson as a robin's.

SOPHIA: (*forgetting shyness a little*) Is that true? The blackbird can't be true!

ALEX: (*fierce*) Everything about my island is true. The flowers, the sun, the Great South Sea.

Pause. He's dreaming. She's watching him.

SOPHIA: Did you have curlews?[28]

ALEX is startled, stares.

She is my favourite bird. Her cry is my favourite cry.

ALEX: Birds a plenty. But no curlews . . . And no folk!

SOPHIA: (*moving away*) I never meant to bother you. I come here every day to graze my father's cow. But I take care always not to bother you. If you are up here on the Links, I take my beast home by the shoreline. For my father told me you don't care to meet with folk.

ALEX: I've seen you walking with your cow – and heard you singing to her.

SOPHIA: I would be calling her. That's all. Just calling. She comes when I call.

ALEX: It sounded like a song to me. A very gentle, sweet song.

SOPHIA: Of all the beasts we have, she is my favourite. And she likes it when I sing to her. Where's the harm in that? There's nothing daft about it. Besides . . . well – I have heard them say you sing to Maggie Bell's cats.

ALEX: I sang with my cats on my island – and my goats. And I danced – on the sands . . . I have seen you dance like that.

SOPHIA: Indeed sir, you haven't. That can't be true.

ALEX: I've seen you gathering your skirts in your hand, and running through the waves, laughing at the gulls. That's dancing, isn't it?

SOPHIA: Folk wouldn't call it that.

ALEX: I would . . . I never danced with a lighter heart than then . . . I never knew how happy I was . . . (*suddenly*) I would be glad to dance a spring with you, Sophia Bruce. (*It's as if he means: right now. She's taken aback, but shy rather than afraid.*)

SOPHIA: Why . . . so you may, sir – you may dance with me at the wedding!

ALEX: (*surly*) Wedding? – What wedding?

SOPHIA: The wedding next month of my greatest friend Elizabeth, and your nephew William.

ALEX: (*kind of a laugh, brusque*) I will not dance with you at any wedding. (*He turns away.*)

SOPHIA: (*hurt, confused*) I have to go now. I have to find my cattle beast before it grows dark. (*Retreats.*)

ALEX: (*calling after her*) Sophia Bruce! – Don't go the long way home again so as not to meet me. I would always be more than glad to meet you – up here on the Links – or down on the sands.

She smiles, retreats.

Lights fade, except on ALEX.

(*to himself*) Sophia Bruce! I thought you were a child: you dance with such a light heart. And sing like a blackbird.

Fade.

VOICES OVER:

SOPHIA: Parsley and sithes and feverfew,[29]
Cat's eyes glinting comfort by piemento flames;
Mountains and sunshine and the Great South Sea,
A blackbird with the red breast of a robin.
If the island had been desolate why would you weep for it?

BOY: (*chanting*) Here comes the Governor of Juan Fernandez!

MAN: Eight hundred English pounds! We've never seen the colour of his gold!

WOMAN: He's nae more gold than Tammy Norrie[30] – he'll have to howk his gold from under Largo Law.

OLD MAN: (*slow, pompous*) And what do you do with yourself all day, Mr Selkirk, now that you're a gentleman of leisure?

WOMAN: If you two bairns don't haud yer weesht, I'll feed the both of you to Sandy Selkirk!

SOPHIA: Will you never see your island again? . . . Will you never find your island again? See your island . . . island . . . island . . . island . . .

Scene 5

House in Largo.

SOPHIA *is holding up some lace trimming against the neck of* EUPHAN's *dress for* MAGGIE *to admire.* JOHN, *sitting slightly apart from them, working on a pair of shoes.*

EUPHAN: How do I look?

MAGGIE: Very well, Euphan – very fine. It's a braw bit of lace. The bride'll not have better.

EUPHAN: She'll not be needing it – she's bonny enough without . . . what do you think, Sophia? – you're very silent!

MAGGIE: It's an unco thing, jealousy!

EUPHAN: Jealous of my Sandy's lace!

MAGGIE: Or jealous of the bride.

SOPHIA: Indeed – I'm not! Why should I be? I'm right happy for them both. Elizabeth always set her cap at William. She even bought a charm off Mistress Guthrie. But, och, she never needed it, for William loved her fine. I'm glad they're to be wed tomorrow . . . and live happy here . . . at home in Largo.

MAGGIE: Well, of course they'll live in Largo – where else would they live?

EUPHAN: The Spaniard's disease. That's what seamen call the jealousy. So my Sandy says. But your turn'll come. There'll be plenty carles to dance with you tomorrow.

MAGGIE: So long as you don't sit glooming on the edge of things.

SOPHIA: I was always on the edge of things! And Elizabeth was always in the middle!

MAGGIE: Perhaps it's you that's needing one of Mistress Cuinzie's charms.

EUPHAN: Sandy's jacket trimmed with the same lace. We'll look well together when he walks me to the kirk.

JOHN: Sandy'll not be at the kirk, mother.

EUPHAN: Of course he'll come to the kirk – and he'll gift the couple handsomely, you'll see.

JOHN: There's no reason why he should.

EUPHAN: Oh, but he will.

MAGGIE: What makes you think he's anything left to gift them with?

EUPHAN: He's rich! Eight hundred English pounds. He could buy fine lands – he could buy up half of Largo if he wished.

MAGGIE: He's taking his time over it, then. All he's bought so far is one wee boat. And all he's given you is a wee bitty lace.

EUPHAN: You wait til Sandy weds. Now *that'll* be a wedding!

JOHN: Sandy! Marry! God help the lass that Sandy weds.

SOPHIA: Why do you say that?

MAGGIE: Ach, because the lassies are feared for him, that's why! The ones that aren't gawping and giggling at him.

EUPHAN: That's right! Give a dog a bad name! you're as bad as the others – and you married to a Selcraig – married to the best tanner and shoemaker in Fife – and don't you forget it! Folk round here were always jealous of my seven sons – that's all it is – the Spaniard's disease. And Sandy's the finest –

MAGGIE: The runt!

EUPHAN: – the seventh! They're more jealous of Sandy than of any of my others. Well, he'll show them! Sandy could marry any lady in the Kingdom of Fife.

JOHN: I don't think he will though, Mother.

EUPHAN: What else is there for him to do? He cannot live forever like a hermit. Is he to lodge with you and Maggie always?

MAGGIE: No!

EUPHAN: Of course not! A man of means! He needs someone to live for and care for.

MAGGIE: Ah – you mean someone to love him – who'll live and care for him!

EUPHAN: Well – of course that's what I mean! – is that so strange? Mercy on us – but weddings make you crabbit, Maggie Bell!

MAGGIE: Weddings make me old! . . . And Sandy makes me restless. Wandering God knows where all day, and half the night. Can you see Sandy married –

JOHN: He'd keep his bride up there in his cave, sewing goatskin shirts and dancing with his cats!

MAGGIE: *My* cats!

EUPHAN: That's enough, d'you hear?

MAGGIE: The two of them at the kirk at midnight in the rain, instead of mid-morning godly dressed!

EUPHAN: Plenty seamen marry.

MAGGIE: Plenty seamen aren't like Sandy! He's as restless as the ocean, he should go and live on it again.

SOPHIA: Will you never be done talking, talking about Sandy!

Everyone astonished. SOPHIA's *crushing the lace in her hands.*

There's an ocean now between him and Largo. And every time you speak you make it deeper.

EUPHAN: You'll have my lace in tatters, lass.

EUPHAN *takes the lace.*

SOPHIA: Why don't you leave him be? – It's *you* that's driving him away!

SOPHIA *goes out.*

EUPHAN: Mercy on us – will you look at my lace!

MAGGIE: Mercy – indeed. Mercy on Sophia Bruce! In love with Alexander Selkirk!

JOHN: Och, come on! She's just a bairn.

MAGGIE: She's the very same age as William's bride!

JOHN: She can't be!

MAGGIE: But she is.

JOHN: That wee milk-maid – out on the Links every day, grazing the cow!

MAGGIE: That wee milk-maid – out on the Links every day. And so is Sandy – out on the Links every day.

EUPHAN: Och, it's just a notion – wedding whispers. All the lassies hear them, once there's a wedding in the wind. It's natural – what lass wouldn't hanker after Sandy?

MAGGIE *and* JOHN *exchange looks.*

JOHN: Sophia's right. We're never done talking about him.

MAGGIE: He stirs us up, that's why. He makes me feel dull, old. (*To* JOHN) He makes you seem dull too. All these years we've been married – Sandy's been across the world – gambled and spent two, three fortunes. And what have we done?

JOHN: (*equably*) Cleaned a thousand skins, and cobbled a thousand shoes.

MAGGIE: And reared a handful of bairns.

EUPHAN: Some folk are never satisfied.

MAGGIE: It's Sandy that's never satisfied. That's why he'll go to sea again. That's why he'll never marry.

EUPHAN: Like you just said to Sophia: it's an unco thing, jealousy.

MAGGIE: Jealous! Of your youngest? He's as daft as a Fife Laird!

EUPHAN: Daft, is it? – let me tell you – he's as *fine* as a laird! And that's what he is now – an officer!

MAGGIE: (*with mirth*) A what?

EUPHAN: And a gentleman!

JOHN: That's enough. Enough, d'you hear? Let's have no bargling, not tonight. We've a wedding in the morning.

Lights fading on Largo house.

MAGGIE: (*scorn*) An officer!

EUPHAN: *And* a gentleman!

MAGGIE: A buccaneer – that's all he is – a pirate! And a misfit!

Scene 6

Fiddle music in distance.

ALEX – *island area.*

ALEX: Voices! What made me long for Largo sands – and Largo voices! What made me think I needed salt and linen and nails, and shoes and knives – and people! . . . I fear I will grow mad here. Run mad – and wade in there amongst those voices, screaming at them, like them!

SOPHIA: (*downstage*) Sandy!

ALEX: (*He doesn't hear her. Shouting – to the whole of Largo*) You drive me mad! You are as senseless as a pack of sea-lions!

SOPHIA: Sandy!

ALEX: (*turns to her*) Am I a ghost? I used to think I might be, on the island. Am I talking to you – can you hear my words? I used to think perhaps I merely girned like some beast, and only thought I spoke. But that was when I first lived on the island. I could fight there – for my soul and my survival. I cannot do it now. Why should I still live like a castaway? – a ghost?

SOPHIA: I could not love you, if you were a ghost!

ALEX: I'm not mad – not yet. God would not let you fall in love with madness. Would he?

SOPHIA: No, no.

ALEX: We must leave here, Sophia. We must leave here now, tonight, while they are dancing and drinking.

SOPHIA: (*although she knows it is useless*) Come and dance? Come and bless the bride and groom and dance with me. And then you will see things differently –

ALEX: No!

SOPHIA: – you will feel able to talk to my father – you could even talk to him now, tonight?

ALEX: We've been through all this before.

SOPHIA: See how they all are at this wedding. And they'll be glad for us.

ALEX: They will laugh at you Sophia. And they will forbid you to marry me.

SOPHIA: I have three uncles ministers. Any one of them would marry us.

ALEX: (*a laugh*) They would not. They would not marry you to me! But I do not need a minister to tell me how to marry. Nor your father to tell me how to love you.

SOPHIA: How can I leave them – not yes married? And Euphan – dancing now in her new lace – how can you leave without saying anything to her? How can you?

ALEX: Like I did before. And she'll forgive me, like she did before.

SOPHIA: She will not forgive me. No-one will forgive me.

ALEX: If they don't forgive you they don't matter. It's you and I who matter. We must leave now. You promised – promised me faithfully, and lovingly, that you would leave with me tonight.

Burst of clapping, a few 'hoochs', as music comes to an end.

SOPHIA: Yes.

ALEX: Or has the capering yonder changed your mind? (*pause*) Is that what you want? Dancing and ale, a new bolt of linen and a stocking full of silver? (*pause*) I will go mad if I stay here . . . Must I leave without you?

SOPHIA: (*an assent*) Where will we go?

ALEX: (*embracing her*) Across the Forth. To England.

SOPHIA: But where, in England?

ALEX: It doesn't matter. Wherever it is, we'll make an island, you and I together.

As the lights fade, someone has already started to sing, in distance – first the chorus, and then the last verse, of 'Fife and Aa the Lands Aboot It'.

Scene 7

EUPHAN *very subdued.*

MAGGIE *brandishing* SANDY's *lace-trimmed jacket.*

MAGGIE: And what am I supposed to do with this? The famous jacket! And his kist, still up the stair? With his powder-horn, and his drinking cup? I want them out of here! They're in my way.

EUPHAN: (*taking the jacket*) I'll keep them. I'll keep them til he comes again.

MAGGIE? Til he *what*? Do you think we've to go through all this again! If he comes back he'll get short-shrift from me!

EUPHAN: He never was one for faretheewells. He always upped and left like this. It's just his way.

MAGGIE: He never upped and left with a lassie before! Sophia's mother's near demented. They only have the one lass – and not yet seventeen.

EUPHAN: I was married at sixteen. You were married at seventeen.

MAGGIE: Married – ay!

EUPHAN: They've time yet to be married. He must love the lass to have taken her with him. She was always a god-fearing, dutiful bairn.

MAGGIE: I never thought she was that sleekit!

EUPHAN: If I had had a daughter, I'd have had her be just like Sophia. A bonny, blithe wee –

MAGGIE: wee besom! Well – she's made her bed – and she can lie on it – til he ups and offs and leaves her stranded in some strange city – without a faretheewell – which is 'just his way!'

EUPHAN: You must get John to break the news to his father.

MAGGIE: Why?

EUPHAN: Well, I can't tell him. I tried to. And someone has to tell him!

MAGGIE: Why John? It was John who had to go and break the news to Sophia's folk. Rab Bruce had him by the throat – and Sophia's brothers drummed him out the house. He's black and blue all over.

EUPHAN: John has to tell his father.

MAGGIE: You'll be telling me next it's all John's fault – and mine!

EUPHAN: Ay . . . well . . .

MAGGIE: Well – what?

EUPHAN: He lodged with you . . . but you never made him welcome. And John should have made him keep the Sabbath. He's the eldest brother. If John had made Sandy walk me to the wedding – Sandy would still be here. In Largo.

MAGGIE: (*fury*) Lord, give me peace. Save me from Sandy Selkirk!

EUPHAN: Och, you never wanted peace, Maggie Bell. Now Sandy's gone, you'll soon find someone else to throw your mouth at.

Scene 8

Lodging house in Bristol.[31]

ALEX (*on island area*). SOPHIA *downstage*.

ALEX: . . . all wearing apparel of any kind, all worsted,[32] linen, lace, was counted plunder. All plate, all manner of bedding, buttons, buckles, crucifixes, gold and silver watches – that was plunder. Arms, sea books, and instruments – that goes without saying. Even gold rings – found in any place or on any person . . . But not a woman's earrings. The basest buccaneer would not – should not – remove a woman's earrings . . .

He opens out his hand to show SOPHIA *a pair of gold earrings. Steps nearer for her to look.*

Do you like them?

SOPHIA: They're very beautiful.

ALEX: Then take them.

SOPHIA: But Sandy – these are gold. You should never have bought these!

ALEX: I didn't. They were . . . a gambling debt repaid!

SOPHIA: (*handing them back*) Then they belong to some other woman.

ALEX: A lady? (*laughs*) Not any longer.

SOPHIA: But don't we need the money more? Should you not have sold them?

ALEX: You want more money?

SOPHIA: No, I thought perhaps we needed some.

ALEX: You will not wear them then? . . . In other countries women wear their fortune . . . In South America the Spanish ladies flaunted it. Round their necks and waists – and ankles – dripping from their ears – gold rings like crusts upon their fingers.

SOPHIA: I'm not a Spanish lady.

ALEX: They were very clever women. The ladies of Peru. Clever cunning women! We made an expedition upriver from Guyaquil. The city itself had yielded nothing. The place was stricken with a fever. We routed the men, and broke open the churches, but there was little to be found. Some of us would have taken up the floorboards and searched among the graves for treasure, but the graves were new, the bodies still stank of the fever. An Indian we had taken prisoner told us that the treasure had been hidden in the barklog houses up the river – Forty thousand pieces of eight! The women had been hidden upriver too. All gathered together in one house! In timidity, we thought! Such smiling gracious women! Who thought that once our eyes fastened on the gold they wore, and the wine they offered, we would forget to search the place – and miss our chance of better plunder! Oh, but we behaved like gentlemen! On *that* occasion – we behaved like gentlemen! We left the ladies to their wine – and searched the house – and all the other houses . . . Forty thousand pieces of eight! . . . But they were clever lassies . . . cunning lassies . . . The lassies o St Monans / They curse and ban / The lassies o Pittenweem / They do the same / The lassies o Anster / They drink strong ale . . . But not SOPHIA! . . . How is it that the very gentlest quietest creature will run with me – and watch me drink and gamble and roar . . . and still love me? – Take away the beast in me – and give me sweet South Seas? . . . (*harshly; turned away from her*) Do you still love me, Sophia?

SOPHIA: You know I do.

ALEX: But are you sure you love me?

SOPHIA: I am quite quite sure.

ALEX: (*abrupt*) You do not think too much of Largo?

SOPHIA: (*faltering, afraid of being caught out*) I have never said so.

ALEX: (*abrupt*) You want to go back?

Pause.

SOPHIA: It's where we both belong.

ALEX: You're planning to go back!

SOPHIA: No!

ALEX: Without me!

SOPHIA: No! – I will go nowhere without you – nowhere. Won't you trust me anymore? Don't you believe me? Please – don't stare at me like that – last night I woke to find you staring at me – as if I was a liar – or a stranger.

ALEX: It was a dream that made me stare like that. I thought I dreamt of you. In Largo.

SOPHIA: I'm here, beside you. I sleep beside you . . . while you dream.

ALEX: You will not wear the earrings? . . . You're right. We need the money. We should sell them. Here – take them! – *You* go and sell them. Better you should go and sell them, than I should gamble them and lose them.

The light fades on SOPHIA.

Light on ALEXANDER *in island area.*

. . . Forty thousand pieces of eight! And some of us would have crawled among new graves to find it! . . . I found gold once. On

Juan Fernandez, once, I found three hoops of rusty iron half buried in the sand! I learnt to fashion it. I made new knives! . . . It's a long time since I savoured the colour of that gold.

Scene 9

House in Bristol. CAPTAIN WOODES-ROGERS *and* DEFOE *wear wigs.*
Table: decanter, glasses, writing things; two chairs.

CAPTAIN WOODES-ROGERS: Mr Defoe! I am most glad to see you.

DEFOE: Captain Woodes-Rogers – very glad to be here. Delighted! And Mr Selkirk?

ROGERS: He should be here directly.

DEFOE: Excellent. Excellent. I am very grateful to you for arranging a Sunday meeting.

ROGERS: But I was surprised to hear you were in Bristol.

DEFOE: It seemed best to quit London for a little – a matter of finance. I am known in Bristol – yet again – as 'The Sunday Gentleman!' – Free to walk abroad with the protection of the Sabbath – but courting the debtors' prison if I show my face during the week.

ROGERS: I'm very distressed to hear it.

DEFOE: Oh, fortunes go – and come again. I shall bounce out of trouble – and be back in London soon, God willing. I've been as shipwrecked in my time as our Scotch castaway, and always been rescued.

ROGERS: You have not met Mr Selkirk before?

DEFOE: I was to meet him in London, when the coffee houses first buzzed with his arrival. But he vanished, very suddenly – back to Scotland, so I heard.

ROGERS: He arrived in Bristol, equally suddenly – with a young Scotchwoman.

DEFOE: Ah – so the mariner has married. He is settled.

ROGERS: No – not settled – for he spoke to me of going to sea again. Nor married neither – for he introduced the lady as his loving friend. And so she seemed – most devoted, and delightful. And very young.

DEFOE: All the Scotch are young! Obstinate refractory children.

ROGERS: (*laughing*) I never found Selkirk refractory. We had great respect for one another. But he is much changed.

DEFOE: Four years in solitary –

ROGERS: No, no – the change has taken place more recently. Perhaps since he has been to Scotland – or perhaps since he has left it. When we discovered him on Juan Fernandez, Dampier recommended that I make Selkirk sailing-master – and an excellent one he proved to be. As sober and as honourable – more so perhaps – than any other officer. When we had to set up a fever camp at the Cape, his expertise and knowledge of herbs helped save several of the crews lives. He was never remarkably sociable, certainly. But I find him much changed.

DEFOE: He was thrown into a busy life on board your ship. Since then he has had a lot of money to spend, and very little to do.

SERVANT *enters*.

SERVANT: Mr Alexander Selkirk, sir, to see you.

ROGERS: Selkirk, man, how are you? Come in. This is the man we called the Governor of Juan Fernandez. And this is Mr Daniel Defoe.

ALEX: Sir.

DEFOE: I am delighted to meet you. Delighted!

ROGERS: Now, Gentlemen! The best thing I can do is to leave you both to talk. I recommend my wine. And there are paper and pens upon the table.

DEFOE: Thank you Captain, most kind.

ROGERS *leaves*. DEFOE *pours wine*.

(*Indicating the paper*) We have no need of these. I never forget anything people tell me. I was five when the Plague hit London, six during the Great Fire. I can remember a little of it – but I remember all of what was said about it in the years that followed – by my father and his friends . . . My father's name was James Foe. I improved upon my original name – as light change, but effective. I believe you did likewise?

ALEX *does not care for this remark*.

Sit down, Mr Selkirk, sit down. (DEFOE *hands him a glass*) Now! I must warn you: I am a plain man.

ALEX: (*dry*) You are a man of letters, sir.

DEFOE: (*very amused*) There are those who would deny that. Tell you I write too fast, too carelessly. Ha! No matter – the people read what I write – the people read my pamphlets, satires, histories, panegyrics[33] . . . I have it in my mind now, though, to write something new. And very different . . . (*very excited*) An adventure! (*Remembering* ALEX's *presence*) – *your* adventure!

ALEX: Captain Woodes-Rogers has already written one account of my adventures, sir. I myself have published another.

DEFOE: And you have already talked to many, many people! (*Surveys* ALEX.) I have a feeling that now – what is it – two years later – you might not talk so freely.

Silence.

ALEX: (*with difficulty*) I found that, though they listened, they were not listening to me – but to something in themselves. Speaking to them damaged what I'd found.

DEFOE: Oh, I only want facts, Mr Selkirk. I want to pin my adventures against facts. (*burst of enthusiasm*) I'm fascinated by the lives of those who live by their wits – for I live that way myself. Englishmen are marvellously strong and sensible in adversity. I have always found that to be so.

ALEX: I am a Scotchman, sir.

DEFOE: (*ignoring this*) I have decided to write an adventure – but a moral tale – a Pilgrim's Progress. A pilgrim on an island and a ship! "Providence Displayed!" Was that not what you called your own pamphlet? I never cease to wonder at Providence. It was Divine Intervention (*he speaks with capitals*) that saved you on your island. I was much struck on reading that – and much struck also by the fact that you, like myself, were brought up in a house of dissenting faith – each day bound, like a bible, by prayer.

ALEX *looks at him sharply.*

Oh, yes! There are similarities between your life and mine.

ALEX: That may be true – for you begin to remind me very strongly of my father.

DEFOE: (*off again on his own tack*) A pilgrim! A man of the people – not a savage!

ALEX: Sir – no-one calls me savage!

DEFOE: No, no – Mr Selkirk – forgive me, you misunderstand me . . . I fear this meeting has come too late. I have interviewed people all my writing life – in the taverns, the streets – in Newgate,[34] often the very night before the wretches were to hang. I have stolen the facts from their lives. But this time – for the *first* time – I will write my own invention . . . I already have my mariner – a solid seaman from York city.[35]

ALEX: (*preparing to go*) Then you should question him – not me.

DEFOE: No – no – he isn't real – not yet. He is my fiction. What I wanted from you was – anything! – anything. You have to tell: an involuntary detail, an incident, a clue . . . an atmosphere?

Pause. ALEX *flummoxed. Drinks. Says nothing.*

For example – (*he is watching* ALEX *drink*) – what did you drink out of, eat out of? . . . What vessels did you have?

Pause.

ALEX: A kettle. Some bowls. There is a list of all my effects in my published account.

DEFOE: I was thinking about clay . . .

ALEX *puzzled – and not really interested.*

. . . I thought of – did *you* never think of making pots from clay?

ALEX: No. If I'd needed other vessels I would have used the bladders of my goats.

DEFOE: No. That smacks of the savage. And I know about clay. I used to own a factory that made tiles of clay. Was there clay on Juan Fernandez?

ALEX: I don't know. I have an eye for sea, sir, not for land.

DEFOE: Your life there was a sojourn of discovery. If you had discovered how to fashion clay, then learnt perhaps to fire it –

ALEX: I never knew of any clay!

DEFOE: – discovered how to build a house, and how to till the soil –

ALEX: I never tilled the soil. It was a gentle island, beautiful, bountiful. Mr Defoe: my discovery was greater than making pots, or tilling soil! I learnt to live alone – with God. And God's beasts. I –

He stops. Drains his glass. Awkward silence.

DEFOE: Whatever your strength in the Lord, you must have wished constantly for company. The day the *Cinque Ports* left –

ALEX: The *Cinque Ports* sank! As I dreamed she would! Have you heard what happened to Stradling?

DEFOE: Yes – Captain Woodes-Rogers told –

ALEX: All but seven of the crew were drowned. Stradling was saved. Stradling and six others! Taken prisoner by a Spanish vessel and shut up in a jail in Lima. (*Fury*) Which is too good an end for Stradling! But my dreams will kill him yet!

Pause. DEFOE *taken aback.*

DEFOE: . . . However – you searched the sea night and day for a sail? Your own pamphlet tells us so.

ALEX: I longed at first for a ship – yes – and then I continued to believe that I longed for a ship. Yes. But I see now: I was happy – as happy as I'd ever been. Then the good ship *Duchess* arrived and I found myself with plenty of companions – three hundred men, four boys and two negroes – on one little wooden island.

DEFOE: (*off on his own again*) A companion! But a companion to arrive *after* you had conquered the island – and the solitude!

ALEX: What!

DEFOE: A boy . . . a cabin boy – or a negro! – young and very fearful. In need of Christian education.

ALEX: (*a kind of a laugh*) *What* did you say?

DEFOE: I was pondering on loneliness.

ALEX: (*to himself*) One time I saw footprints, on the sands.

DEFOE: *What* did you say?

ALEX: From the height of the cliff I thought them footprints. When I reached the shore they were the marks of seals. I wept. And then I laughed. Seals make better company than Spanish buccaneers!

DEFOE: (*attracted by the idea*) Footprints! There are no inhabited islands near?

ALEX: No islands of any kind near.

DEFOE: I thought not – (*very cheerful*) But no matter! . . . Your island can be shifted! The Captain has promised to lend me atlases . . . He tells me a negro had been stranded on Juan Fernandez some years previously to you?

ALEX: He was an Indian, so I heard. A Mosquito Indian.[36]

DEFOE: (*excited*) From a ship! That's it! A second shipwreck, perhaps.

ALEX: (*baffled, angry*) There was no shipwreck – not a first, nor a second!

DEFOE: A Moral Tale cannot be founded on a quarrel, Mr Selkirk. But it can very well be founded on a shipwreck.

ALEX: I was right to quarrel with Stradling! God showed me I was right. Not once – but several times!

DEFOE: Divine Intervention delivered you to the safety of the island, and divine intervention released you later from it.

ALEX: *Released* me!

DEFOE: And rewarded your faith and endurance with a fortune! Eight hundred pounds! Do you realise that at this moment, Mr Selkirk, you are a richer man than I!

ALEX: To hell with rescue! Reward? I've lost my reward – forever. Don't you understand? I would forfeit seven fortunes to live – to find – (*tries very hard to control himself*) How will you end this moral "adventure"?

DEFOE: How would you have it end?

No answer.

It must have a moral ending. And the people will prefer it to be a happy one also.

ALEX: Don't you understand? I want my island back again! I want to be there now. I have lost everything – except for Sophia's love, I have lost everything! Will this (*meaning himself – he stands, arms held out to each side of him a little*) be your ending? This happy moral!

ALEX *is about to leave.*

DEFOE: Mr Selkirk –

ALEX: I envy your mariner from York. God's blood! I envy him his happy ending!

DEFOE: Mr Selkirk!

ALEX *goes (to island area).*

At the same time WOODES-ROGERS *enters* – ALEX *leaves without even seeming to notice* ROGERS.

DEFOE *is taking it all philosophically.*

ROGERS: (*sadly*) I wanted him to dine with us.

DEFOE: My fault. My fault. I'm old. And selfish – selfish at this moment with excitement. I have my own story already in my mind. I didn't listen.

ROGERS: We have hurt his feelings. I should have stayed with you, and listened to him.

DEFOE: What he was trying to say would destroy my own mariner. Although I need facts, this time – this time it is different – I need them for inventions of my own. This is not a history, this is to be a fiction.

ROGERS: He has a look of prison on him . . . Richard Steele[37] met him when he first arrived in London.

DEFOE: (*tetchy*) Yes, yes, I know.

ROGERS: He wrote about him in the *Londoner*.

DEFOE: I am aware of that.

ROGERS: He told me afterwards that Selkirk made him think of a bear on a chain.

DEFOE: (*reluctant admiration*) Excellently put. I'm bound to say so: excellent. Though his essay in the *Londoner* was dull.

ROGERS: I saw one here in Bristol recently. A bear matted with rain and mud – shambling before a street crowd . . . dancing on a chain. (*Pause*) Shall we dine?

DEFOE: Delighted. Delighted. Captain Rogers! (*He stops the captain, determined to gain full attention.*) Now: what do you think? What do you think of this? (*Recites – watching* ROGERS *for reaction, approval*) "The Life and Surprising Adventures of Robinson Crusoe, of York, mariner: who lived eight and twenty years all alone in an un-inhabited island on the coast of America, near the mouth of the great river of Oroonoque;[38] having been cast on shore by shipwreck, wherein all the men perished but himself. With an account of how he was at last as strangely delivered by pirates."

ROGERS *thinks the title is over, prepares to exit with his friend, but* DEFOE *stops him again, triumphant emphasis:*

"Written by himself."

ROGERS: A very rousing title. Very stirring!

He puts his hand on DEFOE's *shoulder to persuade him to move on and dine.*

The lights are fading.

DEFOE: (*exiting*) Taylor of Pater Noster Row[39] will print it. Oh, how I wish my debts were paid and I were back in London!

CHILD'S VOICE: (*off*) Poor Old Robinson Crusoe
Poor Old Robinson Crusoe
They made him a coat of an old nanny goat
I wonder why they should do so!
With a ring a ring tang
With a ring a ring tang
Poor Old Robinson Crusoe.

Scene 10

ALEX *on island area.*

ALEX: . . . Sophia? . . . Sophia? . . . I want to run – RUN – hell for leather – like a savage? – yes! – by leagues and leagues of empty sands – til my body pounds like the very breakers on the shore. RUN. I want my island back again . . . Sophia? . . . Once, when I was still raw to the island, not yet the Governor – and hungry! – I chased a young goat along a clifftop. The poor brute, wild with fear, leapt over the edge! And just as wildly, so did I! We both plunged into blackness . . . Three days later, by my reading of the moon – I woke – half-woke – to find myself resting on a soft mattress of dead goat. (*Laughs*) That's Providence – Mr *De* Foe – that's your Providence Displayed! God laughing! . . . I was not afraid. And not in pain. Stunned. Content: like a child lying sick in his mother's dark box-bed, knowing he is comforted and cared for. The wind soughed in the cabbage palms, and the sea soughed over the shore – and willed the strength back into me, until I felt able to crawl home to my piemento bower and my kind cats . . .

And after that, I regularly broke the legs of several newborn kids, in case I should be forced to find my meat more slowly.

I drank with my head spluttering in the running stream – Mr Defoe – I ate flesh with my fingers, tore at it with my teeth. I killed my friends for food. That does not make me savage.

Dreams make me savage. God send me no more dreams, I cannot read them. They weigh me down. Every night a woman walks in Largo. Sophia? – walks in Largo. Without me. Rings on her fingers. Hands like claws . . . Dreams make me savage.

Father: I broke a man's head tonight more easily than if he'd been a new-born kid. And if it were I lying senseless now in some dark alley, I could not find the will to get up again and live. I have not the strength I had in Juan Fernandez. There is nowhere to run! Sophia is not strong enough to run with me. It used to be so easy. The horizon held the prayer . . . God! Send me a ship! . . . One little wooden island . . . God? . . . Father? . . . Sophia?

Lights up on SOPHIA *downstage.*

SOPHIA: I'm coming. I'm here.

ALEX: Where have you been?

SOPHIA: It grew so late –

ALEX: Where were you?

SOPHIA: It grew so late, I was afraid. I went to look for you.

ALEX: You're weeping.

SOPHIA: So are you.

ALEX: What made you look for me? At night? I thought you were terrified of city streets!

SOPHIA: There were men here looking for you. Sandy – the law is looking for you.

ALEX: (*laughs*) Is it!

SOPHIA: They wouldn't listen to me. I told them you were with the Captain and Mr Defoe – that you must certainly be still there even now. But they said they have witnesses!

ALEX: Have they!

SOPHIA: Sandy – please, you must listen! They say you assaulted a shipwright, a man named Richard Nettle, and that you meant to kill him.

ALEX *ignores this.*

I told them you were with Mr Defoe. But they will come again to find you. I told them – Sandy you must make Mr Defoe tell them where you were. They said they have witnesses and that you were drunk.

ALEX: Richard Nettle wished to pick a fight with the Governor of Juan Fernandez – so I fought him.

SOPHIA: Oh, no. Please, God, no.

ALEX: I wasn't drunk, Sophia. And I never tried to kill him! I'm hardly drunk at all. (*Pause*) Don't leave me!

SOPHIA: Of course I will not leave you.

ALEX: We must quit Bristol first thing in the morning. At first light.

SOPHIA: Oh, yes – praise God! I sometimes thought I'd never see my home again.

ALEX: Home? That's where the heart is.

SOPHIA: Yes – indeed – and that is where we must go! I have known that all along. I will get things ready now.

ALEX *catches her arm as she, excited, goes to get ready.*

ALEX: Sweetheart: we'll go to London.

SOPHIA: London?

ALEX: I can join His Majesty's Navy – in London.

SOPHIA: A moment ago you begged me not to leave you. Now you would go to sea again and leave me alone in London?

ALEX: I have friends there. We can lodge with them, and they'll look after you while I'm at sea.

SOPHIA: I had friends a plenty in Largo. I left them to be with you. Don't leave me alone in London. Don't leave me please, not ever. I think you need me. Don't you need me?

ALEX: I've no more money. The only work I know is on the sea.

SOPHIA: We ran away to be together. You said we were an island, you and I together. I love you.

ALEX: I love you too – so do as I bid, and come with me to London, we will stay with Richard Mason and his wife.

SOPHIA: Do your dreams tell you to do this thing?

ALEX: No. My dreams have told me only what I mustn't do. And we must not go to Largo.

SOPHIA: What tells you to go to London?

ALEX: Good sense – and the Royal Navy – and the law officers of Bristol.

SOPHIA: If you will go to sea, then will you marry me first? And take me home to Largo? I will wait for you as your wife, I will wait . . . But let me go home as your wife!

ALEX: We are already man and wife.

SOPHIA: But not in name.

ALEX: Name! You can take any name you choose – Bruce, Selkirk, Selcraig.

SOPHIA: But in the name of God, also.

ALEX: We are married in the sight of God. I held a bible – and your hand – and we swore our love for one another. What could mean more than that? To need more than that is blasphemy! Sophia – before I go to sea we will go to a notary[40] and I will bequeath you all I have . . .

SOPHIA: I do not care about what you have – I care about what you are.

ALEX: I have lands in Largo – orchards . . . the house by Craigie Wall.

SOPHIA: Those are your father's, And your brother John's.

ALEX: There are people owe us money.

SOPHIA: And we owe other people . . . It's all gone, Sandy, the silver, and the lace. My darling Sandy, we only have each other.

ALEX: So – I must go to sea.

ALEX is on island area – looking down at SOPHIA.

Lights are fading on SOPHIA, *but remain on* ALEX.

If we cannot find an island, then I must find a ship . . . In the name of God, Amen, I Alexander Selkirk, of Largo, in the shire of Fife, North Britaine, mariner, calling to mind the perils and dangers of the seas, do publish and declare this my last will and testament: give and bequeath unto my loving and well-beloved friend, Sophia Bruce, all and singular my lands, gardens, orchards, lying and being in Largo. My sum and sums of money, gold, silver, I hereby give unto my said loving friend Sophia Bruce, making void and of none effect all former wills,

Laughter from FRANCES CANDIS. *Her laughter punctuates the rest of the will.*

testaments and deeds of gifts by me at anytime or times heretofore made. In witness whereof I here set my hand and seal the thirteenth day of January 1717 in the fourth year of King George.[41]

Scene 11

Public house in Plymouth.

FRANCES: Mr Selkirk! – Frank – bring ale for Mr Selkirk. On the house!

ALEX: You're very gracious, Mistress Candis.

FRANCES: I'm very proud – to have such a famous lodger – and very sorry that he leaves so soon for London. We'll drink your health before you go, my dear! We always celebrate the rich and famous in my lodging-house!

ALEX: Why not celebrate the down and out – who otherwise might get no ale at all?

FRANCES: D'you hear that, Frank? – that's what Scotchmen call "a joke"! (*To* ALEX) Come and sit here. You always seem to me to be the sort of man who either should not drink at all – or should drink a little more.

ALEX: I'll have some more.

FRANCES: That way you will sleep better nights! Why don't you sleep? I've never known a lodger pay for bed and board before and not to use the bed!

FRANK *guffaws,* FRANCES *quells him with a look, or shove.*

I heard you roam the house last night. Thought you were after my best port!

FRANK *guffaws again.*

Why can't you sleep?

ALEX: I'll sleep better when we go to sea.

FRANCES: That's what my husband used to say. Poor Ned! He's sleeping now all right. Somewhere under the sea. Still – he'd rather feed the fishes than the worms of Plymouth. Died soon after they set sail. Two years to wait for news of a man already two years dead – and only a few weeks wages due.

FRANK: You're well provided for!

FRANCES: I provided for myself, didn't I? I made this place what it is. This is my ship – this house – it's full of seamen – sea-tales and fights and loves.

FRANK: And seamen's profits.

FRANCES: Women must privateer[42] as well as men. What do you think a sailor's wife should do? Sit by the shore and sew a fine seam and sigh and moan for two, three years, til her man comes home – if he comes home? A woman made like that must marry a butcher, a baker, a chandler[43] . . . If I were a man, I'd go to sea.

FRANK: But would you go to an island, like Mr Selkirk here?

FRANCES: (*laughing*) If Alexander Selkirk was still on it – yes, my dear, I would! What was your island like? I've heard the others talk – of you and your island, but you say very little.

FRANK: It's too long ago! He can't remember. Perhaps he doesn't want to.

ALEX: Eight years ago. Four years on the island. Four more long years voyaging home . . .

FRANK: And making a fortune.

ALEX: . . . and four years back here in Britain.

FRANK: Losing it again?

ALEX: Four years! It took some months – fourteen perhaps, to learn to live alone . . . In four years here I've learnt – (*laughs*) – how not to live!

He gets up.

FRANCES: Mr Selkirk – you aren't leaving us? What – this very minute?

ALEX: Yes.

FRANK: You haven't paid your bill.

FRANCES: It's no matter. Pay it when you come again. You aren't saying goodbye? – only farewell, til you come again! Remember – when you come again to Plymouth – Francis Candis sells the best ale, and keeps the finest lodgings. And has always room for Alexander Selkirk!

ALEX: You're very gracious, Mistress Candis.

ALEX *goes to island area.*

FRANCES: Wipe that smile off your face, Frank Hall.

FRANK: You won't catch that one.

FRANCES: Frances can land any fish she chooses.

FRANK: That fish drinks too much!

FRANCES: (*laughing*) So do I!

FRANK: He'll be away at sea too long. The same as your poor Ned.

FRANCES: So? I'm used to that. I even thrive on it!

FRANK: You wouldn't be thinking of eight hundred pounds – now, would you? Frances!

FRANCES: He's a great fine Samson[44] of a man.

FRANK: Down on his luck!

FRANCES: A lord, they say.

FRANK: *Who* says?

FRANCES: *He* says!

They both laugh.

Once when he was drunk, he called himself a 'Fife lord runaway' – a 'daft Fife lord'!

FRANK: He talks Scotch mist when he's drunk! And when he's sober he says nothing at all.

FRANCES: He's a challenge. Worth the landing.

FRANK: I've heard he has a woman back in London.

FRANCES: Haven't they all!

FRANK: A wife he brought from Scotland. That's what some say!

FRANCES: I didn't hear you, Frank!

Scene 12

Lodgings in London.

ALEX *(glooming on island area) is slightly mad/slightly drunk.*

SOPHIA *downstage.*

SOPHIA: Sandy, won't you sleep? In a few hours you sail for Plymouth – and after Plymouth, set sail for God knows where. Will you not sleep with me before you go? Won't you love me?

ALEX: I love you and leave you! I leave you now.

SOPHIA: It's not yet light.

ALEX: And when you get to Largo, tell them I curse them .

SOPHIA: What do you mean? – How should I – how could I – get to Largo?

ALEX: You'll get to Largo!

SOPHIA: I have not the money, nor the courage, nor the will – unless you take me there.

ALEX: I see you back in Largo with another man.

SOPHIA: You're ill.

ALEX: You mean I'm drunk? Drunk or sober, the dream's the same.

SOPHIA: You're ill. Sandy, you cannot go to sea. You're ill. You must stay here.

ALEX: Desert His Majesty's Ship Weymouth!

SOPHIA: You are deserting me! We ran away together – we could run back there now – the Navy would not look for you in Largo. It's far too far away.

ALEX: Didn't you hear what I said? You'll go to Largo with another man.

SOPHIA: Your dreams are evil. There's an illness in you makes you dream such lies.

ALEX: I see you in Largo with rings on your fingers.

SOPHIA: I have no ring.

ALEX: You have my will – I signed it in your name. My good and chattels[45] – and another man. Your hands are claws!

SOPHIA: Your dreams are devils!

Lights fading on ALEX. *He turns his back on* SOPHIA.

SOPHIA: Sandy! Don't leave me like this. Come back to Largo with me and prove your dream a lie. You have been wrong before. Stradling is alive! Don't leave me. At least say you'll come back. Tell me: "God be with you til I come again . . . and love you." Sandy!

ALEX *is in darkness.*

(*After a pause*) When you come back you'll see – I'll still be here. I said I'd never leave you. I will not leave you. I'll wait here in this wretched stinking city . . . but you must come back to me! . . . Oh, God in heaven, Our Father which art in heaven . . . please! . . . I must be strong . . . help me . . . he will come back . . . help my loving well beloved, help him, I know he will come back . . . we were an island for such a little while only . . . (*as light fades, low, by note, in despair:*)

Let my cry come near before thee, O Lord: give me understanding according to thy word;

Let my supplication come before thee: deliver me according to thy word;

Let thine hand help me; for I have chosen thy precepts;

Let my soul live, and it shall praise thee;

Let thy judgements help me . . . help him . . . help him, Oh Lord . . .

Scene 13

Public house in Plymouth.

    ALEX *and* CANDIS *drinking together.*

FRANCES: A dream? . . . You mean to say you left your mistress – for a dream?

ALEX: I shall be dead soon, Frances – I shall die at sea.

FRANCES: Rats, my dear! Only the good die young! For God's sake – let the sea rule your life – and ships too, if you must – but not dreams! I never dream – or if I do, God damn me! – I don't think about any of it after – not once morning's here . . . (*amused and astonished*) You must have been already dead, then, in this dream? If she was claiming what was in your will? So – what do you care what happens when you're dead?

ALEX: We were an island . . .

In my dreams her hands were claws. Talons dressed with rings . . . She was my island . . .

FRANCES: Your island days were over long ago, my dear. Why, if it bothers you so – there's an answer stares you in the face! A babe in arms could see it! All you have to do is make yourself another will . . . then your Scotch wench can't go to Largo – not for *your* fortune, anyhow. And you won't die! (*Kissing him*) Not yet . . . Alexander . . . If I fetch some more ale, won't you smile for Frances: Um? And more? For Frances? . . . You have a month – or more – before the Weymouth sails. I'll show you that you're still alive – and why you mustn't die. A man needs more than dreams to live with – much more than that before a long sea voyage. And so does a woman . . . If a man's word is only as good as his dream – a woman needs much more! . . . I hope Frank's remembered to lock up. We want no more customers tonight. No other mariners on shore – like great wild Samsons with their manes cut off – struggling for strength!

Lights fading.

ALEX: In the name of God, I, Alexander Selkirk of Oarston[46] in the Parish of Plymstock[47] in the County of Devon, mate of His Majesty's Ship *Weymouth*, recommend my soul to God that gave it, and my body I commit to earth or sea as it shall please God to order. And as for and concerning all my worldly estate, all such sum and sums of money, lands, goods, chattels: I do give and bequeath the same unto my well beloved wife Frances Selkirk of Oarston. And I do hereby nominate and appoint my said wife Frances the whole and sole Executrix[48] of this my last will and Testament . . . hereby revoking all former and other wills, testaments and deeds of gift by me at any time heretofore made.

Scene 14

Some office at The Admiralty.

MAN: NEXT! . . . come along now, move forward quickly. There are others waiting . . . Well? What petition is this?

SOPHIA: Sir . . . I – I come to you in very great distress.

MAN: Yes?

SOPHIA: I . . . am in sore distress . . . alone and destitute here in this city . . . while my husband is at sea.

MAN: Your husband serves His Majesty's Navy?

SOPHIA: Yes.

MAN: What name?

SOPHIA: He is Alexander Selkirk. Sometimes called Selcraig.

MAN: What ship?

SOPHIA: He is mate of His Majesty's Ship *Weymouth*.

MAN: The *Weymouth*? The *Weymouth* is still lying in Plymouth. She is being refitted . . . And you say already you are in distress. (*Suspicious*) You are the wife of Alexander Selkirk?

SOPHIA: Yes, sir.

MAN: (*wearily*) Have you proof of this? When, and in what place was the marriage solemnised?

SOPHIA: We are married. In the sight of God.

MAN: Had you witnesses?

SOPHIA: We are married! By God!

MAN: Have you issue by the marriage? Have you children also destitute?

SOPHIA: No. No children.

MAN: You do not wear a ring! Have you papers? Deeds? Bonds? Nothing? (*Consults his lists*) I'm sorry. But the Admiralty lists show Alexander Selkirk to be already ma—... to be still in Plymouth. And there is nothing further I can do. You must move along now – there are others waiting. (*Angrily*) Next! Move forward quickly, there are others waiting – NEXT!

Scene 15

Public house in Plymouth. Laughter.

FRANCES: God damn me, man, what ails you? There's fresh pork roasting. Frank's gone to fetch another hogshead.[49] Alexander? God, but you're a melancholy man – can't you make merry the night before you sail? You've sat like thunder these two days – *and* nights! Alexander?

ALEX: I've seen your face before.

FRANCES: Well, well – now fancy that! Just fancy! You're married to this face!

ALEX: (*grabs at her hand*) You and your sweet friend Frank.

FRANCES: Let go!

ALEX: What makes you wear those rings?

FRANCES: I said let go. (*Calling*) Frank!

ALEX: What makes you wear those rings?

FRANCES: One for Ned Candis – God rest him at the bottom of the sea. And one for Alexander Selkirk – and if he sinks like a stone this coming voyage – I'll very likely wear a third. In fact – you can be sure of it! And gladly!

ALEX: (*laughs*) The widow Candis! The widow Candis and her sweet friend!

FRANCES: Oh, Jesus – not more dreams!

ALEX: It wasn't lies. It wasn't Sophia!

FRANK *enters.*

FRANCES: Your dreams shift with the wind, my dear.

ALEX: There were rings on that hand. Your rings.

FRANCES: You dreamt of me before you'd met me – did you? Dreamt of my belongings, even? Which gown was I wearing? This one – or the one I haven't bought yet?

ALEX: How could I understand? How could I? – God – you let me leave her! Almighty God! You never have been with me since I left the island! Are you laughing now? Do you laugh to look at Sophia now in London? Go on – laugh loud at me! Look at what I'm come to! Down to my last shirt again! And one more ship . . . And one clever cunning woman.

FRANCES: One lawful wedded wife. Who would look after you, whenever you were home – and not fret feebly while you were at sea. What more did you ask for? What more did you *want*?

ALEX: (*he's taking off his shirt, shouting*) I want! . . . I want – (*for a moment he's about to explode – but he's beaten*) (*moves to island area*) . . . I . . . climb the high ground for the wild black plums . . . walk home slowly by the sands . . . Looking for hope on the horizon . . . Sophia, dancing in sweet seas . . . singing like a blackbird . . . (*he's on the ground*) Each night . . . light my fire . . . Eat . . . Pray . . . Sleep . . . I want!

FRANK: What do we do with him now?

FRANCES: Lug him down to the ship. Before he gets up and raves again. Like some silly Samson!

FRANK: He isn't fit for the sea.

FRANCES: He isn't fit for the land! Fetch some of the men from their ale to help you. Get him on board the *Weymouth*. Now tonight. She sails tomorrow with the tide. He mustn't desert His Majesty's Navy!

FRANK: He said he would die at sea this voyage.

FRANCES: Everyone dies. Those who want to, they die easy.

Far off: sounds of the sea.

MAN: (*A figure in the darkness.*) His Majesty's Ship *Weymouth*. Sunday 13th December, 1721. On the Cape Coast Road. A deadly fever sweeps the ship; which we contracted when bringing on wood and water at the River Gambia.[50] The men grow fearful: sullen and difficult to control. This Sabbath day we buried at sea Alexander Selkirk, mate. There will be forty pounds wages due to his widow.

GIRL SINGER: (*voice-over, very soft, slow*) Hey, ca thro, ca thro,
See the moon is sporting
On the seas where we
Daily seek our fortune . . .

FRANCES: Born on the Sabbath – buried on the Sabbath!

FRANK: And only forty pounds to show for it.

FRANCES: There's worse news to come – This Scotch Sophia woman claims his wages! And she has been granted a probate[51] of a will in her favour. Frank – we have a fight to wager!

FRANK: It isn't worth it, Frances. What if it should go against us?

FRANCES: We'll see my will confirmed! And sue for any other moneys and securities that might be owing to me!

FRANK: You'll have the girl arrested – and imprisoned for debts? You'll never see your money that way either!

FRANCES: And she'll never see Largo! She should have fought before. Long before. Women must privateer as well as men!

GIRL SINGER: Hey, ca thro, ca thro
We have little for spending
Hey speed on, speed on
We have less for lending

SOPHIA *turns to the man* (*still a darkened figure*).

SOPHIA: Reverend Sir? . . . I being a person much reduced to want, by reason of this hard winter, presume to trouble you, I being the widow of Mr Selkirk, who was left on the island of Juan Fernandez; and besides – I have three uncles in Scotland, all ministers, of the dissenting faith, like yourself – . . . therefore . . . depending humbly on your consideration of my cruel circumstances . . . Reverend Sir? . . . Your petitioner will ever pray? . . .

GIRL SINGER: Hey ca thro, ca thro
Maidens dinna doubt it
There's better fish in the sea
Than ever yet cam oot it.

FRANCES: What do you say we go to Largo, Frank?

FRANK: To *where*?

FRANCES: To Largo – Fife – you great oaf – Scotland!

FRANK: God's blood!

FRANCES: The widow Selkirk must collect her dues – whatever they might be!

FRANK: You're not the widow Selkirk now – you're married to Frank Hall.

FRANCES: We'll go to Largo – you and I together! What do you say? We'll grab a fortune in our hands! Plunder!

GIRL SINGER: Some have tales for telling
Some have sangs for singing
Some have siller for spending
Some have pints for bringing
Hey ca thro, ca thro
See the moon is sporting
On the seas where we
Daily seek our fortune . . .
 . . . Hey, ca thro . . . ca thro . . .

Fade out sound of the sea. Blackout.

THE END

AN ISLAND IN LARGO
– GLOSSARY

aa: all
aboot: about
affronted: ashamed
alane: alone
argle-bargle: argue
auld: old
ay: yes; always
bairn: child
ban: curse
bargle: argue
barklog: tree bark used for cladding
besom: term of contempt, often jokingly used of young girls
bide: stay, live
bield: protection, shelter
birl: whirl round
black-gaitered: wearing black overshoes or leg coverings
bonnie, bonny: pretty
brae: slope, hillside
braggarting: boasting
braw: handsome
busk: dress up
ca thro: work hard
cam: came
canny: shrewd
carle: fellow
compear: appear in court as party to the proceedings
crabbit: ill-tempered
croon: mutter; hum
ding: strike; ding aa: strike all (everyone)
dinna: don't
firth: estuary
flummoxed: baffled
gin: if
girned: groaned
greet: weep

guddling: grope for fish with one's hands; work carelessly
guid: good
hame: home
haud: hold
hipsy: rosehip gin
howff: tavern
howk: dig up
keeking: peeking
ken: know
kirk: church; 'the Kirk': the Church of Scotland
kirkyard: churchyard
kist: chest
laird: lord
lass, lassie: girl; young woman
lee: lie
leear: liar
limmer: rascal, scoundrel, rogue; mischievous boy
links: sandy, uneven turf-covered ground alongside the sea
loch: lake
nae: no
oot: out
perjink: smart in appearance
sangs: songs
saucie: insolent, cheeky
siller: silver; money
sleekit: smooth; sly
sough: drawn-out sound made by rushing water or the wind
speering, speiring: asking
thro: through
unco: strange
wee: little, small
weesht: hush; haud yer weesht: be quiet
yer: your
yon: that

AN ISLAND IN LARGO
– NOTES

1. Firelock: a gun that requires a slow match to ignite the powder charge.
2. Largo: a parish in Fife containing the coastal villages of Kirkton of Largo (or Kirton, or Upper Largo), Lower Largo and Lundin Links (or Lundie Mill).
3. Vittles: victuals, supplies of food, provisions.
4. Tanner: tradesman who turns animal hide into leather.
5. Darien: isthmus in present-day Panama, location of an attempt in the seventeenth century to establish a Scottish colony. Its failure precipitated a financial crisis in Scotland and contributed to political climate that led to the Acts of Union of 1707.
6. Lima: capital of Peru.
7. Piemento: pimento tree, source of allspice.
8. Papism: Catholicism.
9. *Cinque Ports*: here, a ship named after a historic group of ports on England's south-east coast
10. Plymouth: English port.
11. Yawl: ship's small boat.
12. Pintado: species of seabird, the pintado petrel.
13. Juan Fernandez: group of islands situated 416 miles east of Chile; one is now named Alejandro Selkirk island, after its famous castaway.
14. Fife: historic county in Scotland, situated on the east coast, between the Firth of Tay and the Firth of Forth.
15. Dysart: coastal town in Fife.
16. Buckhaven: town on the east coast of Fife.
17. Leven: coastal town in Fife.
18. Lundie Mill: old, local name for Lundin Links, one of three villages in the parish of Largo. Kirkton: a village in the parish of Largo in Fife, also known as Kirkton of Largo or Upper Largo. Keirs: a settlement in Fife. The Law; Largo Law, a distinctive conical hill to the north-east of Largo. Pittenweem: a coastal village in Fife. Anster: a local name for Anstruther, a fishing port on the Fife coast. Crail: a coastal village in Fife. Arncroach: an inland village in east Fife.

Auchendinny: a village in Midlothian. Clackendinny: name of a small settlement. Balmain: a settlement near Largo, in Fife. Pitcairnie: diminutive of 'Pitcairn', a notable Fife family that gives its name to various places in the county. The Ferry: South Queensferry, a coastal village in West Lothian, and the southern end of a ferry service across the Firth of Forth dating back to the eleventh century. Elie, St Monans, Cellardyke and Crail: coastal towns and villages in Fife.

19 Esau: older brother of Jacob in the Bible, Genesis 25.25, notable for his hairiness.
20 Careen: the act of cleaning a boat's hull.
21 Tallow: solid fat of cattle, used in making candles, soap, etc.
22 Balsam of Peru: an extract of the Santos mahogany tree from South America, used for flavouring, perfumes, and in medicines.
23 Quince: fruit of a central Asian tree.
24 Guyaquil: the main port and largest city in Ecuador.
25 Firth of Forth: the broad estuary separating Fife, on the north shore, from Lothian, on the south.
26 Papists: Roman Catholics.
27 Dumbarnie Links: coastal area in Fife.
28 Curlew: species of migratory wading bird.
29 Feverfew: medicinal flowering plant in the daisy family. Sithes: chives, a plant used in seasoning.
30 Tammy Norrie: a proverbially slow-witted person.
31 Bristol: English port, a common point of departure for voyages to the Americas.
32 Worsted: wool fabric.
33 Panegyric: text written in praise.
34 Newgate: prison in the City of London, that remained in use from 1188 to 1902.
35 York: English city in north Yorkshire.
36 Mosquito Indian: Miskito people, who live in Central America, along the Mosquito Coast.
37 Steele: Sir Richard Steele (c. 1671–1729), an Anglo-Irish writer, playwright and politician; co-founder with Joseph Addison of The Spectator magazine.
38 Oroonoque: Oronoque River in Guyana.
39 Taylor: William Taylor, publisher active in the early eighteenth century. Pater Noster Row: street formerly at the centre of London's publishing industry.

40 Notary: public official who certifies documents.
41 King George: George I of Great Britain (1660–1727), ruled from 1714 until his death.
42 Privateer: armed private ship, licensed to attack enemy shipping in time of war.
43 Chandler: supplier of provisions and specialised equipment.
44 Samson: character in the Old Testament Book of Judges; he was divinely granted superhuman strength on the condition that he did not allow his hair to be cut.
45 Chattels: personal property.
46 Oarston: Oreston, a village in Plymstock parish, Devon.
47 Plymstock: a parish in Devon.
48 Executrix: female appointed to execute a will, that is, to ensure its provisions are honoured.
49 Hogshead: large cask or barrel.
50 Gambia: major river in West Africa.
51 Probate: legal determination of the validity of a will.

WHITE ROSE

by Peter Arnott

First performed at The Traverse Theatre, Edinburgh, 23 May 1985

Cast

Lily Litvak *Kate Duchene*
Ina Pasportnikova *Tilda Swinton*
Alexei Salomaten)
   The Director) *Ken Stott*
   The German)

Inspired by the book *Night Witches: The Untold Story of Soviet Women in Combat* by Bruce Myles (Mainstream, 1982)

AUTHOR'S INTRODUCTION

Peter Arnott

White Rose had a pretty tangled history for me in regard to Scottishness, law, personal ambition, poetry, Oxbridge et al . . . and I'm not sure I really want to go into any detail about that . . . as it would be self-serving and inevitably partial to do so. So I won't . . . except to say that I was tremendously lucky with most of it and that life as a playwright turned out to be a damn sight more complicated than I thought in between the time the show was on from when the show was commissioned.

The brief was absolutely ideal . . . write something for three actors for the studio space at the Traverse (the studio space downstairs at the Grassmarket) and it's on in May and can we have something epic, please?

So that was good. Oh, as was the Festival revival in August, seeing David Steel turn up to see the show in a white dinner jacket . . . and Derek Jarman wearing overalls to offer Tilda Swinton a part in his Caravaggio film. And the party in from some Russian State Theatre, with their KGB handler, all in floods of tears.

I had no idea, really, what heady stuff it was . . . but with Jo Clifford's *Losing Venice* and Chris Hannan's *Elizabeth Gordon Quinn* both being on in that festival too, knowing that something very special was going on, and true enough I've never known a time as acutely full of feeling.

Then I was young . . . very young. I went from a fresh-faced twenty-two to a haggard twenty-three while this was going on.

And bliss it was in that dawn to be alive . . . and to be young was very heaven.

Cast

LILY LITVAK

INA PASPORTNIKOVA

ALEXEI SALOMATEN

The characters of the DIRECTOR and the GERMAN are played by the ALEXEI actor.

WHITE ROSE

Act I

Newsreel One

Music. LILY *and* INA *pose for a propaganda film. The voice of the* DIRECTOR *is heard.*

LILY: (*as if ready to run to her aircraft*) We are the women air fighters of the 586th Division, 73rd Fighter Regiment; the Free Hunters of Stalingrad.[1] We kill lots of Germans! Na zdorovje![2]

She runs. The DIRECTOR *stops her.*

DIRECTOR: Again!

LILY: (*reluctantly doing another take*) We are the women air fighters of the 586th Division, 73rd Fighter Regiment; the Free Hunters of Stalingrad. We kill lots of Germans. Na zdorovje!

(*to* DIRECTOR, *angrily*)

Better?

DIRECTOR: (*impatient*) Carry on!

INA: We engineers salute our pilots. We salute the men and women workers in the factories and our glorious soldiers. We salute our courageous Russian People. We also salute the Comrade General Secretary[3] for his direction and inspiration in the struggle. We promise we will help to drive the fascist beast back into his hole, and come home and breed happy healthy children!

(*to* DIRECTOR, *eagerly*)

All right?

The DIRECTOR *enters with a light meter.*

INA: Is this going to get shown everywhere? I want my parents to see it especially.

DIRECTOR: Not your boyfriend?

LILY: Come on, Ina . . .

INA: I haven't got a boyfriend.

LILY: Will you put that in your film? That she hasn't got a boyfriend?

DIRECTOR: Have you got a boyfriend?

LILY: You've taken your pictures, now take them away and show them to people who don't care about our boyfriends whether we've got them or not.

DIRECTOR: But they do care, Comrade Captain. These pictures are being distributed to raise morale in the munitions factories so that we can win the war all the sooner. Are you saying we should deny these workers the pleasure of wondering about you, wanting to know about you? They will, you know. People are like that. It's a tribute to your accomplishments as a pilot, nothing more.

LILY: You are very correct.

INA: I told you, Lily. You're famous. People want to know about you.

LILY: There are other pilots . . .

INA: But they want to know about you.

LILY: Then you tell them, Ina.

> LILY *exits*.

DIRECTOR: (*to her back*) Thank you so much, Comrade!

(*to* INA) She's tired, probably.

INA: She's sensitive about outsiders.

DIRECTOR: Outsiders? We are all in this together, Comrade. That's the point of my film.

INA: Well, people from outside the unit, you know . . .

DIRECTOR: Ah, yes, my apologies, comrade, the unit . . . of course . . .

INA: You ought to make a film about Lily. A special film all about Lily. I think people would like that.

DIRECTOR: With respect, I'm not sure that Comrade Captain Litvak appreciates the role of cinema in the war effort. Still, it's a thought. The beautiful huntress of the night . . . we could do with a little romance . . .

INA: Romance?

DIRECTOR: Oh, it's not frowned on any more, you know. Nothing really is, so long as it's cheerful. She is lovely. She'll photograph very well. She's not at all severe looking.

INA: No.

DIRECTOR: Well, give me your thoughts, comrade. I'm only here while there's a battle. Our troops are on the point of victory. Soon I'll be filming their triumphal entry to the ruins of Berlin.

INA: She's a woman fighter pilot. She flies at night. Most of her life is at night, more or less. Did you see her roses? I paint a rose on her fuselage for every fascist she shoots down.

DIRECTOR: Red Roses?

INA: No, white. There are some white roses she likes near the hangar.

DIRECTOR: Pity . . . I might have been able to shoot in colour . . .

(*thinks*)

Hold on, though . . . White Rose . . . Lily Litvak, the White Rose of Stalingrad. It's got possibilities. A pale Soviet[4] flower that rises from the ashes of the city . . . Could be . . . could be. I'll let you know.

INA: When?

DIRECTOR: Might take some time. There are committees . . . you know . . .

INA: We might not have time. That's why I want you to make this film.

DIRECTOR: Have no fear, Comrade. Our troops are on the point of victory. Soon I'll be filming their triumphant entry to the ruins of Berlin.

INA: You said that before.

DIRECTOR: It's my line in the film. I wrote myself in. "The War Workers Promise the Motherland Victory" Don't you believe that promise, engineer?

He exits. INA *turns to the audience.*

Newsreel Two

INA: I'm nineteen, Lily is twenty-one. This airfield is eight weeks old.

LILY *re-enters, accompanied by the male actor now as* ALEXEI. *The* INA *and* ALEXEI *actors narrate the newsreel.*

ALEXEI: Stalingrad, formerly Tsaritsyn, monument to the sacrifice of thousands, monument to the acceleration of history . . . reduced to rubble, a waste of burning stone.

INA: They've said they will bomb us into slavery. Into nothingness.

ALEXEI: Six hundred fascist planes raided the city on August the 23rd, 1942. They killed forty thousand civilians, made six hundred thousand homeless.

INA: It was those civilians who built this airfield, and fifty-one others like it, on this side of the river, within three weeks of the tanks reaching the suburbs.

ALEXEI: Three divisions with their backs to the Volga,[5] bombarded night and day. Stalin[6] has instructed them to stand. And they stand.

INA: The monster Hitler[7] has told his fascists to take Stalin's city no matter what the cost. So they stand too.

ALEXEI: History will picture two great wills, contesting every street, every building, every broken room. But history is the people.

INA: And we're here too. Making history. And eating and shitting and falling in love. And killing too, sometimes.

ALEXEI: In these six months in Stalingrad, eight hundred thousand people will die and the tide of fascist victories will finally be turned.

INA: In these four years of war, twenty three million of our people will die, more than half of them civilians. Only one out of every three men between the ages of seventeen and twenty-three ... will survive this war.

ALEXEI: Whose anniversary we mark with reverence and celebration.

INA: We in the Soviet Union remember, whether we are faithful to the Party,[8] to the country, our families or even just ourselves. We remember that our current allies all invaded us in 1919, and that they refused to join a common front against the fascists, some of them hoping, perhaps, the fascists would destroy us for them. We remember everything. And let you remember too.

ALEXEI: We took a quarter of a million prisoners in Stalingrad. Less than seven thousand of those prisoners ever got home, alive or dead.

The actors go back into character as LILY *talks about herself.*

LILY: I used to tell my parents I was going to drama classes. By the time they knew the truth, I was a qualified pilot.

Targets of Opportunity

ALEXEI *briefs the squadron while* INA *and* LILY *recount how they came to join it.*

ALEXEI: Targets of Opportunity! Divisions 580, 584 and the two new ones 587, the lady bombers . . . and 589 are to protect the Volga Ferries, and it is our job to protect them. It will be hairy enough for you, I promise you.

INA: I got a telegram from Marina Raskova[9] . . . my girlhood hero, I don't mind admitting. She said I was to come to Moscow for an interview. "Bring suitable clothing," she said, "you won't be going home."

LILY: Moscow was in disguise when I saw it last, on my way to meet Raskova. Sandbags on the roofs, tank traps on every corner. A young man singing to keep people's courage up. On his own! The police didn't bother him. Wooden painted boards being hauled up over the dome of St Basil's[10] to disguise it from the air. I used to listen to Raskova's broadcasts on the radio.

ALEXEI: We'll take off with the bombers, sweeping the city from North to South and back again. It's a big place, so keep breathing on your fuel gauge. Groups of sixteen, pilot wingman, pilot, wingman.

INA: Raskova's got this hard face. Years of concentration have made her skin tight. It'll sag if she ever retires. She was very kind. More than ever I wanted to be like her, I told her . . .

LILY: (*interrupting*) Now look, Marina Mikhailovna, I wasn't built to be a railway worker or anything like that. My Dad used to introduce me to his workmates, and get me little jobs sweeping out the waiting rooms . . . but every hour that I'm not in the air is wasted as far as I'm concerned. I used to follow the members of the flying club around and eventually I talked them into letting me join a year early. I showed them what I was made of. I knew the Yaroslav trainer better than they did. Every lead and screw. They were quite taken aback.

INA: They made me train as an engineer at the Academy. I didn't mind as I still managed to get a hundred hours or so flying. I didn't want to push my luck with them. I thought they might not let me fly at all if they thought I was too big for my boots.

She glances at LILY.

ALEXEI: Here's a little bonus for those of you who were with as at the defence of Moscow. Von Richthofen's[11] flight are here, flying the new Fokker-Wulf 190s.[12] It's a mean bitch of an aircraft, comrades, so let's get up there and kick his arse. We are here to kill Fascists, comrades ... on the ground and in the air ... the best and simplest, busiest job in the Airforce. I trust you'll seize these targets of opportunity with sweaty hands, brothers!

INA: Of course, Comrade Raskova, I'll serve in any way I can. I mean the war is everything, isn't it. There just isn't anything else. It's a bit like looking down a long tunnel ... don't you think ... or into a cave ... a long, dark cave.

LILY: I mean, I'm good enough. Just look at my papers. You'll never see better references. Look, I know they're worried about discipline and all that, but I'm a pilot, Comrade Raskova. And any man who doesn't recognise that determination and match it will get nothing out of me. Oh, if I miss an opportunity like this, I'll just kill myself.

ALEXEI: Oh, and you can kiss goodbye to your Yak Sevens. We've been assigned thirty spanking new Yak Nines[13] ... got a rate of climb faster than the ME 109,[14] 37mm cannon, 12.7mm machine gun. Just wait till you've got a monster like that between your legs.

INA and LILY: Then Marina Raskova said:

INA: Your engineering skills are in great demand.

LILY: Do you think Hitler invaded us just that you could show off your skills as a pilot?

INA: Think of how you'll be able to help the other women, as well as the men.

LILY: You might get your way at the Moscow Flying Club, but this is the Army.

INA: It's far more difficult being an engineer, and the fact that you're experienced as a pilot will make you invaluable on the ground.

LILY: I asked her if that meant she'd turn away a first class pilot. She scowled and said "Wait and see." That's fine by me, I thought. I know the answer. I know just how good I am.

ALEXEI: Finally, a sober word, comrades. Never in the history of warfare have so many aircraft been concentrated on a single battlefield. We are pioneers, comrades. We are on the frontier of a new kind of war. And for the sake of all humanity . . . we have to win.

(they raise their glasses) For the motherland!

LILY and INA: For the motherland!

They drink. INA *crosses to* LILY. *This is their first meeting.*

Members

INA *is exhausted and lonely.* LILY *is fresh and eager.* INA *introduces herself.*

INA: Pasportnikova.

LILY: Litvak.

INA: I know. How did you get your uniform to fit you so well?

LILY: Oh . . . I stayed up a couple of nights. Made some alterations.

INA: You must be clever.

LILY: How's that?

INA: Only, I never thought of altering my uniform. I just reconciled myself to looking like baggage, you know.

LILY: I'm proud of my uniform.

ALEXEI *approaches.* LILY *lights up with ambition.*

ALEXEI: Litvak? Is that right? I've heard of you. Salomaten. How was your flight in?

LILY: Just fine, Captain. When do I go into action?

ALEXEI: I see you've made friends with Pasportnikova here. That's fine.

LILY: When do I fly, Captain?

ALEXEI: You don't, I'm afraid. Extraordinary no-one's told you. Some of the lads are a bit unhappy about the idea of having a woman as a wingman. Completely unreasonable I know. You'll be going straight back when we get papers through for your replacement. Strikes me as extraordinary with all the strides that women have made . . . well . . . that these attitudes still exist. But there we are.

LILY: I've been flying for five fucking years, Captain. Longer than most of your lads. Look at my commendations.

ALEXEI: I understand, comrade, you don't have to tell me . . . I'm on your side . . .

LILY: Then . . .

ALEXEI: But a fighter squadron is a jumpy, superstitious sort of animal, Litvak. Your ability is not in question, but I have to consider morale . . .

LILY: What about my morale . . .

ALEXEI: Well, I'm sorry. I understand your disappointment, believe me, but . . .

LILY: Are you speaking for yourself? Do you think there's anything wrong with women pilots?

ALEXEI: I'd fly with a dog if I could teach it to hold a control column . . .

LILY: You are losing four pilots a week, Captain. Don't talk to me about dogs. I am the best pilot you've ever seen.

ALEXEI: I don't need you to tell me about losing pilots, Litvak.

LILY: Then you take me up. Let me fly one sortie as your wingman. I'll stick to you, Captain, you just try and shake me off. If you can spin me out, you can send me to sew shirts in Sebastopol.[15]

ALEXEI: I wouldn't do that. The Germans have occupied it.

LILY: Take me up, Captain. There are half a million fascists twenty miles away.

ALEXEI: I'm not sure we have a free aircraft.

INA: Lieutenant Domkin is still injured sir. I can have his aircraft ready in an hour.

ALEXEI: You're off duty, Pasportnikova.

INA: There are half a million fascists twenty miles away, sir. Besides, Litvak has been specifically assigned here by the High Command, sir. I read it on the notice board.

(*she quotes verbatim*)

"Exception has been made in the case of Pilot Officer Litvak and twenty other women throughout the Soviet Air Force to be assigned to male fighter units because of their exceptional skill and aggression", sir. Litvak is an outstanding pilot. I've seen her fly. You are countermanding the express orders of the High Command to preserve the ambience of your boys flying club. Sir.

LILY: I want to talk to the commander . . .

ALEXEI: Oh, I'll talk to the commander, Litvak.

LILY: And what will you say?

ALEXEI: Wait and see.

LILY: Will you tell him . . .

ALEXEI: Pilot Officer Litvak. Insistence is one thing. Insubordination is quite another. There are limits to my sense of humour.

LILY: I don't see what's funny, sir.

ALEXEI: Don't give me a reason to have you grounded. I can see to it that you never get to fly anywhere at all, Litvak, here or anywhere else. There are lines drawn in this Boy's Club, Comrades. Be careful where you tread.

He exits. LILY *pulls closer to* INA.

LILY: Do you smoke?

INA: No.

LILY: Neither do I. I think I might start. How do they expect me to fight two wars at once. I just want to be useful.

INA: Hmn.

LILY: Oh. Thanks for sticking up for me.

INA: That's all right. I've seen you fly, like I said. At Engels.[16]

LILY: Oh, were you in Engels?

INA: Yes.

LILY: I feel like a nagging wife or something.

INA: I know. You can waste a lot of energy that way. You insisting that you fly is just you doing your job. You must fly.

LILY: How are your engines? You're an engineer, aren't you.

INA: Engines are all right. They keep you occupied. They have logic as well as temperament. You can get fond of engines.

LILY: Look at your hands. Isn't there any hot water?

INA: I know. I don't think about it much. Some of the men make remarks. I mean, I'm up to my eyes in grease so that they can fly around being heroes and they complain about how I look. I don't care now. But it used to make me self conscious and stupid. And I'd make mistakes, and end up working longer than the others. Which amuses them.

LILY: I had a friend who worked as a mail carrier in Siberia.[17] And he told me he used to drain water from his engine when he landed. Had a wash and a cup of tea. He called his plane "the Samovar".[18] You should try that.

INA: Not in the time we have to turn them round . . . we don't have time . . .

LILY (*not listening*): Confidence. That's all you need. Confidence. Being clear in the head is a habit, like riding . . . or flying. It's a skill you have to acquire. But you never lose it. All you need is a bit of confidence.

INA: Confidence. That's what my grandmother said the great ladies had in the old days. She said you could always tell a real lady by her quiet confidence. Of course they were fucking quiet. They had nothing to do all day. It was my granny did the work. A princess had nothing to distract her from getting on with being a princess. But do you remember how at Engels . . . how calm and purposeful everyone was . . . even me? When it was just the women. How surprised everyone was there was so little bitching going on. The instructors just got in the way. It was just us . . . just us being together with a purpose we shared.

(LILY *has stopped listening*)

Lily?

LILY: Sorry. I was thinking about something else.

INA: It's nothing.

LILY: No. What were you saying?

INA: Nothing important. You're waiting for news. You don't have to listen to me.

ALEXEI *enters.* LILY *jumps up.*

LILY: Well?

ALEXEI: You fly with me on dawn reconnaissance tomorrow. Don't show off and you'll be fine.

(*thrilled,* LILY *turns to* INA, *who smiles equivocally*)

Now, say thank you.

LILY: What for?

(*softening immediately*)

Thank you, Captain.

ALEXEI: No need to thank me. Just doing my duty. Welcome to the boys and girls club. See you in the morning.

He goes to exit. LILY *catches him.*

LILY: What time?

ALEXEI: Stupid of me. Five Thirty. Here.

LILY: Sounds fine.

LILY *is beaming with excitement.*

ALEXEI (*to* INA): Tell you what, Pasportnikova. It's a real pleasure to see people looking happy.

INA: Yes, sir.

ALEXEI: You two will bunk together . . . so do try to buck up, Pasportnikova. You have a little hut all to yourselves, you two. With a guard on the door. To protect you . . . from the Germans.

A slight pause as he and LILY *look at each other and* INA *looks at them, holding* LILY's *bag.*

LILY: I'm sorry if I've given you any trouble.

ALEXEI: Well . . . you've had a bit of trouble yourself.

LILY: See you later, then.

ALEXEI: Yes. In the morning. Good night.

ALEXEI *salutes rather self-consciously and exits.* LILY *smiles after him.*

LILY: He's really quite shy, your captain.

INA: Yes, he is.

LILY: You wouldn't have thought that.

INA: Suppose you wouldn't.

LILY: That he'd be vulnerable. (INA *stares at her.*)

INA: Vulnerable, Pilot Officer Litvak? Vulnerable to what?

LILY: What's wrong with you?

INA: Nothing, Comrade. Allow me to take your baggage to your hut.

LILY *exits angrily.* INA *turns to the audience.*

INA: Women. When you come to struggle
For yourselves, struggle as yourselves,
As women. And when you win
Remember how. Love yourself by loving them
Think of fire, and do not glow at a man's desire.

Do not love how he loves to look at you
Love yourself. You are lovely.
Then think of loving him.
Not back, but forward.

Accounts of the Battle

ALEXEI *and* INA *quote accounts of the battle for Stalingrad.*

ALEXEI: Crawl, get in close, use the ruins . . . said General Chiukov[19] to his men. Dig your trenches in the night, cover them with tarpaulins, bricks and dust. Attack without noise, machine gun on your shoulder, ten or twelve grenades. Now two of you get inside the house together, grenade in first, and you after. Room by room. Grenade in first, and you after. One strict rule. For God's sake give yourself room. You're in danger putting one foot in front of the other. A grenade in each corner of the room . . . short fuse . . . one, two, three, four . . . then the machine gun, rake left to right, rake up, rake right to left another grenade in the centre, then into the room, always on watch for what's left of the fascists. An alcove? Grenade. A corridor? Grenade. Then on.

INA (*reads from a captured diary*): We have fought for fifteen days for a single house, writes the German Lieutenant in his diary, with mortars, grenades, machine guns and bayonets. By the third day, fifty-four German corpses are strewn in the cellars, on the landings and staircases. Faces black with sweat, we bombard each other in the middle of explosions, clouds of dust and smoke, fragments of furniture and human beings. Ask any soldier what half an hour of hand-to-hand fighting means in such a fight. And imagine Stalingrad. Eighty days, and eighty nights of hand-to-hand struggle.

(INA *reacts to the book*)

Well, you weren't invited. German Poet.

ALEXEI: Into the corridor, three machine guns, one to the far wall, one in the doorway, one looking back, firing continuously. Turn the air inhospitable. Now get a move on. Inside the objective of attack, the enemy may go over to counter attack. Act with greater ruthlessness. Use your initiative. It is in your hand. Machine gun, dagger . . . spade. Fighting inside a building is always frantic. Be prepared. Look sharp for the unexpected.

(*to the audience*)

This is what we are flying over.

INA (*reads*): Stalingrad is no longer a town. By day it is an enormous cloud of burning, blinding smoke. And when night arrives, one of those screaming, howling, burning nights . . . the dogs plunge into the Volga and swarm desperately to reach the other bank. Animals flee this Hell. The hardest stone cannot bear it for long. Only men endure.

(INA *puts down the book, and speaks to the audience*)

Where is the purpose in these foreigners? Where is the commitment? This is observation, like he was in a balloon, like he wasn't really here. Like he wanted to be somewhere else. Pain. Terrible pain.

(*to the book*) Why did you come? Did you ever know what you were doing? You were beaten before you got here.

(*to the audience*) Fools. Fools.

Ina's Hands

LILY *is asleep.* INA *comes in, her hands injured. She attempts to bandage them silently. But she moans, and* LILY *wakes.*

LILY: Ina . . . what's the matter?

INA: Nothing, Lily. You go back to sleep.

LILY: Ina. Are you going to tell me what's wrong?

INA: I hurt my hands a little. That's all. Nothing to worry about.

LILY *crosses to her and looks at her hands.*

LILY: Let's have a look. (*she sees that it's bad*) Oh, Ina! (*she takes over the first aid*) So what happened?

INA: I left my gloves off. Some skin froze. Got stuck. And came off on the engine.

LILY: Oh . . . Ina!

INA: Look, don't bother . . . you need to rest.

LILY: It's no bother.

(*she treats* INA's *hands in silence for a moment*)

Why on earth did you take your gloves off?

INA: I was having an argument.

LILY: Were you having an argument, little Ina?

INA: I took my gloves off, and threw them on the ground to make a point.

LILY: And hurt your hands?

INA: Yes!

LILY (*finishing*): There's my brave girl. Who were you having an argument with?

INA: One of your flight. Meklin.

LILY: What did he say? I'll sort him out for you.

INA: He wouldn't let me work on his aircraft. I mean, he wasn't doubting my ability or anything like that. He just didn't want me touching it. Like I had a disease or something.

LILY: How stupid of him.

INA: So I said to him, have I got the plague or something. Scared I'll put a curse on your engine, are you?

LILY: Well, Ina . . . a pilot does have the right to choose the engineers they want to work on their aircraft. After all, it's the pilot who has to fly the thing.

INA: That's what he said. Before he said I was getting hysterical.

LILY: You're tired, that's all.

INA: Don't be an idiot, Lily. Tell Meklin he's tired.

LILY: The men . . . will take time to adjust.

INA: Oh yes. Let's all be reasonable about it. It's fine for you. They've adjusted to you flying all right.

LILY: You know how long that took. You know the time I had.

INA: I know that I stood up for you. I supported you. But you will still not choose to stand for me against one of your precious bloody pilots. Because you're a pilot. And it is too much of me to ask you to show me some support . . . too much to expect a little solidarity.

LILY: I'm a pilot first, Ina. They all know that. I'm not married, I've got no children, so it doesn't make any difference.

INA: You're such a fool sometimes, Lily. You think you know when you're well off. But you don't know that you're insulted. When they insult me. And you pretend to yourself it isn't there.

LILY: What isn't there?

INA: You don't hear the things they say. The things I hear when I finish work and they're all drunk. And you didn't see the disgust in that little boy's eyes when he thought of my hands on his engine. You've forgotten what it's like. To hate yourself. The way men can make you hate yourself. Because you think you're just like them, don't you? One of the lads? Well, you're not. You're not. No matter how normal they pretend to be. You've started hating me now, haven't you. You're sitting there thinking what a bloody woman I am.

LILY: What do you want from me?

INA: I want you to support me. I want you on my side.

LILY: Do you want me to go on strike? Look . . . you should go and see the Women's Commissar[20] at Division. This is her job. She'll tell you . . .

INA: She'll tell me what Lenin[21] said. She'll tell me all about Lenin and Krupskaya[22] and the partnership of men and women in revolutionary struggle.

LILY: I don't have time for this conversation.

INA: I bet you that's what Lenin said.

LILY: Look . . . there is bound to be residual prejudice . . .

INA: Residual prejudice! You know that doesn't sound too bad. I'm sure Meklin can cope with being a victim of anachronism. I'm sure he'll correct this tendency as soon as he has a spare moment. We all go to the same schools, everyone keeps telling us how equal we all are . . . all he has to do is understand it properly . . .

LILY: Settle down for God's sake. We haven't fought before, so why do you want to spoil things now.

INA: Oh, am I spoiling your war for you, Lily . . . how selfish of me, just when it was going so well . . .

LILY: Don't be so stupid!

INA: Don't be such a stupid woman?

Pause.

LILY: We can't do this, Ina . . . we've got to settle . . . .

INA: Settle for what?

LILY: For what there is! This isn't the place for this conversation, Ina.

INA: Where is the place for this conversation?

LILY: (*pause*) I'm sorry if you think I'm behaving like a man, if that is what I'm doing, but man woman or beast I've got to fly a mission with the rest of them in three hours' time. I'll be facing a squadron of Messerschmitts[23] . . . with them . . . in three hours. I don't have time to think about it.

INA: Just try . . . for me . . . just try not to be so proud. That you are too busy . . . there is no time to think about it. Because that . . . is thinking like a man.

Pause.

LILY: How are your hands?

INA: They're all right.

LILY: I'm sorry.

INA: That's all right. War brings out the best in people. (*shrugs*) I chose a bad moment for a crisis.

LILY: Well . . .

INA: What?

LILY: I had a bit of a crisis myself today.

INA: You did?

LILY: Why not? I'm entitled to a crisis too.

INA: I didn't say you weren't. Tell me.

LILY: Today . . . tonight . . . I was flying with Salomaten, and we passed a flight of Heinkels.[24] We passed them. We let them go and bomb our men in the tractor factory. I broke radio silence to protest, and Alexei was furious. He said we'd get them on the way back when they were short of fuel. We got two of them. And it cost maybe a hundred . . . two hundred Russian lives. He fights so cynically, Ina. All he wants to do is shoot down Germans . . . like it's a game. He isn't fighting for his homeland or anything else. That's his homeland, up there . . . shooting down Germans. I don't know, Ina. It scares me. It seems like . . . indiscipline. I think that we're fighting not to lose, Ina . . . not to be wiped out. I don't think I can think about it any further than that. I'm the trigger on a flying gun. I just fire where I'm pointed.

INA: Lily . . . are you in love with Alexei Salomaten?

LILY: Yes. Are you?

Assignation

ALEXEI *drinks, and repeats words from a funeral oration he has just given.*

ALEXEI: Barnarov was my friend, as well as my commander. We fought in many a campaign together. Spain. That was the warm one. Finland, Moscow, Leningrad. All bitter. And now here. As an officer and as a man, his loss will be sorely felt.

(*he stops quoting*)

This war has gone and touched me. No. It has. And now I can hear the guns. All the time. Before, I could shut them out, most of the time, but now I'm listening to the guns. And, oh yes. I'm getting the message. You don't fool me, you clapped out old fraud. You're fucked. You're past it. On the slippery fucking slope for absolutely sure. Old Barnarov would have understood. When you've been in this business for a while, you come to recognise it in your comrades. This little distance behind the eyes . . . not all there. And there isn't long to go, when you slip into the sheets with death . . . and the bastard's still there in the morning. Killing people is just flirting with it death. This, however, this is an engagement . . . when you're inviting your bullet . . . when you just don't care for just one second . . . you are setting a date for the wedding. So, I will drink, to make my marriage to death more bearable, and I will make love to Lily Litvak. I will betray death with her, and conceal from myself my thinness on this earth. I do hope it's nothing catching. Lily. I need you.

LILY *enters.*

LILY: You sent for me?

ALEXEI: Oh no. I hope I didn't send for you. I sent word I'd like to see you. There's a difference. Please. Sit down.

LILY (*sitting*): Thank you, sir.

ALEXEI: Well, Lieutenant Litvak. How are things with you now?

LILY: Not so bad, thanks.

ALEXEI: You're pleased with your promotion?

LILY: Yes, sir. I'm just sorry . . .

ALEXEI: For what?

LILY: The circumstances.

ALEXEI: Well . . . that's how it is.

LILY: Yes, Sir.

ALEXEI: Good. So, you're feeling more settled in with us now. I can imagine what you've been through.

LILY: Can you, sir?

ALEXEI: Well, I hope so. I'd be a poor excuse for a flight leader . . . or a squadron commander . . . now . . . if I didn't notice these things.

LILY: Yes, sir. I'm sorry, sir.

ALEXEI: Yes. Well. Would you like a drink?

LILY: Oh. Yes, thank you.

ALEXEI (*pouring two drinks*): I couldn't have asked you that a few weeks ago, could I?

LILY: Couldn't you? Why not?

ALEXEI: It would have been tactically unsound. But now that I've been informed that the Fourth Tank Corps have shaken hands with the Twenty-Sixth, and that the enemy are now encircled, with no means of getting away, I didn't think that you would resist the urge to celebrate.

LILY: This has just happened?

ALEXEI: Yes.

LILY: Then we must celebrate. What's the toast?

ALEXEI: You choose.

LILY (*stands*): Marshall Zhukov.[25] Saviour of Moscow. Liberator of Stalingrad.

ALEXEI: Here's to the old Cossack.

(*they drink,* ALEXEI *takes the glasses to refill them*)

I would throw our glasses in the fireplace. But I've only got these . . . and I haven't got a fireplace.

He gives her a glass.

LILY: Your turn.

ALEXEI: Oh. Very well.

(*he raises his glass*)

To us. May we see the summer.

LILY: Yes. I suppose that's right. To us.

They drink. ALEXEI *pours another.*

ALEXEI: Here. No toasts attached. This one is purely for purposes of leisure.

LILY: Shall I fetch Ina? I'm sure she'd like to celebrate as well.

ALEXEI: No. Don't do that.

LILY: Why not?

ALEXEI: You used to make me feel very uncomfortable, you know. You used to scare the life out of me. You're a wonderful pilot. Everybody says so.

LILY: Do they?

ALEXEI: Oh, yes. Everybody.

Pause. They are very close.

LILY: Tell me about Barnarov. You and Barnarov.

ALEXEI: You'd like that, would you?

LILY: He was your oldest friend. It's only natural to be upset. But if you don't want to talk about it . . .

ALEXEI: You're very beautiful, Lily. That's no reflection on your abilities as a pilot, by the way.

LILY: Oh. Well. Thanks.

ALEXEI: They made you cut your hair, didn't they?

LILY: It has to be practical. But some of the other girls have never cut their hair at all. And the men all like it. That annoys some of the rest of us, I can tell you.

ALEXEI: I imagine.

LILY: There's nothing inconsistent about caring how you look.

ALEXEI: Inconsistent with what?

LILY: Killing fascists. So long as it doesn't interfere with what's important..

ALEXEI: Well, there's no looking good by accident. Besides, it makes you accessible. Makes you a good comrade.

LILY: Am I a good comrade?

ALEXEI: Yes. Have another drink.

LILY: No, really. It concerns me.

ALEXEI: What can I tell you? Who's telling you you're not . . .

LILY: Well . . .

ALEXEI: People of your generation continually astound me. You are all so serious.

LILY: Our situation is serious.

ALEXEI: Yes. We know that. We know that. So you don't need to continually demonstrate it. All right? It's a waste of energy, and it's bad for morale. Hang the sense of it and fly. Just fly, damn it. Flying is what we are good at. Leave the ideology to the ideologists. That's what they're good at. Lily. Serious people are serious because they enjoy it, in my experience. And good luck to them. Not me. Not everyone can be a philosopher, which is obvious to everyone except philosophers. Be honest with yourself. You know what matters to you. And to me. And it's up there. Lily. You are a pilot, yes? Well I am a soldier, and all soldiers are the same deep down. Thick as pig shit and grateful for it. Oh, we can deploy a smattering of Marxese[26] whenever we might need it, but we have to concentrate on doing our job. Which is not a job for philosophers. It's a job for professionals. We are here to kill Germans. The rest is decoration. Cheers.

He drinks and pours another.

LILY: Don't you think there will be Germans fighting for Hitler who think exactly the same way?

ALEXEI: Course there are. I've trained with them. Back in 1940. Why?

LILY: Doesn't that worry you?

ALEXEI: No. I don't think so. If you're asking me whether I think I've got more in common with a Luftwaffe[27] pilot than I do with a commissar, yes, I should think I probably have. Monstrous, of course. But as long as the philosophers insist on proving their philosophies in wars, they'll just have to put up with barbarians like you and me fighting their wars for them.

LILY: I believe in what I'm fighting for.

ALEXEI: I know. That's why you upset me. Because you are a real pilot and a real philosopher . . . all at the same time. It's people like you, pioneers like you who have made it possible for clods like me to fly at all. You're an original. Blériot,[28] Lindbergh,[29] Raskova . . . Litvak. Well . . . it sounds a little Jewish, possibly . . .

LILY: It is Jewish. My grandfather was Jewish.

ALEXEI: You mustn't pander to egalitarianism, Lily. It ill becomes angels to be democratic. And be honest with me. You don't believe that you're "just another pilot" any more than I do.

LILY: You're impossible.

ALEXEI: Drunk. Don't confuse excess with originality . . .

LILY: Ina says . . .

ALEXEI: Oh . . . Ina! Ina is an engineer. The salt of the earth, no doubt. But you are a flier. Lily Litvak is a flier first and last. It is different for you. You know it is. So don't worry about Ina, don't worry about anything, just . . .

LILY: Fly.

ALEXEI: Fly.

He goes to pour another drink.

LILY: Don't drink any more.

ALEXEI: Just you try and stop me.

She kisses him. A long kiss. They look at each other.

ALEXEI: How old are you, Litvak?

LILY: I'm very young.

They kiss again. Sealing the deal. Pause.

ALEXEI: I'm a worn out old heretic, Lily. You're going to have to accept that.

LILY: Nothing's changed, Alexei.

ALEXEI: Hasn't it?

LILY: No. There's no reason for us not to be lovers, as long as it fits in with killing as many Germans as possible. We must be sure we're consistent in what we're doing.

ALEXEI: Well, that's right.

LILY: I feel very positive about it.

ALEXEI: Yes?

LILY: Hmn. Very confident.

ALEXEI: Good.

LILY: I've got to get back. Come to my quarters tomorrow night. We won't talk on the field in the morning. We've got to be careful. We can't lose strength in love. It's got to be part of our strength. We mustn't see each other as a retreat from the struggle.

ALEXEI: No, of course not.

LILY: Let's just concentrate on getting down safely and finding somewhere to make love. I'll check Ina's duty roster.

ALEXEI: All right.

LILY: Good night then.

ALEXEI: Good night.

LILY exits. ALEXEI pours another drink and drains it.

ALEXEI: Girl scouts. Junior bloody girl scouts. What do you think, Barnarov? "We mustn't see each other as a retreat from the struggle". I am wet from the smell of you, Litvak. And I can't hear the guns at all.

Act II

Lily Meets a German

A captured GERMAN *airman, in handcuffs.*

GERMAN: They've been almost human so far. Then, they are pilots, aren't they? Like me. The one who shot me down though. Reckless. Complete disregard for his own safety. I bailed out. I thought I was behind our lines. They'd moved. What comes of losing wars.

(*pause*)

That pilot! They don't have any regard for human life. We've slaughtered millions of them. Millions. I heard there were a million in Leningrad alone. They're like animals. How else can they stand it?

(*pause*)

Perhaps we haven't behaved entirely as soldiers. I've seen the villages. They'll have seen the villages too. The livestock. Women. Children. Terrible, terrible things . . .

(*outburst*)

We've bitten them . . . By God we have. They won't forget us in a hurry. Bombed them into the stone age. And now I'm in their hands.

(*pause*)

I've heard stories. About their women. What they do to the men they capture. My God, I've seen pictures . . . now Be calm, Erich . . . you are among aviators. Professionals. Who will understand. That orders are orders, duty is a categorical imperative. We can all live together in peace and harmony . . . (*suddenly fierce*) They'll fear us till the end of time. The end of time . . . and the next time, Ivan, we will have the world on our side. England and America will waken to their danger, and then next time we will have the world behind us and your Jewish, Bolshevik[30] poison will pollute the world no more.

(*he laments*)

I am a stricken wolf. In a cage of rats.

INA *enters with a tray of food, followed by* LILY *carrying a rifle.*

GERMAN: Now, Erich. Calmly. Do nothing to provoke them. (*to the women*) Vielen dank.[31]

INA (*with difficulty, speaking a foreign language*): They tell me you want to meet one who shot you down.

GERMAN: Yes. Yes, he was a real ace, whoever he was. I'd like to shake him by the hand.

LILY: Well?

INA (*translating*): He says he wants to shake your hand.

LILY: Does he? Hold on to this.

LILY gives INA the rifle and goes to shake the GERMAN's hand. He shrinks from her, smiling nervously.

Tell him.

INA: She shot you down.

The GERMAN decides that they're kidding, and to go along with it. He smiles and takes LILY by the hand.

LILY: He doesn't believe it. He's humouring us. Tell him he's a stupid pig and he flies like an ox.

GERMAN (*to INA*): What does she say?

INA: She says you do not think she shot you down and that you fly like . . . you're not a good pilot.

GERMAN (*withdraws his hand in disgust*): Tell her I will no longer speak with her.

INA: He doesn't want to speak to you any more.

LILY: Tell him he flies like an elephant.

INA: You fly like a . . . cow.

LILY: Isn't that "cow"?

INA: I don't know the German for elephant.

GERMAN: Elephant?

LILY: It's the same, see?

GERMAN: I fly like an elephant?

INA motions him to be still.

LILY: He's a coward. He pulled up to avoid the poplars near the river and I got right on his tail.

INA: She got behind you at the trees.

LILY: Near the river, left bank.

INA: Near the river, left bank.

GERMAN: You?

LILY: Jawohl. Ich.[32]

INA: Do you believe she is the pilot?

GERMAN: No. Somebody told her.

LILY: I picked him up at two fifteen. I came out of the sun.

INA: Did she come out of the sun?

LILY: I chased you down the river, south.

INA: Down the river? South?

LILY: One hundred and fifty feet.

INA: One hundred and fifty feet?

LILY: You turned west.

INA: You turned west?

LILY: You turned west, and then you nearly hit the trees.

INA: You were close to the trees?

LILY: And didn't I hit you as you climbed, and broke out of your roll, and I yawed right to avoid you, and then you lost me till I fired my cannon through your starboard wing, and didn't you go into a spin, and didn't I perform a perfect stall turn to follow you down, firing one more burst that cut your propeller shaft? And didn't you bail out then? And didn't he see the white roses on my tail plane as he fell?

INA: I can't keep up! (*to the* GERMAN) Five white flowers.

GERMAN: Flowers? Roses?

INA (*recognises the word*): Yes! Roses.

GERMAN: Lily Litvak? You're Lily Litvak? Oh, thank God! I thought you were just some woman.

LILY: What's he saying Ina?

INA: He knows who you are now.

GERMAN: Lily Litvak! I don't believe it! I am honoured.

LILY: Why is this pig so happy?

INA: He thought you were just some woman.

GERMAN: But you are Litvak. You are Lily Litvak!

Pause.

LILY: What are today's orders on prisoners, Ina?

INA: They're to be handed to the NKVD.[33] They're already on their way.

LILY: He'll be shot immediately. That's what that means. Doesn't it? We're advancing too fast to be bothered with prisoners.

INA: Yes.

LILY: Tell him.

INA: Why?

LILY: Give me the gun. I'll save them the trouble.

GERMAN: What is she saying?

LILY: The gun, Ina.

INA hands her the gun. LILY points it at the GERMAN's head.

This is the enemy, Ina. I've got him. Why don't I just squeeze. In the air, I didn't hesitate. I thought he was dead anyway.

LILY moves behind the GERMAN, forces him to kneel, the gun at the back of his head.

In the neck. That's what they do, isn't it? Hundreds of them at a time.

INA: That's what they do.

LILY: The state takes its revenge for the people.

INA: Yes.

LILY: What's to stop me taking mine? Tell me, Ina.

INA: There's nothing to stop you.

LILY: I promise you, Ina. I don't care. It doesn't make any difference to me.

The GERMAN whines and shuffles terrified towards INA. His hand touches her foot. She pulls back and kicks him in the face.

INA: You're an animal. A fucking animal.

LILY: Ina . . . look . . . he's pissed himself. I can't do it. I'm a pilot.

LILY exits, handing INA the gun. INA turns to the audience. The GERMAN exits during her speech.

INA: Do not think only of what the oppressed must contend with;
   Think also of the lives they must invent as they struggle.
   Struggling, as they do, from the necessities of their oppression,
   They must reinvent their lives out of those same necessities.
   Do not think only of the prejudice that Lily has had to overcome.
   Think also of the life she has invented as a means to that end.
   For if her means are not her end, then the end will escape her.
   Our hope is that it will not escape us, in our new dark times.
   From out of the necessities of the struggles of today
   Spring the inventions for the shape of tomorrow.
   Necessity is the mother of invention,
   And invention is the life and form of revolution.
   Even if we lose a battle, the shape of our excitement
   And the pleasures of invention bring the war's end a little closer.
   This is the meaning of consciousness, indissoluble and enduring.
   Our defeats are only partial. Each one painfully builds our victory.
   Block by block our awareness rises till our inventions reach
   That height of quality, wit and scope that will finally
   Bring us freedom, and let us live peacefully.
   If we need a new world, we are certain, finally, to invent it.

Ina and Alexei Discuss the Future

INA *pours* ALEXEI *a drink.*

ALEXEI: No. Thank you.

INA: Take it. It's there.

   ALEXEI *drinks. Then takes a letter from his pocket and starts to read.*

INA: How many times are you going to read that? It is my letter.

ALEXEI: You let me read it, didn't you?

INA: Once.

ALEXEI: Then if I read it again it makes no difference.

INA: Hang on to it. You might as well.

ALEXEI: She sounds ghastly. Miserable.

INA: She will be. Being away. I'd be miserable away . . . if I knew she was here . . . and that I had to come back. Her poor mother.

ALEXEI: She doesn't say anything about her mother.

INA: I know. That's the point. She's devoted to her mother. Her mother's taking care of her.

(ALEXEI *looks puzzled*)

What can she tell her? How she got wounded? How do you tell your mother it just happened? That there you were flying happily and then there was a piece of engine sticking through your leg.

ALEXEI: Ina . . .

INA: There's no explaining this experience in an apartment flat in Moscow. There's no place there for it. You're supposed to tell your parents your news. Our news is in the papers. How do you explain that this cramped hostility is the same thing every day . . . and the same for the fascists as it is for us? Her mother must feel like she's feeding soup to a stranger.

ALEXEI: You do ramble on, Ina.

(*pause*)

INA: She's going to get a medal . . .

ALEXEI: Yes. I suppose so.

INA: How do you feel about that?

ALEXEI: I'm pleased for her.

(*pause*)

I wouldn't be in Lily's shoes. They're going to make a meal out of our White Rose. There'll be invitations to Party functions for the rest of her life. Presentation dinners, speeches to women's groups . . . school kids. Christ it makes me shudder.

INA: She'll be greatly honoured.

ALEXEI: She'll be greatly patronised.

INA: They've got her age wrong in the papers. It says she's seventeen in Isvestia. Maybe they'll give her some Hero of Youth medal.

ALEXEI: She won't like that. She wants to be an adult.

INA: She won't mind. She is an adult.

(*pause*)

Are you missing her?

ALEXEI: Of course I am. I fly better with her. I'm well past enjoying it for its own sake. But I enjoy her flying. Lily still flies like she means it. I just push my Yak around the sky. But Lily actually flies. Lily Litvak on her wings of steel. I'd like to marry her.

He looks at INA.

But maybe that's not a good idea. And anyway she might say no.

INA: I'm not contradicting you.

(*concedes*)

Perhaps she wants to wait.

ALEXEI: But why? This is the perfect time . . . right now. I mean, if one of us got killed what difference would it make if we were married or not? And I love Lily . . . here. Now. But in some veteran's apartment for retired heroes? With Lily looking after the kids?

INA: What makes you think she'd look after the kids?

ALEXEI: Well she wouldn't. Of course she wouldn't. How could I ask her to be my little wife? When I've seen her do what she can do? No. She'd want children, I think, but then she'd hand them over to some stone-faced hag with immaculate ideology while she went off on lecture tours and flying transport missions in Kirghizstan.[34] How could I stop her? I wouldn't want to. It's stupid to even think about it.

INA: I thought you were thinking about the future. Marriage. Children.

ALEXEI: I want her now. Right now. It's not that I don't want to think about the future. I just can't see it . . . So I don't know if I could be in love with her in it.

INA: So it's a battlefield romance, then?

ALEXEI: That's not what I said, Ina. It would be a marriage made in hell . . . and lived out back on earth. I don't know.

INA: Marriages have to be made somewhere. My great grandmother never approved of a marriage unless it was made in her kitchen. She was a village matchmaker. It was a good system, I think. A village is a fragile thing, and who is married to who is very important. Love is for the movies. Or for cities . . . where it doesn't much matter who you marry.

ALEXEI: What happened to your great grandmother?

INA: She remarried and retired. Lost her objectivity. I like that. People retiring when they lose their objectivity.

ALEXEI: Ina Pasportnikova. As you are so notoriously thoughtful, you have been appointed as matchmaker for the 586th Airborne Village of the Red Army. Though we are currently plagued by a tiresome horde of Tartars[35] your work must go on.

(ALEXEI *raises his glass*)

And here's to a society organised by unmarried women who retire when they lose their objectivity. Let's go back to the good old days, poor and shitten, but comprehensible. Here's a suggestion for you, Ina. After the war, you become the General Secretary. Give Stalin the push. He won't mind. I'm sure you're capable of it. And he's known to be understanding. Then you can brood over old Russia like an observant grandmother, while we hatch good socialists in our native, peasant straw. And I'll marry Lily. And we can make a start under your supervision.

INA: I don't know about that.

ALEXEI: Ach. You've no ambition. You're a good socialist already.

INA: I don't see myself at Party functions, toasting myself. I can see you there. And Lily. One day I'd like to fly again. We'll see what happens.

ALEXEI *takes hold of her around the waist and pulls her to him. Pause.*

INA (*level*): Why are you drinking so much tonight?

ALEXEI: Am I? More than usual?

INA: Yes.

ALEXEI: Well why are you being so serious? I think you should have another drink.

INA: I get more serious when I drink.

ALEXEI: Well I get even stupider . . . and I think that's the right way round.

(*he releases her*)

For Christ's sake, engineer, have a drink and at least be company. Celebrate, why don't you? There is a war on and you are a non-combatant. So celebrate. If you won't do anything else, at least you can celebrate that.

INA: Are you scared, Alexei?

ALEXEI: Well of course I'm scared, Ina. I have been relying on my wingman more than was good for me. The hell with her and the hell with you. I gave her two presents to go away with. A golden dagger to remind her of me . . . but she asked me for a book of poetry. Love poetry. Awful stuff. She has personally killed a dozen

Germans... and she's reading this... shit... You talk about her mother feeding soup to a stranger? I've been sleeping with one. Am I really as stupid as you think I am? Am I really so selfish? Is Lily really all that strange? Really?

INA: Time was the matchmakers' cure for philosophy.

ALEXEI: Good for you, Ina. Always cool. Always contained.

INA: I'm selfish too. I don't feel your pain. I don't feel the pain that brought you and Lily together. I can see it, but I don't want it. You wanted her to share your pain... and now you find yourself saddled with hers as well. You didn't anticipate that she would have pain of her own.

ALEXEI: Why does it still scare me? I've seen more of it than you have. Why aren't I used to it?

INA: Because you think there's something behind it. Some lesson to be learned. Some meaning to be drawn from who gets killed and who doesn't. You can't hap thinking there's a story in it. So you're not capable of giving yourself over to the struggle completely. There's still a part of you that you want to keep safe. But you can't. You know you can't. That's why you're exhausted. That's why you're scared.

ALEXEI: You think I should relax more? Get into the swing of things?

INA: I think you should keep quiet about it. It's hard for everyone. You should read bad poetry, like Lily does. If you still want to do something irrelevant.

ALEXEI: So what do you do with your leftover consciousness?

INA: At the moment, I'm talking to you. I'm wondering what it is that people like you might want out of life.

ALEXEI: Any ideas? That you can share with me?

INA: Mirrors. You want mirrors. Flattering ones, everywhere you look. Multiply your vanity by a few hundred million, and that's the world you've made.

ALEXEI: I've made? Me personally.

INA: Men generally, and the women helping them. You do your part.

ALEXEI: So now I'm responsible for men generally.

INA: Not at all! I hold men responsible for you. Men are so fond of looking at themselves in the mirror of the world they've made that they've made themselves all alike.

ALEXEI: Men aren't all alike.

INA: That's the beauty of the mirror system. Men don't know they're all alike.

ALEXEI: You know what you are? You are a smart arse.

INA: That's right, boy. You put me in my place. Make me a proper woman, looking at you in your mirror, rapt in wonder at your beauty, standing right behind you so that you can look at me without taking your eyes off yourself.

ALEXEI: We're all on the same side, Pasportnikova.

INA: I know what side I'm on. I'm not so sure about you. You should let other people talk more often.

ALEXEI: You talk well. For a woman.

INA: That's a start, comrade. Maybe we will be able to talk about the future one day. The real future. And you won't try to dig around in me when you want to marry someone else entirely.

(*she pours them another drink*)

Cheers.

ALEXEI: What's the toast?

INA: What else, comrade? To the winning of the war.

Newsreel Three

The actors narrate the beginning of the end of their story.

LILY: My wound wasn't serious. All I needed was to build up my strength. I rejoined the unit at Rostov-on-Don[36] in May of 1943.

INA: She'd lost a lot of blood. By rights she should have fainted, been smashed to pieces on the ground. It was miraculous that she had landed safely.

ALEXEI: Lieutenant Litvak was promoted to Captain and recommended for the highest commendation. Really, I was pleased.

INA: More and more the press turned up to take her picture . . . doing embroidery between missions. She had shot down eleven German planes in less than six months active service.

LILY: When I was in Moscow on sick leave, an artillery captain mistook me for a secretary and demanded I come to a meeting to take notes.

ALEXEI: The bluntness of her reply took the captain by surprise.

INA: He must have thought she was in the secret police. It was only ever the secret police who got away with screaming at artillery captains. She was always lucky like that.

LILY: I was apprehensive, coming back. A whole month at home. I felt flabby and distracted. Loose inside my head.

ALEXEI: The performance anxiety of the professional.

INA: Things had changed when she came back. Fewer missions to fly, and the guns mostly quiet. Summer sun. After Stalingrad it was as quiet as the moon.

LILY: Lack of activity went to my head. It was terrible. Another world.

INA: A world with time to think, where you felt you could see the war, see the world. A bit like from the moon. See the world there in space. Whole and beautiful. It's only whole things, considered as a whole, that can be beautiful. Planets. Lives. From here on the ground, it's all too hard to see. The world is fragmented and you have to be practical. But from the moon, suddenly you could see that what we were doing was making history. History shaping itself out of every move we made. The world being reinvented as it turned.

LILY: I hated it.

ALEXEI: Our losses fell away, the flowers bloomed and the roads dried out. We were flooded with supplies.

LILY: Air superiority. Our supply lines were secure.

ALEXEI: While the invincible fascist war machine was strung taut and frayed from the Vistula[37] to the Don,[38] its path strewn with wreckage.

LILY: Our vanguard found pits of bodies, masses of white tormented limbs, tangled in a covering of sweaty, bloody earth. Jews. Like my grandfather. Like my father. Like me, they would have said. We knew who they were now. We knew what we were fighting. This was not repelling invaders. Not for me. They had be crushed, wiped out, utterly without mercy. So they would never dare to rise again.

ALEXEI: Lily and I went walking in some woods one night. We found the naked, rotting, mutilated carcass of a teenage girl . . . perhaps a partisan . . . perhaps not . . . tied upright to a tree.

INA: Whole towns and villages had been erased, emptied for slave labour, extermination, reprisals against partisans. We were given fiery, tearful lectures by our commissars. They seemed to relish this moment of moral superiority. They shook with hatred and righteousness and terrorised the ones who were to do the actual fighting with calls to greater and greater sacrifice. While any crimes they commited . . . or ordered to be committed . . . were expiated. Like they were stealing the war away from the fighters. Using it. For themselves.

ALEXEI: And like evangelists we proclaimed universal freedom. No more talk of socialism in one country. This was a crusade. And the grey survivors, Stalin's bureaucrats, became fervid and eloquent, demanding of the fighters justice and purity in voices mean and twisted by the war.

INA: The war went mad. We went mad. Officially, at any rate.

(*she looks over at the others*)

As for Lily and Losha, the Prince and Princess of the night skies of Stalingrad . . .

ALEXEI: Well, we weren't energetic. We were lazy about it. We were tired of who we were. We even stopped making much effort to arrange our duties so that we could see each other. We only flew together sometimes. My caution on her behalf had become embarrassing for her. She would shrug me off. That stopped bothering me quite so much after a while. It wasn't often that I woke in the night from a dream that I was burning alive in my cockpit, and I needed her to talk nonsense to me for an hour, till my sweat went cold and hard.

INA: I worried for them. It took a rare courage to be lovers on a battlefield. And to be honest with each other. It was an invention . . . that made such demands on them. That's what I thought. (*starting to set up the final scene*) In Rostov, I taught Lily to play chess. It seemed an appropriately tactical way for her to pass the time. We were waiting for Alexei to come back from training his recruits. It was the last day of our war together.

The three hold a pose, as for a portrait of a moment in time. Then ALEXEI *exits.*

Lily and Ina Play Chess

The women are playing chess outside on a summer morning. LILY *paces.* INA *concentrates on the board.*

LILY: It's quiet. I can't hear anything.

INA: The guns are on the move again. You're not concentrating.

LILY: Six hours on standby. It's unheard of.

INA: It's a long way to Berlin. It's a matter of wearing them down from now on. Pursuing them. Isn't it better this way?

LILY: If you like chess.

INA: And you don't.

LILY: I want to do more with the pieces. They're boring.

INA: Of course they are. Check.

LILY: What?

INA: Knight to queen's bishop three. Check.

LILY: All right, all right.

She moves out of check. INA *puts her back in check.*

INA: Check. No room to move. You'll make a mistake soon.

LILY: Then you'll pounce. You fiend.

INA: A little foresight, a little planning. Want to concede?

LILY: That'll be the day.

LILY *moves.*

INA: All right. *(she moves)* Check.

LILY *(moves)*: This could go on all day.

INA: If you say so . . .

INA *moves.* LILY *stares at the board for a moment. Then looks up and grins at* INA. INA *panics.*

INA: Shit.

LILY: Can't take it back . . . *(moves)* Check, I think.

INA: Yes.

LILY: A little planning, a little foresight.

INA *(moves)*: Shut up.

LILY *(moves)*: A little flair and imagination . . .

INA: Yes. (*takes* LILY's *queen*) That's your queen. Sorry. I've told you. You can't play this game just by instinct. Sorry.

LILY: I didn't see that.

INA: No.

LILY: Oh well . . .

LILY knocks over her king. They sit back, squint at the sun. Pause. INA looks up.

INA: Where's Alexei?

LILY: Up there somewhere. With the new boys.

INA: He seems to be very fond of them.

LILY: He likes being a big brother to them. They like it too.

INA: I don't see the attraction myself.

LILY: You could try to be more friendly.

INA: Nasty little boys. Playing with their toys.

LILY: Bitter. Bitter.

INA: What do you expect? I've twice the flying hours that any of them have, I know the machines inside out and they treat me like a servant. They do. Then one of them had the arrogance to offer me a drink. Some little squirt.

LILY: He might be good for you. You know how you like to be lecturing somebody.

INA: I wouldn't have the patience. And they'd never listen to me anyway. They're having too good a time with their Uncle Alyosha. I don't mind the engineers so much but the pilots are cold-blooded babies.

Pause.

LILY: Have you thought about what you're going to do? When it's over? When things are back to normal?

INA: I'll teach. Mechanical engineering.

LILY: Would that be good enough for you?

INA: Why not? It'd be all right.

LILY: Not like you not to be . . . focused. I'd have thought you'd have had a whole campaign planned out.

INA: There's no point in planning what you can't control. You did say "back to normal"? I would have thought my teaching engineering would be normal for someone who never stood out in the boy's flying club . . .

LILY: You're very cynical.

INA: It's the time on my hands. And you did ask.

LILY: I'm going to marry him, Ina. I decided to last night.

INA: Right. Have you told him yet?

LILY: No, I haven't.

INA: But you've decided anyway. Good. That's good. You wild impulsive thing. Good.

LILY: "Good". That sounds a bit final.

INA: It is a bit final. Congratulations.

LILY: Thank you. And I hope you can cheer up a bit and that you'll get to fly again. You can if you really want to. If you try hard enough.

INA: Sure.

LILY: You do still want to fly, don't you?

INA: For Christ's sake, Lily . . .

LILY: What?

INA: Nothing. It's your faith. It's a little hard to swallow.

LILY: My faith in you?

INA: No. No. Never mind. How's the lucky fellow?

LILY: I don't know. I think he's fine.

INA: Yes. He does seem happier.

LILY: How do you know?

INA: He told me. We do talk sometimes. We talked a lot while you were away.

LILY: About me?

INA: It's not likely he'd talk to me about anything else.

LILY: So . . . does he ask you things? Does he ask you what I tell you about him?

INA: He tries not to be too obvious. It's quite charming in a way.

LILY: So do you tell him?

INA: No. And no, I'm not going to tell you what he says about you. There is such a thing as solidarity.

LILY: You sit there and soak us both up?

INA: I think of it as maintenance. Attending to flying machines when they've got a screw loose.

LILY: Really?

INA: Well there's no scope for gossip. For a pair of secret lovers you've been pretty public about it. I'm told that "Love in the Air" is the new divisional motto.

LILY: Don't mock. It's not right to mock.

INA: We all need a part to play, princess. Something we can call our own. It's just my way of coping. It helps me to get up in the morning, the prospect of snooping and superiority.

LILY: You don't seem to like yourself very much today.

INA: Not something with which you have a problem.

LILY: That's not fair.

INA: You better get on with it. He's going to propose to you any minute.

LILY: Did he tell you that as well?

INA: No. But I heard him practising last week in his cockpit before take-off. He saw me and went as red as pickled beetroot.

LILY: I hope he concentrates and doesn't get distracted.

INA: He won't. He's a professional.

LILY: Why do you keep saying that like it's a dirty word? What is wrong with you today?

INA: Nothing. Nothing you want to know about.

LILY: I'd like to understand. I'd like to know what you're thinking.

INA: Would you really like that?

LILY: Yes. Tell me what you're thinking.

INA: I'm thinking that you're blind. I've always thought that about you. I think that everybody is blind. And that professionals like you . . . and him . . . you choose to be blind.

LILY: Blind?

INA: You wander about in a dream. You're going to get married. You're going to fly forever and have roses round your door . . . and all the world will love you . . . and you deserve everything you've got.

LILY: What does that even mean?

INA: You are privileged. With talent and stupidity. You see? I told you didn't want to know.

LILY: I'm good at what I do.

INA: And you think that's enough? You think you can drift along happily being "good at what you do" while you're spouting rubbish?

LILY: You're right. I don't think I do want to hear this.

INA: You haven't got a mission now, princess. So you are going to listen to me.

LILY: Am I?

INA: It's easy up there in the sky. It is! Why do you think those boys have such a wonderful time up there? Why do they act like royalty down here? Like they do? Because it's easy for all of you. Oh, ask any of you why you're doing it and you'll spout some pre-digested crap about the motherland. Ask you what you'll do after the war, and you'll dribble out some shit you've got memorised about reconstruction and the forward march of socialism . . . because you just see the world from up there . . . where it looks like a map . . . with clear directions and targets of opportunity . . . well it's not like that for most of us, it's a mess . . .

LILY: I know it's a mess . . .

INA: And that's just the way it is, and there's nothing you could do about it even if you wanted to . . . which you don't. You really don't.

LILY: Ina, I'm as engaged in all these questions as you are . . .

INA: Engaged, Lily? You're incriminated, and especially when you're up there looking down on the rest of us. When you are free of all the tedium and complications you have to put up with when you're stuck down here! In the mud.

LILY: Are you jealous?

INA: Probably! I'd love to be an expert! I'd love to be a genius . . . a master of the world! This war is a dream come true for the likes of you. Never mind the cost, never mind the complexity. We are flexing our minds and we never stop to ask ourselves why.

LILY: We are pilots, Ina, not Gods . . .

INA: But that's how it feels . . . up there, with it all laid out below you. That's the power and the joy of it. Can't you imagine the leaders up there, looking down at us, sticking paper flags into the world, obsessively plotting and planning their strategies?

LILY: The war has to be won, Ina. So that kind of power needs to be given to these people.

INA: But they'll never let it go! Can't you see that? Can you see them ever relinquishing control of such big, bright engines? When they love them so much, when they love what these machines can do for them, and they love making them perform for them, better and better all the time, when they've had five years with this kind of power? Don't you remember . . . the boys didn't mind you flying . . . but Meklin didn't want my dirty hands on his big bright engine? They have all got your faith, Lily. Your blind faith in the machine, in the righteousness of ability and energy, in the unquestionable correctness of being good at what you do. When you don't know what you're doing and you just don't care. Don't let them tell you lies!

She chokes into silence, unable to be clear. Pause.

LILY: You're right, Ina. I don't understand you. I don't know what's become of you. I think you've maybe gone a little mad.

INA: Yes. I know. I have. I'm sorry.

(*suddenly she cries out*)

I love you, Lily. I wish I could fly like you. Fly out of all this shit.

She breaks down. LILY *holds her, uncomprehending. Eventually . . .*

LILY: Ina . . . I don't know what to say.

INA: Doesn't matter. It doesn't matter. Don't say anything, Lily. Just be the princess of the air. Be Alexei's own best girl. Don't listen to me. Be whatever you want to be. Whatever you want.

(*embraces her*)

Oh, Lily. Promise me you'll have lots of kids for me to play with. I want to be their eccentric Auntie Ina, and go for picnics by Patriarch's Pool.[39] And you and I can have terrible arguments on our way home.

LILY (*they recover. Then* LILY *looks up*): Look Ina . . . there's my prince now, flying over the mill house.

(*she looks back to* INA, *who keeps looking beyond her into the distance*)

We will have time, Ina. We will.

INA (*looking*): He's gone.

LILY (*turning to look*): What?

INA: The nose dropped. He's gone.

LILY *keeps looking into the distance.* INA *steps forward and talks to the audience.*

INA: We jumped onto the truck that went speeding to the accident. It was an accident. Alexei's flight had made no contact with the fascists. The free hunters had liberated the Soviet skies. Accidents happen sometimes. They were already playing hoses over his aircraft by the time we got there. But Alexei was a good pilot. He knew the danger from fire, and he'd already switched off his engine when he'd seen there was no way of landing safely. I wish that he hadn't given himself that chance. I wish he'd burned and been lost to us completely. His head was perfect, but his plane had collapsed like a concertina and crushed his body with it. His perfect head and face, his eyes closed, were perched on a body that would have fitted in a shoe box. I had to hold Lily back from taking hold of him. His head would have come off in her hands, and she would have gone mad. We all knew. One of the firemen . . . he just knocked her out and heaved her onto the truck that took us back to the bunker. I didn't look round when I heard the head fall. I never really spoke to her again, after that afternoon. She seemed to fade into the war after that. I lost her. She wasn't really concentrating, the comrades told me, even when she was flying. Her love for flying, for me . . . for everything . . . was gone. You recognise it, when you've been in combat, in your comrades. That little distance behind the eyes. We'd been in combat for less than eleven months when her aircraft disappeared over the Don Estuary. I think of her, often. And I am strong.

(INA *says her farewell in the manner of the propaganda film*)

Ina Pasportnikova. 586th Division, 73rd Fighter Regiment. Still living in hope. Never flew, never married, never joined the Party.

(*she salutes*)

Dosvedanya.

BLACKOUT

WHITE ROSE – NOTES

1. Stalingrad: a large city on the Volga river in Russia. Formerly called Tsaritsyn, it was renamed in honour of the Soviet dictator, Josef Stalin, in 1925. In 1961, it was renamed again, and is currently called Volgograd. From July 1942 to February 1943, Stalingrad was the site of a major siege and bloody battle between the Soviet forces and those of Nazi Germany. The battle is regarded as the bloodiest example of urban warfare in human history. It ended in a victory for the Soviet Union.
2. Russian: You're welcome!
3. General Secretary: General Secretary of the Communist Party of the Soviet Union. From 1924 until 1991 the person holding this post was effectively the leader of the Soviet Union.
4. Soviet: relating to the Soviet Union, or the Union of Soviet Socialist Republics (USSR), which lasted from 1922 to 1991. The political structure of the USSR was nominally based on workers' councils, or 'soviets'.
5. Volga: the river on which Stalingrad/Volgograd stands.
6. Joseph Stalin (1878–1953): the General Secretary of the Communist Party of the Soviet Union, from 1922 to 1952, during which time he became a dictator, or sole ruler. He led the Soviet Union through the Second World War.
7. Adolf Hitler (1889–1945): dictator who led Nazi Germany from 1933 to his death by suicide.
8. Party: the Communist Party of the Soviet Union, which governed the USSR from 1922 to 1991.
9. Marina Raskova (1912–1943): the first woman in the Soviet Union to become a qualified air navigator. She commanded a bomber regiment in the Second World War, and died in 1943 when her aircraft crashed making a forced landing on the banks of the Volga river.
10. Saint Basil's: Russian Orthodox cathedral situated in Red Square in Moscow, characterised by its colourful onion-shaped domes.
11. Von Richthofen, Wolfram (1895–1945): a German fighter pilot during the First World War who rose to the rank of Field Marshal in the Luftwaffe (the German air force) during the Second World War.

12 Fokker-Wulf 190: the Focke-Wulf 190, a German single-seat fighter aircraft used in the Second World War.
13 Yak Seven/Nine: Russian fighter aircraft used during the Second World War, designed by Alexander Sergeyevich Yakovlev.
14 ME 109: the Messerschmitt 109, a German fighter aircraft commonly deployed during the Second World War.
15 Sebastopol: the largest city in Crimea, and a major Black Sea port.
16 Engels: a Russian city and port, located on the Volga river, home to a military airbase.
17 Siberia: an extensive and sparsely populated region in North Asia, notorious for its long and severe winters.
18 Samovar: characteristic Russian metal container used to heat and boil water for the brewing of tea.
19 Vasily Chiukov (1900–1982): a Soviet general and military commander, who commanded the 62nd Army during the Battle of Stalingrad during the Second World War.
20 Commissar: a Russian political officer, responsible for the political education and organisation of the military unit to which they are assigned, in order to guarantee political control of the armed forces.
21 Vladimir Lenin (1870–1924): a Russian revolutionary and leader of the Soviet Union from its inception in 1917 until his death. In 1898 he married fellow revolutionary, Nadezhda Krupskaya.
22 Nadezhda Krupskaya (1869–1939): a Russian revolutionary who in 1898 married fellow Communist, Vladimir Lenin. She was influential in the development of Soviet education and librarianship.
23 Messerschmitt: a make of German aircraft, usually fighters, commonly deployed in the Second World War.
24 Heinkel: a make of German aircraft, usually bombers, deployed in the Second Word War. Manufactured by a company founded by Ernst Heinkel.
25 Georgy Zhukov (1896–1974): a Marshal of the Soviet Union who, in the Second World War, directed the Red Army in some of its most important victories.
26 Marxese: a type of discourse expressing the political, social and economic principles of Karl Marx, a nineteenth-century German philosopher whose work influenced the Communist revolutionaries of the Soviet Union.

27 Luftwaffe: the German air force during the Second World War.
28 Louis Blériot (1872–1936): a pioneering French aviator, inventor and engineer. In 1909, he made the first aeroplane crossing of the English Channel.
29 Lindbergh, Charles (1902–1974): a pioneering American aviator and military officer, who in 1927 made the first non-stop flight from New York to Paris.
30 Relating to the Bolsheviks, the radical faction of the Marxist revolutionary party that seized power, under Vladimir Lenin, in Russia in 1917.
31 German: Many thanks.
32 German: Yes. I.
33 NKVD: the Russian interior ministry and feared secret police from 1934–1946. The acronym is based on the Russian for 'People's Commissariat of Internal Affairs'.
34 Kirghizstan: former state of the Soviet Union in Central Asia, now the independent Kyrgyz Republic.
35 Tartar: people from Tartary, a region in Central Asia.
36 Rostov-on-Don: a Russian port on the delta of the Don river.
37 The Vistula: a major river in Eastern Europe; the longest river in Poland.
38 The Don: the fifth longest river in Europe, flowing from central Russia to the Black Sea.
39 Patriarch's Pool: a large water feature and park in the downtown Presnensky district of Moscow.

PLAYING WITH FIRE

by John Clifford

*First performed at the Traverse Theatre, Edinburgh,
11 June 1987*

Cast

Justina *Celia Gore Booth*
Fernando *Richard Williams*
A Beggar *Kathryn Hunter*
The King *Simon Donald*
The Constable *Annabel Arden*
The Devil *David Gant*

Author's note:

When I wrote this play I was living as a man and known as 'John Clifford'.

I am now living as a woman and am known as Jo Clifford.

I am proud of what I achieved as 'John', and although I no longer go under that name, I do not want it erased from the record.

But I am John no longer.

Now I am Jo.

AUTHOR'S INTRODUCTION

Jo Clifford

1987 was a hard year. I'd had a huge hit with *Losing Venice* two years before, but it had left me destitute. I'd had to go back on the dole. A bursary from Thames Television briefly rescued us but, after *Lucy's Play* in 1986, I was broke again. We both were. My partner Susie was a writer too. We were sharing care of our two daughters – Rebecca who was six and Katie who was two – and I was taking on too much work to try to get by. The note above the cast list tells the story: '1st draft: Lintonburnfoot, 12th–17th April 1987'. Five days to write the first draft. And just three weeks before the start of rehearsals. In those days, the Traverse would commission me to write a script, and then schedule it before it was written. And they didn't in any way dictate what I was to write about. I should have appreciated their courage and trust at the time; but just took it for granted.

Looking back, it's clear that those two things, trust and courage, were part of what made it such an exciting artistic time for the theatre. As for me, it was stressful. But productive. The intense pressure of time meant I had to trust my instincts; and my characters. They told me what to write. And there was no time to question it . . . The only way I could get a script written was to escape to this remote cottage, lent me by a friend, where I could wear women's clothes in safety and just get on with writing. There was a beautiful Calderon play about a female Faust called *The Amazing Magician* I wanted to translate, but couldn't get anyone to commission me. That's where the name 'Justina' came from. I'd read a book the year before by the historian Barbara Tuchman called *A Distant Mirror: The Calamitous Fourteenth Century*. It was about war and plague and disaster in France at the time feudalism was breaking down and capitalism was painfully being born. I saw it as a metaphor for our calamitous times. It was also a metaphor for our calamity: me and Susie were stuck in poverty, unable to escape it, and stuck in a cottage that, for all its beautiful location, was damp and squalid. We believed the personal was political and were trying to live our lives as if the feminist revolution had already happened. Which was one reason I was also very concerned with trying to right gender imbalance in casting: which is why there are three women and three men; and why the lead character is female. I was still living as a man in those days, and there seemed to be no way I could ever escape the closet. But intense childcare and intense writing enabled me to enter parts of my psyche that had been forbidden up to then: and eventually led to me being able to live openly as a woman. As for the production, it was amazing. The design was extraordinary – Paul Brown went on to have a glittering career designing opera – and all the cast were wonderful. I went on to work with Kathryn Hunter in *Celestina* in the Edinburgh International Festival, and in *Bernarda Alba* at the Manchester Royal Exchange. She and Annabel Arden and Celia Gore Booth became core members of Complicité. Richard Williams is an actor who has since disappeared. He was a white magician who believed that if you needed something and focused on it, it would manifest. He was a kind man, too. Rebecca was being bullied at school for using an *Asterix the Gaul* lunchbox. He made a magic object for her, a kind of fetish, for her to carry with her. And the bullying stopped.

Characters

JUSTINA: an alchemist

FERNANDO: her husband

A BEGGAR

A KING

THE CONSTABLE OF FRANCE

THE DEVIL

The play is set in the workshop of a medieval alchemist.

In the first production, the whole theatre was transformed into a crypt, leading off from the cloister of the Cemetery of the Innocents[1] in fourteenth-century Paris. JUSTINA and FERNANDO use it as their home and alchemical workshop. The Dance of Death was painted on the walls. The room was dirty and very untidy. A big stove against one wall. Various retorts and alembics scattered about the place. Old books.

There were three doors: one to the outside world, through which the audience also entered, a second to a kind of store room, and a third concealed in the fresco. In the script, this is referred to as 'Death's Door'.

To enter the theatre, the audience had to squeeze through a narrow door and climb down a stair. To take their seats, they had to be part of the scenery.

There were candles everywhere. An old smell of incense.

PLAYING WITH FIRE

As the audience enter, FERNANDO *is at work. He is preparing the experiment. He brings in the container for the lead, and the acid to pour into it. There is a circle traces out on the floor, with alchemical symbols at the cardinal points. He fetches the symbols of the elements: a bowl of water, a bird cage, a fire burning in a dish.* JUSTINA *enters with a plant, to symbolise earth, and the play begins.*

JUSTINA: Shall we begin?

FERNANDO: Can't we wait?

JUSTINA: Why?

FERNANDO: I'm nervous.

JUSTINA: It'll be all right.

FERNANDO: Are you sure?

JUSTINA: Yes. Ready?

FERNANDO: Yes.

An opening ceremony

JUSTINA: May the earth give us shelter.

FERNANDO: May the air give us life.

JUSTINA: May fire give us strength.

FERNANDO: May water be our friend.

JUSTINA: Help us, you spirits trapped in every stone.

FERNANDO: In every tree.

JUSTINA: In every cloud.

FERNANDO: In every scrap of sky.

JUSTINA: Help us complete this work.

FERNANDO: This transformation.

JUSTINA: Help us turn this lead to gold.

They pour acid on the lead. FERNANDO *starts to stir.*

FERNANDO: Let's hope it works.

JUSTINA: Don't doubt it. Just keep stirring.

FERNANDO: I'm tired of explosions.

JUSTINA: There won't be any explosions.

FERNANDO: Are you sure?

JUSTINA: Of course I'm sure. Don't think about it. The lead is sick.

FERNANDO: Very sick.

JUSTINA: Like everything in the world. Everything and everyone. Lost in darkness. And so we take the lead.

FERNANDO: We take the lead.

FERNANDO *takes the lead to the stove.*

JUSTINA: And we kill it in the fire. The first stage. The beginnings of transformation.

FERNANDO: It hasn't changed a bit.

JUSTINA: It's got to die first. It says so in the book. "Except a seed fall to the ground and die it shall not bear fruit."

FERNANDO: It's not a seed. It's a lump of lead.

JUSTINA: It doesn't matter. It's like a seed. It can change. It can be transformed. That's the whole point of alchemy.

FERNANDO: It all sounds fine in theory.

JUSTINA: It's not just a theory. It's a fact. And it's not just fine. It's beautiful. A beautiful fact. Think of it.

FERNANDO: I'm trying.

JUSTINA: The seeds are everywhere. In every plant, every pot, and every stone. In everything that makes the world. And in every person too. Each and every one. Full of seeds. The possibilities of change.

FERNANDO: I wish it were true.

JUSTINA: It is true. I know it is. The world is dark. A dark and bitter place. Everything is locked within impurity and filth. Like a prisoner locked inside a jail. And there's our hope. There's always a door. Even if it is locked. A doorway to endless possibilities. Every prisoner can be set free.

And we are looking for the key. The Philosopher's Stone.[2] That will end all want. Meet every need. Cure the sick. Make the old young. Turn evil into good.

Bring freedom to the world.

FERNANDO: Which way am I meant to stir this?

JUSTINA: To the left.

Fierce bubblings from the pot.

FERNANDO: I don't like the sound of this.

JUSTINA: Don't be such a pessimist.

FERNANDO: It's going wrong.

JUSTINA: Nonsense.

A massive explosion. FERNANDO *and* JUSTINA *are half buried in a deluge of soot, bones, and dubious alchemical substances. There is a stunned silence. The dust settles.*

JUSTINA: Fuck.

FERNANDO: Yes.

JUSTINA: It didn't work.

FERNANDO: No.

JUSTINA: Your fault.

FERNANDO: I knew you'd say that. I knew it.

JUSTINA: It's true.

FERNANDO: It's not. It is not my fault. I refuse to take the blame.

JUSTINA: You stirred it wrong.

FERNANDO: I stirred to the left. Like you said.

JUSTINA: I said right.

FERNANDO: No you didn't.

JUSTINA: Yes I did.

FERNANDO: No you did not.

JUSTINA: Well I meant right.

FERNANDO: Then why didn't you say?

JUSTINA: You wouldn't listen anyway.

FERNANDO: That's not fair.

JUSTINA: Well this isn't fair.

FERNANDO: No.

JUSTINA: This time I thought we'd got it right. We said all the prayers.

FERNANDO: Perhaps we got them wrong.

JUSTINA: We can't have. I got them from the book.

FERNANDO: Perhaps the book was wrong.

JUSTINA: Of course it wasn't. It was Maria's. Maria the alchemist. Best alchemist there ever was.

FERNANDO: Anyway we've wrecked the workshop.

JUSTINA: Yes.

FERNANDO: Again.

JUSTINA: Yes!

FERNANDO: So what do we do?

JUSTINA: We start again. We do better.

FERNANDO: Must we?

JUSTINA: Yes. Come on. Let's get organised. Let's make a list.

FERNANDO: Can't.

JUSTINA: Why not?

FERNANDO: We burnt the pen.

JUSTINA: Then we find another one.

FERNANDO: And the paper.

JUSTINA: Why is life so complicated?

FERNANDO: We keep blowing up the workshop.

JUSTINA: Can't be that simple.

FERNANDO: Why not?

JUSTINA: It's all part of a bigger picture. A planetary phase. A stage we're going through. Nigredo.[3]

FERNANDO: Oh yes. Of course. Nigredo.

JUSTINA: Darkness. Disharmony. Discord. Doubt. And this endless quarrel between us. That's part of it. Part of the picture. And that's what we're about. Trying to find the cure. The cure for a sick world. Torn to pieces by wars. At the mercy of ignorance and greed.

Ragged. Hungry. Starving. Sick and exhausted. Crying out for the cure. Crying out for the Philosopher's Stone.

Enter the BEGGAR.

BEGGAR: Alms for the poor.

JUSTINA: Shut up.

BEGGAR: Why?

JUSTINA: I'm trying to think.

BEGGAR: And I'm trying to beg. We've all got to make a living. Alms for the poor. Alms. Alms for the poor.

Alms.

FERNANDO: I thought you cared about the poor.

JUSTINA: I do.

FERNANDO: Well then.

JUSTINA: I don't have anything. Besides she smells.

BEGGAR: So do you.

JUSTINA: That's different. I'm working.

BEGGAR: So am I.

JUSTINA: You're begging.

BEGGAR: I'm working at begging.

JUSTINA: You'd have to. You're hopeless.

BEGGAR: You try it then. Go on, you try it. It's a skill, begging. A skill like anything else. There's not many can do it.

JUSTINA: Then why don't you do it somewhere else?

BEGGAR: It's your turn. Alms for the poor. Alms.

I've got my rounds to make. And I've got to make a living like everyone else. I've got to pay the rent.

FERNANDO: But you sleep on a tombstone.

BEGGAR: Under it in cold weather.

JUSTINA: You shouldn't have to pay for it.

BEGGAR: Well I do. Same as you.

FERNANDO: But we live in a crypt.

BEGGAR: Still church property. You still have to pay.

FERNANDO: It's wicked.

JUSTINA: Yes, wicked. Everything's corrupt. That's why I won't give you anything.

BEGGAR: Why?

JUSTINA: Because it wouldn't change anything.

BEGGAR: I could get a meal.

JUSTINA: That's beside the point.

BEGGAR: No it isn't.

JUSTINA: Go away.

BEGGAR: No.

FERNANDO: All right then, don't.

A pause.

FERNANDO: Look I'll give her something.

JUSTINA: What?

FERNANDO: I don't know. There must be something.

BEGGAR: Make up your minds. I've got clients waiting.

FERNANDO: Take this. With my blessing.

BEGGAR: What is it?

FERNANDO: An implement. It'll come in handy.

BEGGAR: I'll take the blessing.

FERNANDO: What about the implement?

BEGGAR: You can keep it, Fernando. I don't need junk. I need alms. Alms for the poor. Alms. Alms for the poor.

Exit BEGGAR.

BEGGAR: (*off*) Alms for the poor. Alms.

FERNANDO: She could have found a use for it. Just takes a bit of enterprise.

JUSTINA: It all goes to show.

BEGGAR: (*off*) Alms for the poor. Alms.

FERNANDO: What?

JUSTINA: That people are ignorant.

BEGGAR: (*off*) Oh thank you.

JUSTINA: Charity is useless. We have to find the Stone.

FERNANDO: But how?

JUSTINA: We'll just have to read more books.

FERNANDO: Books are useless.

JUSTINA: How can you say that?

FERNANDO: Easily!

JUSTINA: Books are all we have. Our only guides.

FERNANDO: Then we're lost.

JUSTINA: They've taught us everything.

FERNANDO: And look at us. Look at the state we're in.

JUSTINA: We're a bit untidy.

FERNANDO: We're ragged. We're hungry. We're covered in soot.

JUSTINA: We're seekers after truth. We're suffering in the cause of science.

FERNANDO: Then I'd rather not.

JUSTINA: Don't say that. This is just a phase. A time of trial.

FERNANDO: Then when does it end?

JUSTINA: That's not for us to say.

FERNANDO: That's because it never will.

JUSTINA: You don't know that. It could happen tomorrow.

FERNANDO: It could. But it won't. That beggar's right. We stink.

JUSTINA: We've no time to wash.

FERNANDO: That's not what I meant. I mean we smell of failure. We stink of it. The foulest stench in the world.

JUSTINA: We're doing our best.

FERNANDO: Then it's just not good enough.

JUSTINA: You're just upset. Go and get some mercury.

FERNANDO: I don't want mercury. I want food.

JUSTINA: Same thing.

FERNANDO: You can't eat mercury.

JUSTINA: But you can transform it. Everything can be changed. That's the whole point of alchemy.

FERNANDO: Why can't we do something simple?

JUSTINA: It's not that difficult. Just a matter of changing a few atoms.

FERNANDO: You call that simple?

JUSTINA: In principle, yes. In practise it's a little bit harder. But it can be done.

FERNANDO: I don't believe it.

JUSTINA: Look I am trying not to give up. I am trying not to despair. You are not helping.

FERNANDO: Can't we do something practical?

JUSTINA: Like what, for instance.

FERNANDO: We could make love potions.

JUSTINA: Very practical.

FERNANDO: I could make good ones.

JUSTINA: You're hopeless.

FERNANDO: No. Think of it. A magic decoction of herbs. That fills all who drink it with the strongest, the deepest, the most passionate, most enduring love. Think of it. We'd give it to the beggar woman. She'd smile and fall in love with every passer by. And they'd love her, too. They'd shower her with gold. We'd give it to the grocer. He'd give us credit. He'd send us love letters. Great lumps of cheese, carved in the shape of a heart, parcelled up in red ribbons. We'd give it to the recluse walled up next door. She'd stop moaning. She'd touch herself all over and swoon in ecstasy. She'd say it's all the work of sweet Jesus. Instead of sores and stinks and hairshirts he'd give her pleasure. We'd give it to the prostitutes that wait about after mass. To Teresa. And Maria. And Isabel. They wouldn't have to pretend to the men they service on the tombstones. They'd love them for real. They'd suffer less. And the men would love them too. They'd never have to sell themselves again. We'd give it to the soldiers, every one: they'd walk out onto the battlefield, clanking and groaning under all their ridiculous armour, and instead of bashing each other to pieces they'd open up their arms and embrace each other. They'd swop stories round the campfires, and then go home. They'd kiss their wives. They'd take care of their children. They'd tickle their tummies and make them laugh. They'd hold them tight in their loving arms. They'd stay in their gardens and grow cabbages. And the whole land would be at peace.

JUSTINA: You're dreaming.

FERNANDO: A good dream.

JUSTINA: Yes. Very good.

FERNANDO: We'd put a sign up above the door.

The sign of the double bed.

JUSTINA: Don't spoil it.

FERNANDO: I'm not spoiling it. Just elaborating. We could make something of this place.

JUSTINA: It's a graveyard.

FERNANDO: It's a busy place. Everyone comes here. It's all the rage.

JUSTINA: You have spoilt it.

FERNANDO: I'm sorry. I never meant to. It's just we have to live. In the world.

JUSTINA: I hate the world.

FERNANDO: That makes life difficult.

JUSTINA: I don't care. I'd rather it was difficult.

FERNANDO: I'd rather it was easy.

JUSTINA: And put up with this? I'd rather die.

FERNANDO: Justina. It's this place. Enough to get anyone down. You need some fresh air. And I'm hungry. Let's get out. Into the street. Let's go for a walk.

JUSTINA: I hate walks.

FERNANDO: Just out in the street.

JUSTINA: I hate the street.

FERNANDO: It was just a suggestion.

JUSTINA: The wretched parade. The procession of walking corpses. The filthy rich. Their wallets stuffed with the loot of the world. And still looking miserable.

FERNANDO: We'll walk together arm in arm. People will greet us: Fernando and Justina, the famous alchemists. Makers of love potions. About to pave the Paris streets with gold.

JUSTINA: They'll throw stones at us.

FERNANDO: No they won't. Someone'll smile. A baby. You might like it. You liked it last time.

JUSTINA: Last time I saw a woman beat her child. She did it because his teeth were chattering. They were wearing rags. His hands were blue with cold. His mouth was covered in sores. And when she hit him he started crying. And so she hit him again to make him stop. Which he didn't. And then a fat man came. He was wearing furs. He had a gold chain round his neck. And she knelt on the ground by his feet.

FERNANDO: We've seen worse things. They happen all the time.

JUSTINA: That's why I hate it. Why I hate the world. Why I can't bear it. Why I stay here.

FERNANDO: I'll go then. I'll get some bread.

JUSTINA: What for?

FERNANDO: Isn't it obvious?

Exit FERNANDO.

JUSTINA: No. Why should it be? Who wants bread, when every crumb is stolen from someone who's starving. When every loaf is tainted with blood and with tears so it turns to ashes in the mouth. But then he's right. It's commonplace. Common as cruelty.

So what do I do? Pick myself up. Pick up the pieces. Begin again. Pick up a broom. Look for a broom. Fail to find a broom.

Oh I don't care. I've had enough. I'm too tired. And it's so cold.

JUSTINA *goes across and opens the lower part of the stove.*

JUSTINA: The fire's dying down. I'd give anything to have that Stone.

The DEVIL *reveals himself in the upper part of the stove.* JUSTINA *is frightened. The* DEVIL *pokes his fingers through the grille.*

DEVIL: Something wrong? Did I startle you? Obviously. I'm sorry. But don't be startled. Please.

JUSTINA: Who are you?

DEVIL: An old friend.

JUSTINA: I don't know you.

DEVIL: We've not been introduced. But we have met. Many times. And I know you. Know you very well.

JUSTINA: What are you doing in the stove?

DEVIL: Oh. That. Forgive me. I was trying to get warm.

JUSTINA: Why?

DEVIL: I'm cold. Always so very cold.

Pause.

DEVIL: You don't happen to have any coal?

JUSTINA: Sorry?

DEVIL: Coal. A kind of stone. A black stone.

You put it on fires. To make them burn.

JUSTINA: Stones don't burn.

DEVIL: So you haven't heard of it?

JUSTINA: No.

DEVIL: Pity. This is very unpleasant you know. Like being in the bath when the water's getting cold. You can't stay in, but you don't want to get out.

JUSTINA: Am I dreaming?

DEVIL: You don't know about baths either?

JUSTINA: I must be.

DEVIL: No coal. No baths. What a primitive age.

JUSTINA: Then why don't you go away?

DEVIL: I can't.

JUSTINA: Why not?

DEVIL: I'm stuck in your stove. There's a bolt I can't reach. Would you open it?

JUSTINA: I can't.

DEVIL: Do you really want to?

JUSTINA: Yes.

DEVIL: You don't know your own strength. Try again.

JUSTINA *opens the stove door.*

JUSTINA: How strange.

DEVIL: Very strange.

JUSTINA: It must have been catching.

DEVIL: Perhaps . . . But you've let me loose. Thank you.

JUSTINA: Now will you go away?

DEVIL: Nasty place you've got here.

JUSTINA: No-one asked you to stay.

DEVIL: But you did. I heard you distinctly. I'll give anything, you said. Anything to have the Stone.

JUSTINA: And you have it I suppose.

DEVIL: Of course.

JUSTINA: How could you have the Philosopher's Stone?

DEVIL: Very easily.

JUSTINA: But wise men have given their lives to find it.

DEVIL: They didn't know where to look.

JUSTINA: And you do?

DEVIL: Of course.

JUSTINA: And you can give it to me?

DEVIL: I can give you anything you wish.

JUSTINA: I don't believe you.

DEVIL: Try me.

JUSTINA: All right, I want a broom. A new broom to sweep the room clean.

DEVIL: Easy.

JUSTINA: With the head not too big, not too small. The bristles not too hard, not too soft.

DEVIL: Over there. Look.

The DEVIL points to a corner. JUSTINA goes over and finds a broom there. She picks it up, marvelling.

JUSTINA: How did you do that?

DEVIL: You wanted it. I just showed you where to look.

JUSTINA: It's just what I wanted. Thank you. Now I can start.

JUSTINA starts to sweep. The DEVIL watches.

DEVIL: You disappoint me.

JUSTINA: Do I?

DEVIL: Is that really all?

JUSTINA: What else could there be?

DEVIL: What else do you want?

JUSTINA: Can I ask?

DEVIL: Of course.

JUSTINA: And you'll give it?

DEVIL: Naturally.

JUSTINA: Who are you?

DEVIL: I told you. I am a friend.

JUSTINA: So you say.

DEVIL: It's true.

JUSTINA: You don't feel like a friend. I'm not sure I should listen to you.

DEVIL: Should. Shouldn't. Everyone is ruled by should. Should go to work. Should go to fight. Should go to church. Should love each other.

Doesn't stop them being perfectly vile. Doesn't stop them hating each other. Doesn't stop them being thoroughly miserable. Doesn't make the world one ounce better. And why are they so unhappy? Because they think they should be.

Don't listen to 'should'. Listen to 'want'. And who wants to suffer? Do you?

Of course not. You want the Stone. Of course you shouldn't want it. You should want a husband or a lover or a child. Or silk on your skin. Gold on your arms. A new house, perhaps, or an expensive grave. But you reject all that. Very wise. And why? Because you want the Stone. You want it more than any husband or lover. More than any miserable child. And why? Because you want to change the world. Of course. What could be more natural?

JUSTINA: Are you laughing at me?

DEVIL: Of course not.

JUSTINA: People do. In the street, children throw dirt at me.

DEVIL: Forget them. Dirt cannot touch you. And what people say is their affair. You want the Stone. Want it, you shall have it.

JUSTINA: And you?

DEVIL: Me?

JUSTINA: What do you want?

DEVIL: Nothing. Nothing at all.

JUSTINA: You want nothing in exchange?

DEVIL: Do you take me for some merchant, that buys and sells? Do you think yourself a mere commodity?

JUSTINA: It is the way of the world. People give, and people take.

DEVIL: I do not belong to this world. I am an exile. And I am too old to want. I need.

JUSTINA: What do you need?

DEVIL: Your soul. Just a little thing. Of no consequence. You'll never know it's gone.

JUSTINA: My soul?

DEVIL: And what's a soul? A bag of air. A little wind. Sign here.

JUSTINA: Now I know who you are.

DEVIL: Very astute.

JUSTINA: I should have nothing to do with you.

DEVIL: There we go again. Should. What an ugly word.

JUSTINA: You are evil.

DEVIL: Me? Evil? What do you know about evil?

JUSTINA: Enough.

DEVIL: You know nothing. You and your petty little crimes.

Shall I tell you what I know of evil? Shall I show you its true face? That makes you feel afraid. As if it came from me.

People give me many names. Prince of Evil. Lord of Darkness. Its origin and source. They know nothing.

If it were true this earth would be my home. I'd be a citizen of the world. Close kin to you. I'd be the marrow of your bones. A citizen of France. With all you other citizens. Living in this grubby little city. This scabby dunghill. Huddled on the banks of a muddy little river, filthy and polluted with your dirt, on the far northern fringes of the civilised world.

You clutch your pitiful rags to cover your nakedness and build your wretched little hovels of stone. Your god is an instrument of torture that night and day you meditate upon to devise new means of tormenting each other. Your people are starving. In every alley, every street, every square and every hedgerow you can hear the cries of your hungry children. And they could be fed. They could be. But you choose otherwise.

Life lies all around you, Nature would welcome you with open arms, if you would but let her.

But you choose death. And you honour most of all those butchers most adept at lies, those whose only art is to perfect the instruments of war.

And your king sits in his tower and he sees it all. But thinks instead of the cut of his robe. And your constable looks nowhere but over her shoulder at the rivals she fears will attack her. She fortifies her castle. She sharpens her sword. And you call me the Prince of Darkness. What gall. What pitiful presumption. Where is the darkness? Not in me.

It is in yourselves.

JUSTINA: So you, too, hate the world.

DEVIL: I loathe and I detest it with every fibre of my self.

JUSTINA: Then you are my brother.

DEVIL: Perhaps

JUSTINA: And you have the Stone?

DEVIL: In my pocket.

JUSTINA: Then give it me.

DEVIL: Sign.

JUSTINA: I have no pen.

The DEVIL *produces a pen.*

JUSTINA: Nor ink.

DEVIL: Blood will do.

The DEVIL *hands her a knife.*

JUSTINA: Do you think me afraid?

DEVIL: What have you to fear?

JUSTINA *cuts her arm. She draws blood.*

JUSTINA: There.

JUSTINA *writes.*

DEVIL: And did your blood freeze up? Did choirs of angels implore you to desist? These days all the angels hide themselves. I am the only one to walk the earth.

There. It's done. Farewell.

JUSTINA: But the Stone!

DEVIL: Oh the Stone. I was almost forgetting. Here.

The DEVIL *gives* JUSTINA *a very ordinary looking stone.*

JUSTINA: What do I do with it?

DEVIL: Throw it into the fire and see.

JUSTINA *tosses the Stone into the bottom of the stove.*

Exit DEVIL, *unseen by her.* JUSTINA *stares into the fire a moment. Enter the* BEGGAR, *who startles her.*

BEGGAR: Alms for the poor. Alms. Alms for the poor.

JUSTINA: Oh go away!

BEGGAR: Bad tempered. As usual.

JUSTINA: You woke me up.

BEGGAR: That'll be right. Asleep as usual.

JUSTINA: I was having the strangest dream.

BEGGAR: When are you ever awake?

JUSTINA: There's nothing wrong with dreaming.

BEGGAR: I've no time for dreams. Alms for the poor.

JUSTINA: Oh shut up.

BEGGAR: How can I beg without asking?

JUSTINA: You could hold out your arms. In silent supplication. Like this.

BEGGAR: Doesn't work so well. I know. I've tried it.

JUSTINA: What have you come back here for? I never give you anything.

BEGGAR: There's always hoping. Besides, it's your turn. I'm doing my rounds. Alms for the poor. Alms. Alms for the poor. Alms.

JUSTINA: I wish I had a door so thick I could never hear your cries.

BEGGAR: Very charitable. Alms for the poor.

JUSTINA: Why don't you go to the rich?

The BEGGAR *cackles.*

BEGGAR: The rich have hearts of stone.

JUSTINA: Don't talk to me of stones!

BEGGAR: I'm not. I'm talking about money.

JUSTINA: I haven't got any. I've got nothing.

BEGGAR: Liar.

JUSTINA: It's true.

BEGGAR: Everyone has something.

JUSTINA *starts to push the* BEGGAR *off stage.*

JUSTINA: Everyone but me. Don't waste your time. Please go away.

BEGGAR: Your time's up, anyway. I'll go. But even stones have souls. And clods of earth and blocks of wood. They'd be easier to beg from than you.

JUSTINA: I haven't even got a soul. I just signed it away.

Exit the BEGGAR, *cackling.*

BEGGAR: (*off*) She hasn't even got a soul! Oh Justina, Justina! Alms for the poor. Alms.

JUSTINA: I can't have. I must have been dreaming. I was going to clean the floor.

But there's that broom. I never had that before. And did I really have the Stone? I'll rake out the ash.

JUSTINA *opens up the grate. The fire burns strangely. She is absorbed. Enter* FERNANDO. *His hands are empty.*

FERNANDO: No bread. Not even a crumb. Everyone ignored me. When I asked, they walked on like I didn't exist. In this town, the only crime is failure.

JUSTINA: Fernando.

FERNANDO: What?

JUSTINA: Look. Look!

FERNANDO: Gold.

JUSTINA: Yes.

FERNANDO: Ow.

JUSTINA: Don't touch it. It's hot.

FERNANDO: It looks like gold.

JUSTINA: Yes.

FERNANDO: You've done it.

JUSTINA: Me?

FERNANDO: Well I didn't.

JUSTINA: I'm not sure.

FERNANDO: It was you. You never lost faith. I did. But you didn't. I'd given up, but you kept on trying. And now you've done it. I think you're brilliant. I love you.

JUSTINA: It was just . . . I thought it was a dream.

FERNANDO: That it doesn't matter. We've got the gold. That's real enough. Now we can be happy.

JUSTINA: Can we?

FERNANDO: Of course we can. We'll buy a house.

JUSTINA: I don't want a house.

FERNANDO: Then we'll do up this place. We'll get a new bed. A feather mattress. Some comfy chairs. Real glass for the windows. Champagne. We can have parties. It'll be lovely.

BEGGAR: (*off*) Alms for the poor! Alms. Alms for the poor.

JUSTINA: We'll give her some.

FERNANDO: No we won't.

JUSTINA: What?

FERNANDO: We'll hide it. Quick.

JUSTINA: Why?

FERNANDO: She'll want the lot.

They hide the gold. Enter BEGGAR.

FERNANDO: Lovely day.

BEGGAR: It's raining.

FERNANDO: Nice rain. Wet.

BEGGAR: What are you being so nice for?

FERNANDO: Just making conversation.

BEGGAR: You look happy.

JUSTINA: Us?

BEGGAR: Makes no difference anyway.

FERNANDO: No?

BEGGAR: When people are happy, they don't want to be made sad. So they don't give.

When people are sad, they've no time for sympathy. So they don't give.

I don't like it.

Pause.

FERNANDO: You're back very soon.

BEGGAR: I smell gold.

FERNANDO: Thought you had a cold.

BEGGAR: Gold clears it. Gold cures anything.

And I'm sure. Got a nose for it.

FERNANDO: Round the corner. A merchant. I saw him as I was coming in. His purse was bulging.

BEGGAR: Where?

FERNANDO: All over.

BEGGAR: Where was the merchant?

FERNANDO: Seeing a priest.

BEGGAR: Which priest?

FERNANDO: The fat one. With indigestion. That always talks of hell.

The BEGGAR *sniffs.*

BEGGAR: But I can smell it. Here. I'm on the scent. On the other hand. Is it likely, I ask myself, that the likes of you could really have found out how to make gold? Is it plausible? No.

FERNANDO: Certainly not.

BEGGAR: With the fat priest, you said?

FERNANDO: Yes.

BEGGAR: Humph.

FERNANDO: The merchant'll be out in a minute. He'll be desperate for a good deed.

BEGGAR: I'll go. On the other hand. My nose is itching. And it never lies. I'll be back.

Exit BEGGAR.

FERNANDO: That's got rid of her.

JUSTINA: Swine.

FERNANDO: Why?

JUSTINA: Deceiving her like that. Not giving her any.

FERNANDO: Neither did you.

JUSTINA: I should have done.

FERNANDO: I didn't stop you.

JUSTINA: And I thought you believed in charity.

FERNANDO: That was different.

JUSTINA: Why?

FERNANDO: We had nothing to give.

JUSTINA: Hypocrite.

FERNANDO: Anyway we couldn't give her this. Not all this. It'd make her miserable. And there wouldn't be any for us.

JUSTINA: We could've given her a little bit.

FERNANDO: And we will. Once we've divided it. Don't worry. Let's be happy.

JUSTINA: How?

FERNANDO: Well I don't know. We're obviously out of practice. But we'll find a way. Won't we? We got what we wanted.

JUSTINA: I thought you wanted love.

FERNANDO: That was before I got gold.

JUSTINA: I'm not sure I like this.

FERNANDO: I do. I'm so tired of being poor. And now it's all over. It's wonderful.

JUSTINA: What are you doing?

FERNANDO: Making a parcel.

JUSTINA: What for?

FERNANDO: To carry it through the streets. I don't want people to see it. I don't want to get my throat cut.

JUSTINA: But where are you taking it?

FERNANDO: To a bank.

JUSTINA: Why?

FERNANDO: So we can live off the interest.

JUSTINA: Is that right?

FERNANDO: Who cares? We'll be rich.

JUSTINA: Shouldn't we give it away?

FERNANDO: Some of it. But not all of it.

JUSTINA: Shouldn't we work?

FERNANDO: The rich don't work. Not nowadays. No-one makes money by working. They make money from having money. They get richer for being rich already. The rich sit on high balconies and look down on the tumult below. They watch the porters coming from the market, staggering to and fro under heavy loads, and they say: the poor are poor because they don't know how to work.

We'll do the same. We'll stay in bed all day. We'll sip exotic drinks from crystal glasses and we'll throw a coin down from time to time. The life of the intellect.

That's the life for me. I'll become a philosopher. Or perhaps an economist.

JUSTINA: Your face has changed.

FERNANDO: Has it?

JUSTINA: Gone a nasty colour.

FERNANDO: The mirror's cracked. Never mind. We'll get a new one.

JUSTINA: The books are wrong.

FERNANDO: What are you talking about?

JUSTINA: They say gold is the noblest of metals. The most lustrous. The most pure.

FERNANDO: Oh but they're right there. I love it.

JUSTINA: But I know what gold is now. It's dull and heavy and it's made you bad.

FERNANDO *has finished his parcel.*

FERNANDO: I'll be off now.

JUSTINA: Don't go.

FERNANDO: But we're losing interest.

JUSTINA: Give me the gold.

FERNANDO: No.

JUSTINA: Please.

FERNANDO: You'll do something silly with it.

JUSTINA: I won't. I promise. I'll do something better. The best thing of all. The best thing for both of us. Trust me.

Please.

FERNANDO: All right.

JUSTINA: Thank you.

FERNANDO: I've changed my mind.

JUSTINA: Too late.

FERNANDO: No!

FERNANDO *gets between* JUSTINA *and the fire. They start to struggle for the gold.*

FERNANDO: You're going to throw it in the fire.

JUSTINA: No. Yes! Please. It's not what we wanted. Look what it's doing to us.

FERNANDO: It's making us happy!

JUSTINA: It's not. And I wanted the real gold. Philosopher's gold.

FERNANDO: You're mad.

JUSTINA: No! I want to change it into something better.

FERNANDO: There's nothing better. You'll see. And you'll give it to me. Now. Or I'll take it.

JUSTINA: Don't.

FERNANDO: I will. I'm warning you.

FERNANDO snatches the gold and throws JUSTINA to the ground.

FERNANDO: You asked for that.

Exit FERNANDO.

JUSTINA: And I sold my soul for this!

Enter the DEVIL.

DEVIL: Aren't you going to thank me?

JUSTINA: What for?

DEVIL: Ungrateful.

JUSTINA: You cheated me.

DEVIL: Unfair. I gave you the Stone.

JUSTINA: That was the Stone?

DEVIL: Where do you think the gold came from?

JUSTINA: That wasn't Philosopher's Gold!

DEVIL: You could have got that as well. If you'd known how to use it.

JUSTINA: But why didn't you tell me?

DEVIL: You didn't ask.

JUSTINA: You made me throw it in the fire.

DEVIL: It was just a suggestion.

JUSTINA: But what'll I do now?

DEVIL: Learn how to wish.

JUSTINA: I don't want to wish. I want the Philosopher's Stone.

DEVIL: Then look for it.

JUSTINA: But where?

DEVIL: Seek and ye shall find.

Exit DEVIL.

JUSTINA: But that's no help!

Where are you? Come back. Please.

All right. I'll manage without you. I'll find the Stone. You'll see.

JUSTINA *opens the stove door. A huge cascade of pebbles.*

JUSTINA: And isn't that just typical. Isn't that just the way life is. You spend your entire life looking for something and when by some miracle you find it what do you do?

You throw it away. And when you find it again what does it do? It goes and gets itself lost.

But I'll find it. It shouldn't be too hard. It's supposed to be miraculous. So where are you, bringer of peace and concord? Fucking Stone. I'll find you.

JUSTINA *rummages frantically through the pebbles.*

JUSTINA: Is this you? No. Too big. Or you? Too small. And you're the wrong colour. And you're too speckled. You're too heavy. You're too light. You?

JUSTINA *licks a stone.*

JUSTINA: You taste horrid. On second thoughts . . . maybe it was that one. Where's it gone?

And what's it supposed to look like anyway? Oh I don't know. I'll look it up in a book. Oh where's it gone?

Anyway, I must have read all the books. And none of them ever said what it looked like or smelt like or felt like or tasted like. Just like books. Never tell you what you want to know. Anyway I've seen it. What did it look like? Like a pebble. Did it rattle?

No of course it didn't. Don't be stupid. It's useless. A waste of time. I'll never find it. Never. I'm fed up. I want to throw the whole lot away. I want to smash them to pieces.

JUSTINA *tries to break the stones.*

JUSTINA: They won't even break!

Enter the BEGGAR, *angry.*

BEGGAR: He wasn't there.

JUSTINA: What?

BEGGAR: The rich man.

The merchant your husband spoke about. Lying swine. He wanted to put me off the track.

JUSTINA: You're right. He did. I'm sorry. There was gold here. But now he's got it and he's gone.

BEGGAR: You're as bad as him. You're trying to put me off.

JUSTINA: I'm not.

BEGGAR: But you don't know me. I told you. I've got a nose for gold. And I can smell it. I can smell it under there.

JUSTINA: It's not there. There's nothing there.

BEGGAR: You've buried it under those stones.

JUSTINA: Look if you like.

BEGGAR: I will.

JUSTINA: You're wasting your time.

The BEGGAR *rummages among the stones.*

JUSTINA: You see? There's nothing.

BEGGAR: It's a cheat.

JUSTINA: Yes. A cheat. We've been had. Both of us. By this rotten, cheating, senseless, lying world.

Help me.

JUSTINA *begins to the load the stones into a basket.*

JUSTINA: I want to get rid of them. The whole lot of them.

BEGGAR: Are you sure they're not worth something?

JUSTINA: They're worthless. They're little balls of shit. And this is what I gave my life for. This is what I worked and sacrificed and struggled for. I gave up my soul for this!

Enter the DEVIL.

DEVIL: Something wrong?

JUSTINA: You cheated me. Again.

DEVIL: You asked for the Stone.

JUSTINA: So where is it?

DEVIL: I gave it to you.

JUSTINA: You just gave me loads of pebbles.

DEVIL: I was feeling generous.

JUSTINA: What?

DEVIL: Generous. I wanted to give you a surprise.

JUSTINA: You mean these are all the Stones?

DEVIL: Useless now of course. They would have worked, but you were so violent. You've broken the spell. Shame.

JUSTINA: Can't I do anything right?

DEVIL: I told you. Learn how to wish.

Exit the DEVIL. *The* BEGGAR *cackles.*

BEGGAR: So. You've got an angel too. I used to have one. Came when I was doing the washing. That's just like them. They get you when you're down. Bastards. Does yours make music?

JUSTINA: No.

BEGGAR: Mine did. That's then I knew there was something wrong. Music between the ears. A bad sign. There I was, bent double over the clothes and my back was aching. And there was the music. Beautiful music. And the sound of gently flapping wings. Kind of humming. It was beautiful. I wanted to look up, more than anything in the world. But I didn't. I just kept scrubbing. You mustn't let them catch your eye. Just let them catch your eye and you're done for. Sanctified. So I just kept scrubbing and waited for it to go away. Which it didn't. It spoke to me instead. Lovely voice it had. It said, "I am an angel sent from God." "I know that," I said, "I'm not stupid. I don't need you to tell me that. It doesn't get us any further," I said, and it still didn't go away, so I said to it, "Look," I said, "Look missus or mister or whatever you are please go away. We don't want you. You'll get us into trouble." And then it never said a word. It kind of shuffled its feet, though I don't think it had any. Anyway.

"We just want to be left alone," I said, "I'm sorry." And then I looked up. The angel was crying. Before I knew it, it was gone. It was getting dark. I was frightened. So I picked up my washing and walked back to the village. Only there wasn't a village. It was gone. Even the smoke had died down, and all the ashes were cold. My man had gone, and so had my child. I walked all night, calling their names. No-one came. In the morning, I walked on. Every village was the same. It was the angel. I was following the path of its wings.

JUSTINA: That wasn't the angel. That was troops. You shouldn't have sent it away.

BEGGAR: What should I want with an angel?

JUSTINA: It might have brought you something good.

BEGGAR: Has yours?

JUSTINA: Well, no. Not yet. But I'll make him. I'll make him bring you justice.

BEGGAR: No such thing.

JUSTINA: There must be.

BEGGAR: Maybe in heaven. Not here.

JUSTINA: Look, I'll help you. Tell me your name.

BEGGAR: Don't have one.

JUSTINA: You must have. Everyone has a name.

BEGGAR: I lost it.

JUSTINA: You can't have.

BEGGAR: Why not? I lost everything else.

Exit BEGGAR. *Enter the* DEVIL.

DEVIL: Won't you cry for me? I lost everything too.

JUSTINA: Even your children?

DEVIL: You can lose worse things.

JUSTINA: But she has suffered a terrible wrong. I want to put it right. I want justice.

DEVIL: Not my department.

JUSTINA: There must be something you can do.

DEVIL: If you insist.

JUSTINA: I do.

DEVIL: There is a risk.

JUSTINA: I don't care.

DEVIL: Very well. On your head be it.

A thunderous knocking on the door.

JUSTINA: Who's that?

DEVIL: Go and see.

Enter the CONSTABLE, *a gigantic and threatening figure in full armour.*

CONSTABLE: I come in the name of the king.

I come in the name of justice.

The king wants gold.

JUSTINA: I don't have any.

CONSTABLE: You are Justina? The alchemist?

JUSTINA: I am.

CONSTABLE: Then you have discovered the secret of making gold.

JUSTINA: No I haven't.

CONSTABLE: Do not deny it. It is a thing we know. We are never wrong. The king needs gold. He is at war. His coffers are empty. He seeks to drive the English from his land.

JUSTINA: But what has that to do with me?

CONSTABLE: You can pay for it.

JUSTINA: No I can't.

CONSTABLE: You must. The English are like leeches. They suck the lifeblood of the land. They are locusts. They strip the countryside bare. Their mercenaries are everywhere. They burn for the sake of burning. They loot everything they can steal. They kill the men and they torture the children. The women they rape. They have turned our fair country into a desert full of corpses.

They have been here so long the people can hardly conceive of being free. But they will be. They will be free. The English will be driven from the land. We have undertaken to do it. But we lack the means. Our country is weak and poor. Our armies must be fed.

JUSTINA: I can't feed your armies.

CONSTABLE: You have the secret of making gold.

JUSTINA: No I don't. I can't give you anything.

CONSTABLE: I will inform the king. In an hour I shall return.

JUSTINA: I'll still say no. I'll still have nothing.

CONSTABLE: Then we will strap you down and strip you bare. We will have the pincers heated. We will burn your flesh. Here. And here. We will peel back the skin. And for every no you give us, we will give you boiling lead. Drop by drop. And then you will say yes. They always do. We will hire a man. He knows his trade.

I am a servant of the king. An instrument of his justice. The Constable of France. You have an hour. The king is merciful.

Exit the CONSTABLE.

JUSTINA: Now look what you've done.

DEVIL: I warned you.

JUSTINA: You never told me this would happen!

DEVIL: You said you'd take the risk.

JUSTINA: I wanted justice!

DEVIL: That's what you said, yes. For the beggar. Don't blame me that you forgot to ask.

JUSTINA: How could I?

DEVIL: You wanted justice. There it is.

JUSTINA: I don't want to be tortured.

DEVIL: That is the justice of the world.

JUSTINA: But what about the other kind? Real Justice. Where is that?

DEVIL: Not here.

JUSTINA: It must be somewhere.

DEVIL: Then look for it yourself. I can't help.

JUSTINA: It's all your fault.

DEVIL: Why blame me? Don't blame me. Blame the world. Blame your husband. He got you in this mess.

JUSTINA: You're right. He did. He stirred the mixture wrong.

DEVIL: If it weren't for him, I wouldn't be here. None of this would have happened.

JUSTINA: And it's just like him. Typical. He muddles everything up. Muddles up my head. Muddles up my life. Muddles up my house. Never puts things away. Always gets things wrong. Confuses things. Never gives me any support. Wants to make love potions.

DEVIL: And look at the trouble he's left us in.

JUSTINA: And it's all right for him. He's got the gold. No-one's going to torture him. Oh no. And he'll be out on the street somewhere spending it. He'll be drunk. Scattering money. Dropping it everywhere. Kissing people. He's very fond of kissing. And then he'll come back with some stupid present and he'll smile and he'll want life to go on just the same. But it can't. It just can't. And I never wanted gold. Never never never. I wanted the Stone. The Philosopher's Stone. And he got me all confused. He always does. I want to see things straight. I want to see things clear. And I'm so tired of him. So tired. Oh I wish he were dead.

The DEVIL *opens Death's Door.* FERNANDO *is inside.*

DEVIL: At last you've learnt how to wish.

JUSTINA: Fernando!

The DEVIL *slams the door shut. Exit the* DEVIL. *Enter the* BEGGAR.

BEGGAR: Your man is dead.

JUSTINA: No.

BEGGAR: It was a cart. Full of dung. Squashed him flat. I wanted to warn him, but he just stepped right out in front of it. He was dreaming. You'd have thought he could have smelt it coming. I'd have picked him up, but I wasn't quick enough. The bakers got there first. They'll make him into a pie. A Scotch pie.[4] These new ones. They're all the rage. They're making millions. I was given one on the way home. I was hungry. But I didn't eat it. Out of respect.

The BEGGAR *produces the pie, and puts it on a tomb. They stare at it.*

BEGGAR: He could still have a service. I could easily get him a coffin. Could tip someone out. One of those merchants. When no-one's looking. Got to get something out of living in a graveyard. And I'll find a priest. A cheap one.

Oh, and I was forgetting. There's this.

The BEGGAR *hands over Fernando's parcel.*

BEGGAR: He had it on him. Weighs a ton. Still, you know how he was. Always had his bit of junk. Thought you might like it. As a keepsake.

JUSTINA: The gold.

BEGGAR: The what?

JUSTINA: We're saved.

BEGGAR: Saved?

Massive knocking on the door.

BEGGAR: Who's that?

Enter the CONSTABLE, *majestically. The* BEGGAR *makes herself scarce.*

CONSTABLE: The King. Make way for the King.

There is no sign of the KING.

CONSTABLE: Your majesty!

Enter the KING. *A weedy figure. His clothes are padded, to prevent him breaking. He comes in through the door with infinite care.*

KING: Sorry if I'm late.

CONSTABLE: Can't you make a proper entrance?

KING: I'm sorry.

CONSTABLE: You are such a disappointment to me.

KING: I do my best.

CONSTABLE: I've half a mind to make you go back and do it again.

KING: Please don't.

CONSTABLE: And where are the trumpeters? I ordered a fanfare.

KING: I think they've gone home. They did ask, and I couldn't bear to refuse. They were terribly tired. And so were their instruments. They said they couldn't play.

CONSTABLE: Your majesty is too kind.

KING: Yes.

CONSTABLE: Have you got your speech?

KING: My speech?

CONSTABLE: The speech we prepared together.

KING: I think I put it down somewhere.

CONSTABLE: The enemy is at our gates. The invader hammers on our door. Our institutions crumble. Old alliances decay. The people suffer untold agonies.

I try continuously to get you interested in affairs of state. I organise these little outings. I strain every nerve to muster the resources to meet the occasion. An occasion that calls for all our reserves of fortitude. For all our resolution. All our courage. All our strength. And what happens? You lose your speech. God give me patience.

And as for you, worm. Alchemist. You'd better have the gold. The torturer is at your door. Heating the pincers. I made no mistake about that. I organised him myself.

JUSTINA *reveals the gold.*

CONSTABLE: What's that?

JUSTINA: Gold.

CONSTABLE: It had better be. The knots are tight, but my blade is sharp. The gold looks pure. For now it is enough. I shall assemble the army. There is not a moment to lose. But rest assured, I shall be back. We shall have need of more. Receive the thanks of a grateful king.

KING: Yes. Thank you. Thank you very much.

Exit the CONSTABLE. *The* BEGGAR *scuttles out of hiding. The* KING *starts to shuffle vaguely away. Very cautiously, he starts to negotiate the door.*

BEGGAR: So. You did have gold. Shame you had to give it away.

JUSTINA: I was going to help you. She never gave me the chance. I'll ask him instead.

She catches the KING, *and prevents him leaving.*

JUSTINA: Your majesty!

The KING *jumps.*

KING: Do be careful. You almost broke me.

BEGGAR: Don't talk to him. It's a waste of time.

KING: That's what they all say. No-one ever wants to talk to me.

JUSTINA: But we do, your majesty.

KING: You do?

JUSTINA: We want to talk about her village.

KING: Oh.

JUSTINA: It was burnt.

KING: How interesting.

JUSTINA: Burnt by troops.

KING: Terrible.

JUSTINA: You think so, your majesty?

KING: War is terrible. Terrible. I never think about it.

JUSTINA: But you should.

KING: Why? It's most unpleasant.

JUSTINA: But you're the King!

KING: Oh that? Yes. Most unfortunate. People have the strangest notions of what is to be king. My father used to feel the same. Terrible man.

Frightened me to death. Always getting onto his horse. Trying to do things. Galloping about. Shouting. All that happened was his throat got sore. And people kept dying. I hated it. And he kept insisting that I do it. And I was a terrible rider. Terrible. Always falling off. Smashing things. Then people would have to come and hoist me up again. On a crane. Most undignified. The risks I ran. That was before I knew what I really was. Before I understood.

Better to do as little as you can. You do less harm.

JUSTINA: But you can't do any good.

KING: I never could do any good.

JUSTINA: Why not?

KING: Too fragile.

JUSTINA: No more than other people. Look.

KING: Don't touch me. I'll break. I am made of glass. It took me years to understand. But then I never rode again. Whoever heard of a vase on horseback? What could be more absurd. Even walking, one must take precautions. That's why I wear these clothes. To protect me. If you carry crystal, do you let it go naked in the streets? Of course not. You cushion it. You cosset it. You protect it from harm. Of course it means I have to cover my glory. Regrettable.

But can't be helped. Wouldn't do to splinter into pieces. Or fragment.

JUSTINA: I suppose not.

KING: It can easily happen, you know. All too easily. That's why I have trouble with doors. Sharp edges. Dangerous. No-one understands.

BEGGAR: Got any gold?

KING: Gold, my dear? No. I never carry gold. Never. Far too great a risk. It might break a bone.

BEGGAR: I'm off then. Nothing here.

Exit the BEGGAR.

KING: Disagreeable person. Dirty.

JUSTINA: She is a victim of the war.

KING: War has its victims, I believe. Though I rarely see them.

JUSTINA: But you are responsible.

KING: It has nothing to do with me.

JUSTINA: It is fought in your name.

KING: So many things are done in my name. I couldn't possibly keep track of them all.

JUSTINA: But it is your duty.

KING: Duty?

JUSTINA: Don't you have duties?

KING: Very few. They disagree with me.

JUSTINA: Don't you ever have to sign things?

KING: Oh that. Every day. For hours and hours. Thank God I can't read. Or I'd have to do that as well.

I would die of tedium.

JUSTINA: Well you should.

KING: You think I should die?

JUSTINA: No.

KING: It is occasionally tempting. Life can be so wearisome. One's curlicues get so covered in dust. But I am obliged to live. I am the state. I am the embodiment of order. That is why I am so fragile. Why I take such care. Why I am so beautiful.

JUSTINA: You're not.

KING: Oh you don't see. You poor poor thing. So many people don't. But I thought better of you. And you're missing such a treat. I feel sorry for you.

JUSTINA: For me?

KING: You have spoken to me. People don't, you know. Hardly at all. I just have to sit on my throne, high above the people, where it's terribly draughty, in these frightful heavy robes. And no-one says a word to me. And they look so sad. They're always quarrelling. And I have to sit up there and watch them. And I think, if only they'd stop. If only they'd stop for a minute and talk to me. Or just listen. They'd hear such lovely music. Can you hear it?

JUSTINA: No.

KING: Oh try. Please try. You'd love it, I know. You have a musical face. Close your eyes, please. Concentrate. Shut off every other sound from your mind.

JUSTINA listens. We can hear the music too: far off, unearthly.

KING: There. Can you hear it?

JUSTINA: Yes. I think so.

KING: The music of my spheres. My spinning crystals.

Pause.

JUSTINA: It's beautiful.

KING: I am so glad you can hear it. It is so beautiful. It is a feature of the finest glass. From Venice. It vibrates in the atmospheres.

It's fading.

JUSTINA: It's gone.

KING: It makes me so happy to share it. You know these days I cannot always hear it. All these wars. So noisy. And that Constable's frightful armour. Why can't he take it off?

JUSTINA: She.

KING: Sorry?

JUSTINA: She. The Constable. She's a woman.

KING: My dear I take no interest in such things. They used to make me try. You cannot believe the frightful things. Frightful things they made me do. They produced some silken creature. Wanted me to touch her. Something to do with an heir. Of course I refused. She then screamed some gibberish at me. In English, I believe. Frightful ugly language. Then she hung about the palace for a while. Apparently she died. But all that was years ago. Before the war.

JUSTINA: Was that how the war began?

KING: Oh I don't know. It really is of no concern to me.

JUSTINA: But this is the war that lays your land to waste. This is the war that burnt the village of my friend. And that doesn't concern you?

KING: Is there any reason why it should?

JUSTINA: You're the King!

KING: Well, exactly.

JUSTINA: I thought I felt sorry for you but now I don't. Don't you want to change things? Don't you want the land to be at peace?

KING: What I want has nothing to do with it. I'm only the King.

JUSTINA: Well I want to change things. And if you won't, I will.

KING: I'm disappointed in you. I thought you were rather nice. But now you've turned into a screeching, querulous creature.

JUSTINA: Kingship. It's such a lie.

KING: It's no lie. You are querulous. Very querulous.

JUSTINA: They tell you the rulers are wise. Infinitely above our heads. That they know what they're doing. Well they don't. I could do a better job than you. I mean look at you. You're useless.

KING: Of course I'm useless. If I were useful I would not be king.

JUSTINA: Then I'll be king. Give me your crown.

KING: No. It's mine.

JUSTINA: Give me your crown. Or I'll take it.

KING: No. Don't. Don't come near me. I mustn't be touched. Or I'll break.

JUSTINA: I don't care.

KING: If you touch me I'll shatter. I'll break into a thousand pieces. Please.

JUSTINA: I don't care if you break into a million pieces.

I am going to be King!

JUSTINA advances on the KING and takes the crown from his head. The KING screams and falls to the ground. JUSTINA runs off to the pantry. The KING does not break into pieces. He sits up and starts feeling himself all over.

KING: Extraordinary. Quite extraordinary. I should be shattered. I should be smashed to pieces. My particles scattered to the four winds. The ground littered with my shards. The air choked with smithereens. Yet here I am. In one piece. Apparently. And I feel lighter. So much lighter. My head feels as though it could fly.

Enter JUSTINA wearing the crown.

JUSTINA: It suits me. It definitely suits me. Gives a certain something to the head. Authority. I think I like it. Can I have your robe?

KING: Of course. With pleasure. Better and better.

JUSTINA puts on the KING's robe.

KING: I feel different all over. What is this? It is a foot. What are these? These are toes. And they wiggle. Extraordinary. And these are hands. Human hands. They don't have to be regal. Not any more.

Nothing else to sign. Nothing else to approve. Nothing. How wonderful. Wonderful. I can be human. Whatever that means.

JUSTINA: I've always wanted authority. Just think. A whole life spent coughing in attics. Choking in crypts. Struggling over smoky substances. Trying to be an alchemist. And now I can be king.

KING: And I can be useful. I wonder what it's like to be useful.

JUSTINA: I'll show you. Summon the Constable.

KING: Me?

JUSTINA: Who else.

KING: But I can't.

JUSTINA: No such word.

KING: I don't know how to.

JUSTINA: It's simple. Walk to the door. You can walk?

KING: Yes. Yes, I can walk. And I can bump into things. Bump into anything I like. Bump. Bump. It's wonderful. Sheer delight.

JUSTINA: To the door.

KING: This door?

JUSTINA: Now stand beside it and say: Constable. The King requires you.

KING: I couldn't.

JUSTINA: Yes you can.

KING: I've never required her in my life. I'd hate to.

JUSTINA: But you don't require her. I do. So summon her.

KING: Constable.

JUSTINA: Again. Louder.

KING: Constable!

JUSTINA: I'll show her who's boss. I wish the beggar could see me.

KING: Constable! Where are you?

Am I getting better?

JUSTINA: Much better.

KING: There's someone coming!

Enter the BEGGAR.

BEGGAR: Alms for the poor!

KING: Oh dear. That's not the Constable.

JUSTINA: It's a start. Don't be downhearted.

BEGGAR: Alms for the poor!

JUSTINA: Give her alms. Go on. What's keeping you?

KING: They won't come off.

JUSTINA: Not your arms. Stupid. Alms.

KING: In that case I don't have any. I think I used to have an alms-giver. But he died.

BEGGAR: Alms for the poor. Come on. Alms.

Justina!

JUSTINA: Yes.

BEGGAR: It's you.

JUSTINA: That's right.

BEGGAR: So. You're king now. Fancy that. I didn't recognise you. And that's the poor soul who used to be king. He's looking better.

KING: Thank you.

BEGGAR: You look human.

KING: And you're not so disagreeable.

BEGGAR: Come and see my graveyard.

Exit KING *and* BEGGAR *arm in arm.*

JUSTINA: But what about the Constable? Still, if you don't want to summon her, I'll summon her myself. I wish to see the Constable!

Enter the CONSTABLE.

CONSTABLE: (*bows*) Your Majesty.

Your Majesty has changed.

JUSTINA: Now I am King.

CONSTABLE: It makes no difference. I deal with the crown. I do not care who wears it.

It is the same with my army. When I pass it under my eye, what do I see? Human beings? No. I see rows of helmets. What is under those helmets is not my concern.

It is the same with the crown. One king is very like another. All are useless.

Your majesty plays chess? The king has no power of his own. The power is in the queen. As in myself. The king is just a cumbrance. He can scarcely move. And yet he is the centre of the game.
Without him, all things fall to pieces. And that is how things are.

JUSTINA: I want justice for my friend. For everyone whose lives have been destroyed by war.

I want to see the land at peace.

CONSTABLE: The army has set out. You cannot call it back. Besides, we fight for peace. What else is there worth fighting for? Observe this map.

The CONSTABLE *picks up a chessboard with a half-completed game.*

JUSTINA: But that's no map. That's a chessboard.

CONSTABLE: You do not see it with the strategist's eye.

To the trained eye, the military eye, each meadow, each field and hillside is a square.

Just a square on the board, each with its own particular traps and possibilities. Here is the position. You be England.

JUSTINA: If you like.

CONSTABLE: Your move. Take care. Your forces are scattered.

JUSTINA: I'm attacking you on many fronts.

CONSTABLE: You are greedy. You are destroying your sources of supply.

JUSTINA: My castle will attack your flank.

CONSTABLE: I'll counter with my knight.

JUSTINA: I can take it.

CONSTABLE: Of course. I knew. It was a sacrifice. I bade them farewell. They rode off in the grey dawn.

Their spurs were jingling, the feathers on their helmets bobbing up and down. Their armour gleamed, even in moonlight. A brave sight.

The next day I rode past the place. They told me the streams ran red with blood. You could not walk five yards without stumbling on a corpse.

You forgot my pawn.

JUSTINA: Pawns are nothing.

CONSTABLE: The people of France. My pawns. They encircle you on every side. I have led you into a trap. You will not so easily escape.

JUSTINA: I take that one.

CONSTABLE: But there are others. Burn one town and ten more are eager to attack you. And you depend on them. You prey on us and yet we feed you.

Destroy us and you destroy yourselves.

I move this pawn forward. Watch. A mere battalion. Not so great a sacrifice. But see all the other forces it brings into play.

JUSTINA: I can't turn back.

CONSTABLE: Yes. You have cut off your own retreat.

JUSTINA: What do I do?

CONSTABLE: You die. See. I have assembled forces here. And here. They burn the villages as they pass. Your men will starve.

JUSTINA: You're killing your own people too.

CONSTABLE: I will do anything to be rid of you.

JUSTINA: You'll destroy your own country to make it safe?

CONSTABLE: If I must.

JUSTINA: That is how the beggar lost her land. Her home. Her children. Her name.

CONSTABLE: Only a beggar.

JUSTINA: She wasn't then. She had a village.

CONSTABLE: Why feel sorry for a village. Bigger issues are at stake. We are fighting for survival.

JUSTINA *overturns the chessboard.*

JUSTINA: I don't want to play.

CONSTABLE: You don't like to lose.

JUSTINA: I think it's wrong.

CONSTABLE: Wrong or not, we have to play it. Right or not, you cannot end it.

Life is warfare. Evil surrounds you on every side. If you turn your back on it, do you think it disappears?

JUSTINA: I don't know.

CONSTABLE: You think that I have never dreamt of other things. I used to have a husband. One I loved.

We lived in Brittany. Our castle was fair. And then the English came. We were besieged. I was expecting my first child. It was a long and bitter siege. My husband led a sortie, and was killed. The rabble fled back in terror. The enemy attacked. What was I to do? Was I to let our town be taken? To be sacked and burnt? To have my people tortured, sold to slavery, or worse? I could not.

I cut my hair. I led the charge. But I felt the child inside me die.

Some days later the corpse was born. There was a new attack, I had no time for grief. I wear the ashes round my neck. They keep me safe.

Where else do you think I find my courage?

JUSTINA: Are you very much afraid?

CONSTABLE: We are all afraid. I have seen men weep behind their armour. Soldiers are not born. They are made.

JUSTINA: And how are they unmade?

CONSTABLE: They die. As we all must.

Exit CONSTABLE, *through Death's Door. Enter* BEGGAR *and* KING, *laughing.*

BEGGAR: What happened?

JUSTINA: I don't know.

JUSTINA *takes off her crown and robes.*

JUSTINA: These are no use now.

KING: It's not so easy being king. Not half so easy as it looks.

JUSTINA: She'll burn your village all over again.

Enter DEVIL *through Death's Door.*

DEVIL: She has gone to lead the dance. Who will join her?

BEGGAR: Oh yes. I'll go.

KING: Don't. Please.

DEVIL: She has to go. You all must. And she is not afraid. The tune's gone round and round her head for years.

The music begins to play.

BEGGAR: I have walked through the dead lands where no birds sing. Where the doors yawn empty and the houses are dark. I have heard that music before.

I have seen the faces. Their teeth were clenched. Their jaws were set. They sat or huddled or lay there in stupid defiance while all around them the flies buzzed and sucked.

They were all that moved in the dead lands, them and I. From house to house I trudged, from village to village, from town to town. And death was everywhere. She had taken the people, the houses she had left intact. And the strangest thing of all: she took all who fled from her, but left me, who sought her out. I entered all the houses. Sometimes I touched their faces, or I closed their eyes. And then she left the land, as quickly as she came, leaving me bereft.

Let me go. Don't be afraid.

KING: I feel no fear. Not now. But when I was made of glass, everything threatened me. Each step I took, each breath of wind. It was always thus.

Men with hammers lay in wait behind every door. No-one touched me. I could let no-one near. My own voice sounded distant, as if I was sitting inside a jar. And then she took away the crown. I thought I'd die. She was the man with the hammer, but she only smashed the jar. I could step free. I walked out into the air. I sat on a gravestone. I felt earth between my toes. The sunlight on my face. Your hand in my hand. My music returned. We laughed. What more could I ask for? I will follow you. Where you go, I'll go too.

BEGGAR: We'll go to a cottage just beside a road. With a fire always burning in the grate, with logs always ready beside it. A table always stocked up with food, and beer from a barrel in the corner. Everyone stops there, and tells a tale or two, and then moves on. And there's dancing on the way there.

KING: Will it be slow and stately?

BEGGAR: No, it'll be like a wedding.

KING: Will you teach me?

BEGGAR: Of course. Come on.

The BEGGAR *and the* KING *begin to dance. They exit through Death's Door, laughing together. The music ends.*

JUSTINA: Where have they gone?

DEVIL: The way everyone goes.

JUSTINA: Why did you make them go?

DEVIL: It wasn't me. They went by themselves. It's your turn next. I see you took off your robes.

JUSTINA: Kingship's just a costume. Why should I want to keep it?

DEVIL: I had a client once. I took him way up a mountain. Showed him all the kingdoms of the world. He turned them down. Did him no good. It won't help you. Are you ready?

JUSTINA: No. I don't want to be alone.

DEVIL: What about Fernando?

JUSTINA: (*sadly*) I had forgotten him. Can't the dead return?

DEVIL: Sometimes. Once my client lost his friend. He wept. And then he said: he is not dead. He is sleeping. And the mourners laughed him to scorn. But he took no notice. He went and he stood before the grave and shouted. "Lazarus. Come forth!" And Lazarus came. He had been in the grave three days. He stank. Imagine it. And the tales he had to tell are enough to freeze the blood.

JUSTINA: I loved him. I won't be afraid.

DEVIL: Then call him. Call him by his name.

JUSTINA: Fernando. Fernando!

FERNANDO *rises from the dead. He is wearing grave clothes.*

FERNANDO: Where am I? Who are you?

JUSTINA: Justina.

FERNANDO: I knew you once. I knew this room. Didn't I live here? But why am I here? I died. What's the point of dying if you just end up at home?

Something's wrong. Something's terribly wrong.

JUSTINA: I called you back.

FERNANDO: I remember now. I was walking. I was frightened. There was something I was frightened of losing. That's all I was thinking. I didn't want to lose it, and now it's gone. There was a crowd. I could see a crowd. Everyone was shouting. There was this . . . thing, this broken thing in the middle of it all, and when I got closer I saw it was a body. A broken body. And I thought: some poor sod's had it, anyway. And then I got closer. And I saw it was me. I was frightened. I was so frightened.

And everyone was shouting, and I thought, why don't they stop, why don't they stop shouting and look after me. I'm dying. Will somebody stop me dying?

But no-one touched me. And it began to fade. It all began to fade.

I struggled, but I couldn't move.

I shouted, but I had no voice.

And then I saw the light. Far far away in the distance. A bright light in the middle of darkness. And I wanted to go. I wanted to go to the light. But it was so dark. And so very far away. And I was so tired. And I wanted to see you, just once, just to say goodbye. I couldn't bear to leave you, it seemed so cruel. So I turned back, and the light was gone.

And now I'm here. I should have followed the light, followed it when I had the chance. But I came here instead.

And now I know. I was married to an alchemist.

We quarrelled all the time. The energy we spent. All the trouble we took to be unhappy. The wasted time. And the garden is still there.

Still there inside our minds. It was never lost. We thought it was. But we walk there, hand in hand. And we are not ashamed.

Why didn't we know?

Why didn't we understand?

Why did we fight?

Why did we hurt each other?

And I loved you. I loved you all the time.

JUSTINA: Can't we go there? Can't we go there now?

FERNANDO: It's too late. The doors are closed. We threw away the key.

JUSTINA: Don't go.

FERNANDO: I must. It's dark, but I can smell the dawn. And I must sleep. I'm tired. Don't call me back. Let me go in peace.

Exit FERNANDO. *He leaves through Death's Door.* JUSTINA *weeps.*

DEVIL: The king sat in her court. She had a soldier, a beggar, a madman and a ghost. And now they've gone and left her.

JUSTINA: All but you.

DEVIL: And I will never leave you. I will stay with you always. Even unto the end of the world.

The DEVIL *moves round the stage, putting out all the candles.*

JUSTINA: You belong to hell.

DEVIL: Where I live. Not where I belong.

JUSTINA: Does it hurt?

DEVIL: It does at first. When we enter it, we cry. We howl with pain and rage. Our skin's so soft, you see. So very tender. But you get used to that.

Besides, we all wear clothes.

JUSTINA: Clothes? In hell?

DEVIL: Of course. It's very civilised.

JUSTINA: But doesn't God torment you?

DEVIL: We don't need God. We all torment ourselves.

JUSTINA: Which pain is worse?

DEVIL: The lack of light.

JUSTINA: Is it always dark?

DEVIL: Of course we have the sun. We have the moon as well. And all the lesser stars. But that is not the light I mean. It is the lack of inner light that hurts. The confusion. The sense of loss.

But you get used to that.

JUSTINA: But that's what it's like here.

DEVIL: Where else do you think we are?

JUSTINA: Is there no way out?

DEVIL: Through the door.

JUSTINA: I won't go.

DEVIL: You will. You must. The seed must die. Your soul is mine.

The DEVIL *has put out all the candles but one. He gives it to* JUSTINA. *He exits through Death's Door.* JUSTINA *stares at her light a while.*

JUSTINA: How frail a light. How easy to put out. I could do it with my hand.

They say to some death comes so sweetly, like a friend. But not to me.

The night is always darkest in the hour before the daylight comes.

Then, they say, the sun will rise and chase away the spirits of the dark.

But, till that hour we have to grope our way through shadows and await the dawn.

JUSTINA *leaves her candle and walks to the door that leads to the outside world. She opens it. Dawn is breaking. We hear the singing of the birds.*

THE PLAY ENDS

PLAYING WITH FIRE – NOTES

1. The play is located in Cimetière des Innocents, which from the Middle Ages to the late eighteenth century was the largest cemetery in Paris. The name was taken from the adjacent Church of the Holy Innocents.
2. An alchemical substance capable of transforming base metals such as lead into gold. It could also be used to make an elixir or potion that would make those who drank it immortal.
3. Alchemical term, referring to blackness or decomposition. In alchemy, this was believed to be the first stage in the process of producing the Philosopher's Stone.
4. A small, double-crust meat pie, filled with mutton or minced beef.

THE WAY TO GO HOME

by Rona Munro

*First performed at the Belgrade Theatre, Coventry,
29 October 1987*

Cast

Liz *Sharon Muircroft*
Sharon *Caroline Paterson*
Maria *Nelly Salas*
Mackenzie *Matthew Vaughan*

AUTHOR'S INTRODUCTION

Rona Munro

The Way to Go Home was written after a life changing trip to Nicaragua as part of a solidarity delegation. At the time, 1984, Ronald Reagan was President of the USA. His government, strongly supported by Margaret Thatcher here in the UK, was in the process of planning bombing raids on this small Central American country. This was because Nicaragua had had the temerity to overthrow the dictator who had ruled for a generations, and replace him with democracy. The democracy voted in was not to the taste of that iteration of the White House. The Sandinistas, named after an early fighter against dictatorship Agusto Sandino, were former freedom fighters turned politicians and their politics were seen as dangerously left wing. Dangerous, because at *that* time the USA saw Soviet Russia as their greatest threat, and the popular struggles of oppressed peoples in South and Central America, the USA's so-called 'back yard', as providing a toehold for that then communist regime, right on their doorstep.

That is a crushed and generalised version of some very complicated history which might be familiar to some of those of my generation, those who attended the same rallies and agitated for the same causes. It is almost completely forgotten elsewhere. The vividness of *our* recollection ('Come on there's a whole Clash album! *Sandinista!*') is an illusion shielding us from a harsh truth. History repeats because history is forgotten. It roils and boils and finds new forms and new geopolitical shapes but most people on this planet still remain at the mercy of a system that concentrates power where power makes wealth.

My own political journey has only changed my opinion about what constitutes effective opposition to that horrible juggernaut. In the 1980s, I was the very passionate epitome of virtue signalling. You can see in this play that I knew where I believed evil lay and I was going to make sure you knew it too. But you can also see that, in the process of writing it, I was learning a humbler (more effective?) kind of solidarity. When I was in Nicaragua (and I would make two visits), the ordinary folk we stayed with or sat up with as they guarded their coffee fields from American-backed soldiers would sometimes ask us how much it had cost us to travel to sit there in solidarity. When they heard the price of our plane tickets, their eyes would widen in shock, enough to keep a whole community there afloat for weeks. We were there to 'bear witness', if I'd needed reminding that I better bear an amazingly effective bit of witness that reaction made it clear.

But I didn't focus on that one goal, I wanted to say something bigger, HUGE, a deconstruction of imperialism, capitalism and the patriarchy, all the three horsemen of the lefty feminist apocalypse.

To that end, with minimal contacts, I then travelled solo into Turkey, at that point in the aftermath of the latest of a series of military coups which had seen a generation of students and activists, my generation, beaten, imprisoned and disappeared. My solidarity with them was, fortunately for me, invisible behind a tourist persona. However, as a solo female traveller in rural Turkey, I received a whole other education in the politics of patriarchy and how they might be acted out on me in particular.

On my return, still processing all that (I'm probably still processing most of that). I was working in community theatre in Wester Hailes and Craigmillar. At that point in history these deprived areas of Edinburgh had earned it the title of the heroin capital of Europe. The level of urban poverty and near total youth unemployment created a charged community, fierce in its survival, horribly bleak in its lack of an imaginable future. This was the sharp end of Thatcher's Britain; that hopelessness visited on urban poor exceeded anything I saw in either Nicaragua or Turkey.

All of these things were, are, connected and so I tried to cram *all* of them into one play. It is far, far too much. Now I believe that political activism is best expressed more directly, as I did with actress Fiona Knowles when we performed, as the feminist double act, The MsFits, comedy skits and songs with clear satire and intent. But in my drama I believe that creating empathy for marginalised characters is more effective in creating change than embedding overt political argument in my narratives.

Far too much is in this play. And when I was told I could only have two and a half performers, that there simply was no budget for anything else, I couldn't rewrite or trim the play's ambitions to make it more effective, instead I shoved one character into a soundtrack and shoved a poor acting assistant stage manager into a burnt Mickey Mouse mask and a job which technically didn't breach equity rules (he had no lines) but basically meant he was under-paid for what became a massive physical role.

But I remain proud of a lot of it. Flawed as it is, its ambitions are huge and the truths it tries to grab, filtered through a female gaze then so rarely given a platform, remain as dangerously relevant as they ever were.

Cast

SHARON: age twenty-two, from Craigmillar in Edinburgh.

LIZ: age twenty-nine, from Glasgow, has lived in London for five years.

MARIA: age twenty-three, from Nicaragua.

MACKENZIE: John Mackenzie, a former lieutenant in the US Marines.

The play is set in Turkey in early Spring, sometime in the present.

The set has three crucial figures. One is a representation of the "Eye of Fatima", the bright blue charm often found on the end of Muslim prayer beads.

One part of the set is used for the "fire" scenes, another for the "water" scenes.

THE WAY TO GO HOME

Act I

Scene 1

Antayla[1] bus station, 3:00 a.m. Blackout. In the darkness we hear MACKENZIE's *voice on tape, he is muttering to himself.*

MACKENZIE: Okay . . . that's it . . . I've got you . . . I've got you . . . (disgusted noise) . . . Aw shit . . . out of the way . . . out of the *way* pal, I can't get a clear shot . . . *That's* it . . . Gotya!

A sudden flash of light at the same time as MACKENZIE's *"gotya!" there is a loud click of a camera shutter,* LIZ *and* SHARON *are flashlit on stage, sitting back to back. They do not move.*

A pause and then sound and lights come up together. The sounds of the bus station buses, a babble of voices, a bread seller calling, ticket sellers chanting their destinations. Grey early morning light reveals LIZ *and* SHARON *sitting exactly as they were revealed by the flash.* SHARON *is looking at everything happening around her, eyes wide, she takes a drink out of a bottle, wipes her mouth and smiles to herself.* LIZ *is slumped forward as if asleep, a large silly tourist hat over her eyes. Both women are wearing grubby jeans and seem to be combatting the cold by wearing everything else they possess on top.* SHARON *starts to sing softly. Fade sound.*

SHARON: Show me the way to go home, I'm tired and I wanna go to bed, I had a little drink aboot an hour ago and it went right to my head[2] . . . Liz?

LIZ: (*under hat*) What?

SHARON: Any raki[3] left?

LIZ: Nup.

SHARON: (*looks at* LIZ *for a moment*) Gees my hat back.

(LIZ *raises her hat and looks at her*) My ears is cauld. (*Grabs the hat and puts it on*) Eh?

Liz?

LIZ: (*eyes shut*) Aye great.

SHARON: Strong stuff that raki. (*Fumbles in her pocket, pulls out a packet of cigarettes and takes one out and looks at it*) Call that a cigarette? Calls itsel a cigarette, it's like a worm wi' dysentry, hingin oot baith ends. Where are the bogs Liz? (LIZ *shakes her head*)

This country'll give me constipation, I'm telling you. (*thinks*) Or worse. (*Nods meaningfully. Offers* LIZ *a cigarette.* LIZ *shakes her head again.*)

Oh that's right you dinny dae you. (*lights the cigarette*) What's he saying? Driving me nuts.

LIZ: (*imitating ticket caller*) Ankara[4] Ankara Ankara, 'stanbul[5] 'stanbul 'stanbul!

SHARON *looks at her.*

LIZ: That's what he's saying.

SHARON: Aye well, what does it mean?

LIZ: It's where the bus is going.

SHARON: Oh aye, right. Where are you going then?

LIZ: I'm going to Ankara.

SHARON: Yeah? Got a ticket have you?

LIZ: Aye. You've no?

SHARON: I wasnae just sure how to dae it I mean . . . Well I'm no just exactly sure where I want tae . . . Look can I chum you there? Ankara?

LIZ: Aye, sure.

SHARON: Good is it?

LIZ: Never been.

SHARON: Right . . . Fuck it I'll go to Ankara. (*she puts out the cigarette she's just lit and puts it carefully back in the packet, she takes out a fresh one*) Right. (*she gets up*)

(*talking front*) 'Scuse me pal. Anyone got a light Eh? No hayir, hayir, Amerika, Iskocya. (*points to herself*) Iskocya . . . En Inglitere? Yeah? You know that? Well I'm no Inglitere, I'm Iskocya, never mind never mind.[6] You're leaving now? This bus? Octobus? Evet?[7] Can you give us a light eh? Come on everyone in Turkey smokes. What's he laughing at? What are you laughing at eh? How much? What do you mean? (*calls back over her shoulder*) Hey Liz, what's he mean?

LIZ *shakes her head at her, to indicate "it's obvious what he means, Sharon".*

SHARON: That's my sister. No it's my sister. You want to meet these guys Liz? She's shy. Okay. That's okay pal, thanks anyway. (*she is patting someone on the shoulder, on the side*) No, I'm getting this bus. No go on, you'll miss it, away you go.

(SHARON *wanders back to* LIZ, *looks round and waves her hand exaggeratedly*) Byeeee! (*sits down*) Wankers! (SHARON *takes out her wallet and looks through it.* LIZ *watches her.* SHARON *looks up, tries to gauge her reaction then removes the money and counts it*) Three thousand Lira, will that do me?

LIZ: It'll get you to Ankara.

SHARON: Great.

LIZ: Better get rid of the wallet though eh?

SHARON: (*grins, looks round then chucks the wallet over her shoulder, looks back at* LIZ, *kicks her affectionately*) I'm really glad I met you ken? Couldnae believe it.

LIZ: (*smiles momentarily then*) You've probably just taken a week's money off that guy.

SHARON: (*winces*) Well he was handy. He shouldnae talk to strange women like that. I dinny take a' the time ken? I never did that stuff till I was here.

LIZ: You're good at it.

SHARON: When I was a kid I'd lift stuff, but no since then.

LIZ: His pals'll maybe lend him some.

SHARON: (*shrugs*) Maybe.

LIZ: Is that how you've been getting by since your money ran out?

SHARON: Aye well . . . It's a long story.

LIZ: Know anything about Turkish prisons, do you?

SHARON: Oh gies us a break eh? We've all seen *Midnight Express*.[8]

LIZ: Go get yourself a ticket.

SHARON: Right. (*gets up*) Eh . . . what it is? . . . Eh . . . Ankara? ya bir . . . beeht . . . iste . . .[9]

LIZ: Forget it.

SHARON: Aye right, say Ankara, look lost, wave your money, universal language eh?

Scene 2

Interior of a bus, 4:00 a.m. The bus lights are off, SHARON *and* LIZ *are dimly lit, nodding as if dozing in their seats. As they speak a light gradually comes up on the blue and black "Eye of Fatima". At the start of the scene we hear the sound of the bus, smokers' coughs and a popular Turkish song, sounding eerily thin and tinny, on a cheap transistor radio.*

LIZ: (*as if talking to herself, quiet and drowsy*) Hiya Susan, see, I did send you one after all. Doing a lot of walking and eating too much. Who's got my typewriter and have they got up your nose yet?

SHARON: I've never been here but it was the nicest picture, weather not so good, food okay but I've got the runs, tell David I saw a camel the other day.

LIZ: Went South and now I'm lost, lost in a bus full of smoke, juddering its way through the Taurus mountains, all that history out there and all I can see is the dark.

SHARON: Weird food. It's barry though, a' meat an spices an stuff. They drink tea oot ae glasses, it's great . . .

LIZ: So much for all that culture and history I was going to soak up for you, I'm sitting in a cigarette fog surrounded by men in hats and men in dark suits with dark moustaches and I feel like they're all . . .

SHARON *has suddenly started to get out of her seat. Lights up suddenly as if they've been switched on.*

SHARON: (*glaring behind her*) He got my bum! The bastard got my bum!

LIZ: (*trying to pull her down*) Sharon . . .

SHARON: (*looking at someone else*) What are you looking at eh? *Eh*?

LIZ: (*gets back into her seat*) Sharon for fuck's sake!

SHARON: I just went tae get a bottle of water, that's all, just got mysel oot ae my seat and had a wee wander up the bus tae get a drink. They all start gawping like I'm a dog walking on its hind legs or something.

LIZ: It's a different culture.

SHARON: (*looks at her for a second*) Nae kidding? And here was I thinking I was on the 15 bus tae Portobello[10] High Street. I don't like it.

LIZ: It's different.

SHARON: It's mental.

LIZ: Have you met any women here?

SHARON: Na. This guy took me tae belly dancing. I'd said I wanted to see that. I'm telling you go go wasnae in it. They were gypsies these lassies, I mean real gypsies ken, sell you a bunch o' flooers if they could, maybe starve if they couldnae. They all looked that fucking hungry ken? An all these guys were shoving money doon their claes . . . This guy says . . . I was talking about the state of this lassie, couldnae have been fourteen even, he says "They are all dirty women, gypsies, they are all very rich, they cheat you", I says "Good luck, good luck tae them." (*looks sideways*) And what are *you* gawping at!?

LIZ: *Sharon.*

SHARON: What?

LIZ: She's trying to give you that.

SHARON: (*looks*) It's a' wrinkled, what is it? An apple?

LIZ: Come on, you canny say no.

SHARON: Eh thanks, tesekkhur[11] . . . Folk are dead friendly here are they?

As SHARON *reaches for the apple, she freezes, there is the sound of a camera shutter, four or five quick shots, plus four or five flashes. Lights down then up again, it is a short time later, we're coming in on the middle of a conversation.*

LIZ: . . . Paris, Leningrad,[12] Moscow, New York, Tokyo . . . I've travelled through most of Europe but you can't count that . . . where else?

SHARON: Where'd you get the money for all that?

LIZ: I temp at home and get work abroad. I don't spend money on much else. This is new, this here. I want to go to Iceland next, I really fancy that, a bit of ice haven't seen any ice for a while.

SHARON: So where's the best then? Best place in the world?

LIZ: Best place in the world? (*smiles*) I don't know.

SHARON: Oh dinny tell me, (*sings raucously*) There's no-o place like home.

LIZ: Estelí.

SHARON: Eh?

LIZ: Estelí, it's a wee town in Nicaragua.[13]

SHARON: Nicaragua? Where's that aboot? South America?

LIZ: Central America.

SHARON: Oh aye, that's them the Yanks keep bombing tae bits eh?

LIZ: More or less.

SHARON: Bastards. See Americans? I hate the bastards.

Lights down, fade Turkish music, bring up Nicaraguan bird noises (well as near as we can get it anyway). We see MARIA, *a Nicaraguan woman of about twenty-three, she is in a spot or other isolated lighting, she is absorbed with the gun she is holding, trying to work the movement, it keeps jamming, she shakes her head, looks up sees that she is being watched, laughs, holds out the gun, "Compañera?"*[14] *She mimes the movement and holds it out again, laughing ("You try"). Lights down on her up on bus again, Turkish music and bus noises, we are coming in halfway through another conversation.*

SHARON: So we were all sitting in the middle of the street, wi'oot a word of Spanish between the three of us and Jean says, "It's only another couple of miles" and I says "Look Jean, I'm nae tortoise, I canny crawl aroond in the dirt wi' my house on my back, me and this backpack are stopping here" and Brian says, "I think we're lost". I wouldnae say Brian was slow but he's the only guy I ken that laughs at the jokes oot o' Christmas crackers. So Jean says, I'll ask a policeman, I says you got to be joking. She's a raj Jean, goes up tae this guy on a horse just aboot waving a joint under his nose. "Where's the campsite" she says. He never looked at her so she shouts at him, "Where's the fucking campsite!". I says "You wouldnae try that in Niddrie[15] and these guys have got guns". Well the horse bit her.

LIZ *throws her head back to laugh, freezes, another series of camera clicks and flashes. Lights down. In the dark the sound of* MACKENZIE *softly whistling, "The Campbells are coming".*[16] *Lights up, still in the bus, later, there is no music. Half way through another conversation.*

LIZ: ... It was one of those journeys when they chuck you from plane to plane like a bit of excess baggage, you know, when you start thinking it must have been easier to travel the world in sailing ships, and I was trying to sleep on a bit of airport floor and I must have nodded off because I woke up and didn't have a clue where I was. Not a clue. All I could hear were airport voices, you know, American with a faint foreign accent and all I could see were the same posters I'd seen in every other airport, James Dean[17] crucified on a rifle trying to flog us all duty free cigarettes and I kept looking round to see what kind of hats the policemen were wearing because that was the only way I was going to be able to guess where I was.

SHARON *nods, yawns and stretches, freezes, another series of camera clicks and flashes. The bright white light stays on after the last flash, like a frozen flame.*

There is the sound of MACKENZIE *loading a gun, a faint metallic clicking, his voice on the tape speaks over this.*

MACKENZIE: I would not do that ... I would not hurt you ... not at all ... not at *all* ... Okay? Why you're ... family ... family, almost ... Ain't ya?

The sound of a sudden gun shot. MACKENZIE *chuckles. The lights return to normal,* SHARON *moves again.*

SHARON: So my mum says "Look you go Sharon or it's a ticket gone to waste" you canny get your money back when there's just a week to go and I said okay 'cause someone had tae use it. I never felt I was daein her oot a holiday, state she was in it was a honeymoon of naething ken? She was as well greiting her eyes oot in the comfort of her ain hame than that poxy hotel in Istanbul, so I just came mysel. Dinny ken who got his ticket. (*pauses, looks sideways at* LIZ) Dinny ken who got mine come tae it. I lost it.

LIZ: You lost your ticket?

SHARON: Aye.

LIZ: Your return ticket?

SHARON: Aye. I went South with this guy see and ... I lost it.

LIZ: Have you told the airline?

SHARON: Aye well, it was a bit difficult see 'cause I lost my passport an aw!

Pause.

LIZ: How will you get home?

SHARON: I'll work something out.

Lights down. Up on MARIA *and her* SON, *a wee boy of about seven or eight. She is pouring water out of her water bottle onto her face, tries to do the same for him, he squirms and yells,* MARIA *is grinning, shaking and teasing him. There is the echoey sound of a gunshot, they freeze and look front. Lights down on them.*

Lights up on the bus, it is later that night. LIZ *and* SHARON *are sitting close together.*

SHARON: You asleep?

LIZ: No. Where did you lose it?

SHARON: What?

LIZ: Your ticket.

SHARON: Don't know. Down south somewhere. You been down there?

LIZ: Aye.

SHARON: Great was it? Fine and hot. I was in the sea, look, (*pulls her sleeve up*) that's nae dirt that, genuine suntan.

LIZ: Did you drop it or what?

SHARON: (*shrugs*) Someone lifted it. Wifey at the place staying just aboot went mental. Sat on the front step wi' her pinny over her heid wailing away tae hersel, "Allah . . . Allah". Think she thought I was away hame tae tell the hale country nae tae go tae Turkey 'cause were a' crooks and she was the worst, I kept saying tae her, "It's nae your fault, I'm no bothered". Carried on like she was ruined.

LIZ: If the tourists stop coming she will be.

SHARON: Aye right enough. Wouldnae be a lot going on would there. No withoot the yachts and cruisers and bams like you and me wi' oor back packs. Guy I went doon wi' took me tae see his family. Couldnae believe it, they lived up the coast a bit, nae road right? Only way in was boat or goat track. Walked for mile over the hills, a' just white rocks and green bushes and goats. The family was living in one room. They got their water oot the burn, their food oot the ground and they made me sit on every cushion in the place and eat all the cake they had. This wee girl had a cold, a'body was makin a big fuss of her, giein her cake and milk and carrying her aboot piggy back, an her treat, her special treat, was turning the light switch on and off. There was nae light, they were waiting on being connected, big event, electricity for the first time ever, they were only getting it 'cause they were building a fucking marina. She kept switching the switch and they kept telling her how great it would be when the electricity came and her wee brothers kept following me aboot, listening tae every word I said, trying tae learn a' the English they could before the summer came.

LIZ: Yeah, yeah I know.

SHARON: I felt terrible ken? Wanted tae pay for the food or something, but I couldnae, they wouldnae take it, couldn't even offer ken? It'd've been that rude. I felt like I came frae another universe.

LIZ: Yeah.

SHARON: Mind you only work I've had last two years has been in the summer, washing oot hotels in the Edinburgh Festival. Nae tourists, nae money. So who's got the money tae be tourists? (*notices* LIZ *is looking out the window*) What you looking at?

LIZ: We've lost him.

SHARON: Who?

LIZ: Whoever was in that jeep. He's been following us for ages.

SHARON: What kind o' car was it?

LIZ: A jeep, an American army jeep, must be from one of the bases down the coast.

SHARON: It's following this bus?

LIZ: Yeah. It's been behind us for miles. It'll probably catch up again in a minute.

Pause.

LIZ: I'm dying of thirst. Do you want another bottle of water? (*she sees* SHARON *is looking blank*)

SHARON: Liz?

LIZ: Yeah what?

SHARON: I need tae get off the bus. I have tae.

LIZ: How? What is it?

SHARON: Take too long tae tell you.

They look at each other.

LIZ: Okay. (*she stands up and picks up her luggage*)

SHARON: What're you daein?

LIZ: Coming with you.

SHARON: (*grins*) I *knew* I'd like you.

Lights down.

Scene 3

The roadside. Silence for a moment then the sound of a jeep approaching, two lights like headlamps swing round to glare at the audience, the jeep stops. The sound of someone whistling, "The Campbells are Coming", it continues with the sound of a jeep door opening and closing, feet on the road, a zip undone, someone having a pee, zip closing, feet receding, jeep door again. The engine starts, headlamps and sound of the jeep recede. Silence. Lights up on LIZ *and* SHARON, *they are crouched in a ditch at the side of the road. Grey light, just before dawn. During this scene the lights slowly come up on the "Eye of Fatima".*

LIZ: What was that?

SHARON: That was Lieutenant John Mackenzie, late of the US Marines, saviour of the world and everything in it, 'specially me if he can get his sweaty wee hands on me.

LIZ: You know him?

SHARON: You could say that.

LIZ: What did you do?

SHARON: Too much. Na, na I did naething, naething me, I'm telling you. I was a lump of wood. Yes John, no John. You want tae eat John? Okay. Want me tae sit and wait John? Okay. Want tae fuck John? Okay. (*taps her head*) Dummy.

LIZ: What's he after?

SHARON: Me. Aye that's right, me. It's the accent, that wee twang, genuine Caledonia, that totie wee hint of urban deprivation in the way I belted back the man's food that put him in mind o' his heiland ancestors and the Clearance[18] ships, that skirl I've had in my walk since I lost the heel off my shoe on the Bosphorus ferry that called back his dear great-granny hirpling up the brae wi' a bucket of coal on her heid. 'Sides that there's my fresh young nubile body in assorted matching shades of skin tone. Drove him mad wi' desire.

The man's a moron I'm telling you. (*She gets out of their hiding place,* LIZ *follows*) Will there be another bus along later?

LIZ: Bound to be.

How did you end up with him?

SHARON: He talked English. (*looks at* LIZ *speculatively*) Listen I don't mean this tae sound cheeky but eh . . . have you had any bother wi' guys here?

LIZ: Bother?

SHARON: You messed wi' anybody?

LIZ: I try not to.

SHARON: (*crushed*) Oh . . . right. (*looks around her*) Dark eh? What's that smell?

LIZ: I think it's wild sage.

SHARON: Barry that.

LIZ: I met this boy on the beach, Beautiful. Just beautiful. I ate raw sea urchins out of his hand . . .

SHARON: An he tried it on yeah?

LIZ: Yeah well I mean I never thought anything, I thought "Okay, so I've talked to him, nice guy," then there he was with three mates in tow . . .

SHARON: Bastards, they are, they're bastards, you cannae get away frae them.

Okay. There was this guy Ali right? Ali got me down from Istanbul. I thought he was dead sweet. Even when he came in my room I thought, Oh well, where's the harm? After that I couldnae call my breath my own. Couldnae move. "Don't move like that everyone's watching", "Aye I can see they are Ali, but I'm just walking doon the road same I always walk." Look. (*shows her arm*) Fucking bruises, dragged me aboot like a suitcase.

LIZ: And not another woman in sight. Not now. They're invisible. You see them in Istanbul yeah? But the further east you go the more invisible they are. The scarfs creep down and the veils creep up, their bodies vanish, it's like they're walking around in their own shrouds, they're not even on the streets anymore just . . .

SHARON: Men. Aye. They're everywhere. An it's that tiring shoving them off a' the time. Tell you sometimes when I'd had a laugh wi' a guy or a drink I'd think, Oh fuck it Sharon, you're on your holidays, but it wasnae awfy nice ken?

LIZ: I sat beside this old woman on the bus down. We had one of those comfortable smiling silences you can find when you know there's no use saying a word. Then these two guys started having a knife fight up the back of the bus and this woman looked at them and looked at me and put her arm round me to take care of me and stroked my face where I should have been wearing a veil. And I knew what she was saying was "You poor silly girl, what are you doing without your armour on?" And I thought, she's got a point.

SHARON: Tell you, I got the feeling like a hoor ken? 'Specially when my money ran out and I needed my breakfast bought for me. I didnae really know what they thought was going on. It was like that was part o' the foreplay ken? Buying you stuff. Tell you something else, coming up wi' the price o' a cup of coffee was the start and finish of their sexual technique, once you'd had the coffee you'd had the best of them.

Anyway, that's how I started lifting things.

Felt . . . cleaner.

LIZ: Honest.

SHARON: Aye. It's daft ken because I've been acting different here to the way I would at hame but you canny seem tae get by like that here.

LIZ: It's not that different. We're just strange women. On our own.

SHARON: It's just how my ma telt me it would be. She's been haein' nightmares aboot this since I was six.

LIZ: Learn the language, keep enough money and always have a return ticket.

SHARON: Thanks.

LIZ: Oh . . . Sorry.

SHARON: No . . . I've messed up. I know I have. Anyway John Mackenzie was going tae get me awa frae a' that. For a start it was just such a rest no tae have tae (*speaks very slowly and clearly*) Talk . . . like . . . that . . . grin a' the time.

I met him in this caff along the coast there, waving a glass aboot – "Is this yoghurt low fat?" Can you believe it? He was a funny guy you know, like his heid was half empty or he was made o' plastic or something. He just wasnae wi' you half the time.

An he had this thing aboot me, aboot Scots right, told me a' this stuff one night there . . . He was lying there wi' that smug look on his face ken, like he'd jist swallowed me doon wi' ketchup.

LIZ: (*smiles*) Smoking a cigarette.

SHARON: Na, he was a health freak, he was chewing sugar-free gum. He says, "I'm a Scot".

LIZ: Just like that?

SHARON: No, mair like (*imitates*) "Eh . . . I . . . I . . . I'm a Scot". He talked like that wee pig in the Bugs Bunny[19] cartoons. I says "You?" He says "Sure, my great-grand-daddy was John Mackenzie from OOist."[20] That's how he said it. OOist. I says, "Nae kidding? My great granda was frae Uist". "Hey," he says, "Maybe we're related." I thought fuck, my genes couldnae mak something like that could they?

LIZ: And now he's chasing you?

SHARON: The man's a moron, I'm telling you . . .

Lights down.

In the darkness MACKENZIE *whistling "The Campbells are Coming", the camera clicks and flashes, they illuminate* LIZ *and* SHARON's *deserted bus seats. The bright white light stays on for a second, the whistling stops abruptly.*

Actually at the bus seat:

MACKENZIE: Shi . . . i . . . i . . . t.

Blackout.

Lights up on MARIA. *It is night. She is sitting back on her heels in a circle of light. She keeps waving insects away from her face. She speaks Spanish, pausing every so often, each time she does so* LIZ *provides a translation.*

MARIA: Este es el hospital. (*points behind her*)

LIZ: This is the hospital.

MARIA: Casi todas las cosas usted vea aca son neuvas.

LIZ: Nearly everything you see here is new.

MARIA: En la lucha revolutionaría, los Somocistas quemaron el hospital mientras la gente estaba todavía a dentro.

LIZ: In the revolution the Somocistas[21] burnt the hospital while the patients were still inside.

MARIA: Ellos lo hicieron para forzar los muchachos parar el attaque y evacuar el hospital.

LIZ: They did it to force the FSLN[22] to drop the attack and evacuate the hospital.

MARIA: Entonces nosotros reconstruimos todito.

LIZ: So we rebuilt it all.

MARIA: Nos quiseremos construir mas pero tenemos muchos gastos en defensa.[23] (MARIA *speaks in english with a strong accent*) Very hard ... very ... (*she shakes her head, smiles*) Habla español?[24]

Lights down. LIZ *speaks her next line out of the darkness.*

LIZ: Sprekenzi deutsch?[25]

Scene 4

A café, still before dawn. LIZ *and* SHARON *are sitting at a table with glasses of tea in front of them.* LIZ *is speaking front.*

LIZ: Français? (*she gets an answer, smiles*) Ah bueno ... I mean bien, vous pouvez nous aider Monsieur? Nous sommes perdu.[26]

SHARON: Tell him we're lost.

LIZ: (*offering a map for inspecting*) Oui? ... Ah merci[27] ... We're South of Sivrihisar.[28]

SHARON: Is that the right road?

LIZ: On peut prendre l'autobus a Ankara ici? ... Merci.[29] Yeah, there's a bus through at eight, (*looks up*) Oui? ... He'll be on it. (SHARON *pulls a face*). Liz, je m'appelle Liz.[30] (*looks at* SHARON) He wants to know your name.

SHARON: Well?

LIZ: Well?

SHARON: You ken my name do you no?

LIZ: Sharon, elle s'appelle Sharon[31] ... He thinks you're beautiful.

SHARON: Tell him to piss off.

LIZ: Elle dit va te ...[32]

SHARON: No, no tell him I'm your sister.

LIZ: Why?

SHARON: It's better eh?

LIZ: How?

SHARON: Just tell him.

LIZ: Elle est ma soeur . . . Comment? . . . He wants to know if you're married.

SHARON: Tell him no. Tell him I'm a career woman.

LIZ: Non, elle n'est pas encore marie, elle travail . . . quelle metier?[33] . . . What do you do?

SHARON: I'm a brain surgeon . . . no, no hud on . . . eh.. I fly helicopters.

LIZ: Elle est pilot, pilot de helicopter . . . He says you're very small . . . Oui, mais ils sont les tres petits helicopters . . . I said they were very small helicopters . . . What do we think of Turkey?

SHARON: (*shrugs*) Tell him.

LIZ: Eh . . . c'est tres beau, le pays est tres beau, tout le monde sympa, tres gentil et[34] . . . Christ I wrote essays like this . . . Comment? . . . He says if we lived here maybe we wouldn't like it so much.

SHARON: He said that?

LIZ: That's what the man said. (*listening hard translating quickly*) He says he loves his country but at the moment he has great . . . honte? C'est ça? . . . he is sometimes ashamed of his country. What music do you like?

SHARON: How does he mean?

LIZ: What groups?

SHARON: Oh go . . . eh . . . Paul Young[35] eh . . . Style Council[36] . . . Talking Heads,[37] they're barry them . . . eh . . .

LIZ: He doesn't know them.

SHARON: Bowie?[38]

LIZ: He loves Bowie.

SHARON: Canny stand him mysel . . . Beatles?[39]

LIZ: Oh yeah, that hit the jackpot.

SHARON: Tell him they're a' deid.

LIZ: He says we are very lucky. Our music is the best in the world, our films are the best . . . he's telling me the titles of his favourite films now . . . Mais ils sont tous les films American . . . Ah bon? . . . I told him those were all American films, he says it's the same thing. Mais non, nous sommes pas Anglaises[40] ... He says we're very lucky to be English.

SHARON: Tell him we're no.

LIZ: Hud on. Non, nous somme écossaises, écossaises ... tu comprend? ... Au nord de Grand Bretagne. Tu comprend? *(laughs)* Oui, oui, c'est ça.[41]

SHARON: *(staring)* What the fuck's he daein?

LIZ: I think it must be the Highland Fling.

SHARON: Aye, very good pal, watch you dinny rupture anything vital there.

LIZ: Elle dit que tu danse trés bien[42] ... He likes to dance. Do you want to dance with him? He'll show you Turkish dance.

SHARON: Get tae.

LIZ: Elle est fatigue. Tu es soldat hein? Depuis de temp?[43] ... He's been in the army a year and a half, he has eighteen months still to do ... *(grins)* seventeen months, two weeks, three days ... Tu compte chaque jour?[44] ... He hates the army ... sometimes he dreams ... Rêve oui, de quoi?[45] ... He dreams he wakes up in his own home but when he opens his eyes he's still in the same bunk in the barracks ... that is a hard time to wake up.

SHARON: What did he join up for?

LIZ: It's military service, all the men have to do it. Et quelle age a toi?[46] He's twenty *(smiles)* nearly.

SHARON: Why doesnae he like Turkey?

LIZ: Pourquoi tu n'aime pas ton pays?[47] ... He says he loves his country ... he loves his people ... but they make him angry, they are very stupid people, in his regiment he is the only one who can read, everyone else ... just looks at stupid things on television ... they don't know anything, they are peasants ... Turkey is full of peasants ... All they know how to do is fight ... All their history with swords and spears, horses ... Non j'ai mal compri ... Ah oui, d'accord[48] ... Eh ... eh ... Scratch the surface of a Turkish man and you'll find a warrior horseman, that's their history. Now they are ready, always ready to fight the Russians and America and England give them guns and missiles to fight the Russians ... but Russia could walk in here tomorrow and America and England ... he means Britain by the way ...

SHARON: Does he though.

LIZ: ... America and England would not protest ... they would not fight for Turkey ... we are ... peasant people ... we are ... not worth a bullet or a war ... only our land, only our sea is important to them. We are (*grins*) a sandwich ... a buffer, he means a buffer. He hopes he doesn't talk too much.

Et que pense tu a 1980, a ce qu'etait arrive en 1980? Le coup et tout ça?[49]

LIZ *looks startled. The soldier has got up suddenly.*

LIZ: Non merci[50] ... Want anything to eat Sharon?

SHARON: I'll hae a cup of tea if he's buying.

LIZ: Tamam, bir chay.[51]

SHARON: No hud on, can I hae a Pepsi?

LIZ: Looks like it.

SHARON: Eh ... monsieur ... What am I after Liz?

LIZ: Pepsi.

SHARON: Aye, right, universal language eh? Bir Pepsi lutfen.[52]

LIZ: Well, he didn't want to talk about that.

SHARON: What?

LIZ: I asked him about 1980, that's when he vanished.

SHARON: How? What happened in 1980?

LIZ: They had a military coup.

SHARON: (*sees newspaper on the table and pulls it towards her, she flicks through it for a second*) Oh look, funnys. (*peers at the page*) Can you make this out?

LIZ: Eh ... I think the man being arrested is asking them to wait till he gets his parachute as so many police suspects seem to fall off windowsills.

SHARON: Ha, ha.

What's this one?

LIZ: Something about strikes ... I think it's saying all strikes are illegal ... miners' strikes are twice as illegal because it's illegal to be a miner.

SHARON: I dinny get it.

LIZ: Strikes in the public sector are illegal here, they've had a lot of hassle with miners in the last few years.

SHARON: So it's illegal to be a miner?

LIZ: No, that's the joke.

SHARON: That's no funny. What's that?

LIZ: Think it's a mother-in-law joke. (*she turns the page*) Oh no. Oh God.

SHARON: What?

LIZ: I think it's bad.

SHARON: *What?*

LIZ: (*calling up to the bar*) Monsieur . . . Vous pouvez traduire ça? (*offers newspaper, waits for reply*) C'était quand? Hier? A quelle heure? . . . Il y a combien mort? Touts American?[53]

SHARON: What's going on?

LIZ: They've blown up a bus. A tourist bus full of . . . Christ, just the Americans, it would be, fucking OAPs[54] . . .

SHARON: Who has?

LIZ: He doesn't know, he says . . . "Libya, Syria, PLO. Abu Nidal[55] . . . who cares?" (*shakes her head*) God.

SHARON: Here we go again. Just as well we're on our holidays eh?

LIZ *does not respond.* SHARON *obviously listening to something the soldier is saying.*

Lights up on MARIA, *standing this time, leaning on her gun. Her little boy is sitting playing with the dirt at her feet. It is nighttime. She speaks shyly, keeping her eyes on her* SON *most of the time as if she is embarrassed by all the eyes watching her. As before* LIZ *translates.*

MARIA: Le mentiria usted si le dijiera que no estaba temerosa.

LIZ: I would be lying to you if I said I was not afraid.

MARIA: No me da miedo morir, pero no quiero una muerto orribleá.

LIZ: I am not afraid of dying, but I don't want a horrible death.

MARIA: Yo no quiere pelear, yo digo, yo auydere, yo cuidare a los niños.

LIZ: I don't want to fight, I say to them, I will help, I will look after the children.

MARIA: Sin embargo, como puedo proteger a los niños si no puedo manejar un fusil?

LIZ: But how can I look after the children if I cannot use a rifle?

MARIA: Ellos estan tratando de asustarnos, estan tratando de matarnos, poco a poco digamos, passito a passito.

LIZ: They are trying to frighten us, they are trying to kill us a little at a time, a little at a time.

MARIA: Hoy, apuntaron a nuestros pies pero pronto apunteran a nuestros corazones.

LIZ: Now they are firing at our feet, soon they will be firing at our hearts.

MARIA: Pero nunca nos rendimeros.

LIZ: But we will never give up.

MARIA: Si hay que comer hierba, hierba comeremos pues.

LIZ: If we have to eat grass, we'll eat grass.

MARIA: Nunca pararemos la lucha.

LIZ: We will never stop fighting.

Scene 5

Hillside.

Lights fade on MARIA. *In the dark the sound of a rain storm beginning on or two drops, loud in the silence then a growing drumming of heavy spring rain. Lights up on* LIZ *and* SHARON. *They are sitting isolated by the tent of a cagoule, staring out at the rain. Each speaks to herself.*

SHARON: Dear Mum, you ken I canny write letters . . .

LIZ: Dear Mark, I'm writing this but I bet I never send it . . .

SHARON: I'm fine . . . No really . . . I'm fine . . .

LIZ: You never know what I *see*. All that time you're not there to see it too.

SHARON: Mind when I left I said "back soon" and you said "See you dinny forget us".

LIZ: I saw an almond tree with the blossom coming on . . .

SHARON: I remember the dug, no really I do . . .

LIZ: Water running in streams down the road like blood in the red dust . . .

SHARON: Sheena and the kids . . . the way Billy puts that face on when he's wanting another sweetie . . .

LIZ: Coming down like a shower . . . Wish you could see it. Wish you were here. (*grins*) Wish you were here in a hot shower with you half slippy soap and nothing to get up for tomorrow.

SHARON: I remember you. I do. I remember when it was just you and me, when I was wee and he wasny aboot. (*grins*) Playing battleships in the bath, do you mind that? Do you though? See I remember fine. I remember more than you mebbe . . .

LIZ: I just . . . I don't know what I feel.

SHARON: Look . . . I miss you, okay? I *do*.

Lights down. In the dark the rain stops. Lights up slowly. LIZ *and* SHARON *have taken off their cagoules. They are watching the sun rise, a light that grows on them throughout the scene. There is a distant sound of the Muslim call to prayer.*

LIZ: It's such a small sound from here, such a small sound to try and fill up all this landscape.

SHARON: (*after a pause*) So anyway after he moved in I moved out. Couldnae tak a' the rowing ken – 'specially when he rowed wi' her, I threw the telly at him one night . . . Aye well, it was only a wee portable one ken? He'd no paid for it yet, he went raj. And she gave him the money didn't she? Oot her pocket. It's a' her money but he spends it, tells her what tae spend it on, she says he doesnae but I ken fine he does. I left, I couldnae take it. Her and me used to go out on a Thursday, me and Sheena would pick her up frae her work, Sheena's my big sister, the three of us would go out on the bevy together. Great times. I mind one night we were a' dancing aboot in the road outside oor house, singing awa' (*sings loudly*) "Stand by your ma-a-an . . .!" Cars driving roond us, and he's got the window up and he's screaming at us . . . Christ I just aboot wet myself . . .

Aye well, he stopped her gaen oot wi' us after that. I says, "Can you no dae what you want? Can you no suit yoursel for once?" And she says, "Oh Sharon, it's too much trouble, let's just keep the peace. Just keep the peace." Well I left. I hate rowing, I dae it a' the time but I hate it.

LIZ: Yeah, me too.

SHARON: Who do you row wi'? Your man?

LIZ: Sometimes.

SHARON: That who you were writing tae? Mark? Is he your man?

LIZ: (*smiles*) Sometimes.

SHARON: Like that is it?

LIZ: I've been away so much . . . There's another woman he sees.

SHARON: Oh aye.

LIZ: Aw come on, fair dos, I'm away half the time, no it's not that that bothers me . . . it's just . . . well last time I was home . . . felt weird. See we were living together when he started seeing her, so he was with me and saw her sometimes, but now, I'm away so much . . . so he sees her every day he sees me sometimes. He'd be better with her you know, she loves him so much and she's *there*. I don't give him anything. I don't even give him postcards.

Pause.

SHARON: I should hae been hame a week ago. I was meant tae sign on, Mum'll be going mental, 'specially if they've had bombs and stuff on the telly. She'll think I'm sitting on top o' it. My auntie was in Italy when that Russian reactor blew up, Mum was trying tae send her telegrams telling her no tae drink the milk and no tae eat lettuce. I says, what are you worried aboot, maist o' it's raining down on us. We're the ones that gonny glow in the dark. Aunty Ina'll just hae a suntan.

Pause.

LIZ: Do you want kids?

SHARON: Kids?

LIZ: Aye.

SHARON: I'm nae sure. I near did once I but I got oot ae it, I was awfy young, would've been stupid.

Sheena had her two by the time she was my age right enough. Never sees their Dad anymair . . . They're great kids though . . . How about you?

LIZ: I don't know . . . I'm three weeks late.

SHARON: Oh nae luck eh? Mark?

LIZ: Yeah.

SHARON: What'll you dae?

LIZ: I don't know . . . It's since I've been away you see, I just don't feel . . . settled about anything anymore.

SHARON: (*looks at the sky for a moment*) It would be awfy wouldn't it? If they blew us all tae bits. That would be just my luck, some bam'll start World War Three and I'll never get hame tae tell my Mum how I'm late. (*shouts at the sky*) Hey you! Tell him no tae push the button till I've seen my Mum . . . As if he ever listened tae anything I said.

Lights down. In the dark the sound of MACKENZIE *breathing heavily as if he was walking or climbing over rough ground, shaky whistling of "The Campbells are Coming". He stops whistling laughs, he starts breathlessly to sing the theme song of "The Mickey Mouse Club".*

As he does so the lights come up slowly on MARIA *and her* SON. *She has her* SON *in a tin bath and is in the middle of washing him.* MACKENZIE's *singing and laboured breathing get louder and louder.* MARIA *stops washing as if she's heard something, walks slowly front with one hand for her gun. Fade lights.*

Lights up on SHARON *and* LIZ. *The sun is now up. They are still sitting as they were in the last scene.*

SHARON: . . . wanted me tae think he'd travelled the world, went on and on aboot a' the places he's been tae, mair than even you. Real big shot American superhero. (*imitates* MACKENZIE) "Baby I can look after you, no-one can look after you like I can, give you a good time in any country in the world." He never gied it a rest ken? "You know what the CIA[56] is baby?"

LIZ: (*suddenly badly shocked*) He was in the CIA?

SHARON: Nae really, (*doesn't notice* LIZ's *reaction*) I think they let him play wi' the guns. Och you want to have seen it, he had a' these wee disguise wigs, false passports, you name it, what a wanker. (*imitates*) "I can get in and out of Syria and not even scare the flies off the shit". If guys like him are running the world we're all deid, I'm tellin you. He says the CIA are wildcats, troubleshooters. "We keep the peace baby, we've got it in our pockets. We're all that stands between your sweet little toes and the black abyss." I says "What's an abyss?" I ken what it is but I had tae shut him up somehow. He says, "Remember who you are, remember what you are, remember where you come from and that's something you can proudly show to the rest of the world." I says, "Christ you sound just like my Grandad," 'cause he was always rabbiting on like that, boring us half tae death aboot the fight wi' the fascists and what his daddy said tae him – "Remember who you are, remember what you are and remember where you come frae and you can hud your heid up alongside your brother workers anywhere on this earth." Went on and on aboot stuff like that and how we should join the Communist party. Well see when I said this, this lieutenant Mackenzie gaes white, I'm telling you, white. "You're a communist?"

I says, "No, dinny be daft. My grandad was though, so was his Dad." Well that shut him up. Kept coming back and back tae it though . . .

"What was it your granddaddy said?" Christ I mean who cares? Oh aye he's been a' over. He'd been tae the place you were talking aboot, that's how I kent aboot that.

LIZ: Nicaragua.

SHARON: No, nae there, near there. Honduras[57] is it? (*she notices* LIZ's *reaction for the first time*) What? What is it?

LIZ: Nothing.

SHARON: Oh *fuck*! Do you see that?

LIZ: (*goes on looking at* SHARON) What?

SHARON: That flash, its binoculars isn't it? The wee bastard's up there watching us through binoculars. Oh *fuck*.

LIZ *looks then looks back at* SHARON.

SHARON: What we gonny dae?

LIZ: Let's get back to the bus station.

Lights down.

Lights up. A figure in partial American army uniform walks on holding a gun. It is wearing a grotesque Mickey Mouse mask, half melted so that it looks as if it is sneering or snarling. Its uniform is battered and dishevelled as if it's been slept in or generally messed around. We hear MACKENZIE *on the soundtrack singing the Mickey Mouse tune more and more raggedly until finally he begins to sob.*

MACKENZIE: (*a sudden howl*) Did anyone ever try and see my point of view! Huh! Did they!

Lights down.

Scene 6

Café.

Lights up. LIZ *and* SHARON *are standing in the road outside the bus station.*

SHARON: I've got it. We look like we're getting on the bus, right? Then we crawl back roon the side and hide in the ditch there, yeah?

LIZ: *(doesn't look at her)* Hey look . . . look I'm sorry but I've got to get back to Ankara.

SHARON: *(stares at her, then it sinks in, she's being dumped)* Oh . . . right.

LIZ: Sorry but . . .

SHARON: Right no . . . that's fine . . . I'll just . . . I'll just hang aboot here eh?

LIZ: Get a bus going somewhere else.

SHARON: Right.

LIZ: Look why don't you tag along with the man a while, you've done it before, what's he gonny do? Shoot you?

SHARON: *(just looking at her feet)* He's weird guy ken? I've had it wi' him.

LIZ: Well . . . I've got to go.

SHARON: Aye. You dae that.

LIZ: Sorry.

SHARON: What for? . . . *(looks up)* Look fuck off will you? Go if you're going. *(she turns away, wrestles with her baggage and pulls out a transistor radio)*

LIZ: *(moves to exit, looks back)* See you again.

> SHARON *doesn't look at her.* LIZ *exits. Sharon is fiddling with the radio muttering furiously to herself. Fade lights. We hear different sounds and music mixed with radio crackle and static. A Turkish folk song, the Nicaraguan song "Estelí",[58] Talking Heads' "Road to Nowhere", someone saying "You get back here right now do you hear me young lady", the shipping forecast, rapid talking in French, German, an American service radio D.J. "Coming right up for you folks . . .", a Scottish "missing my ain country"-type ballad.*

Lights up on MARIA. *It is night. She is standing up with her* SON *by a gate. Again* LIZ *provides a translation.*

MARIA/LIZ: This is the school, they must be walking on the other side, they don't hear me. (*rattles the gate*) Compañero!⁵⁹ He will come soon. So . . . this is the school, we have had to rebuild it, it has been burnt three times, the Somocistas, then the Contras.⁶⁰ They attack the schools and the hospitals because there are new things, the people did not have these things before the triumph, so it hurts them more when they are destroyed. They attack the school, the hospitals, they kill our hope, they kill our children, so we must guard them every night. Where is this man?

MARIA *turns to her* SON, *says something rapidly to him in Spanish. He squeezes through the bars of the gate.*

He will find him. (*smiles*) Yes, that is my son. Now do you see why we bring children on revolutionary vigilance.

MARIA *laughs again and then stands obviously posing for a photograph. There is a white flash.* MARIA *freezes. The sound of flames. The light on* MARIA *changes – it looks like she's on fire. She stands motionless. Fade lights.*

END OF ACT I

Act II

Scene 1

A road side. Morning, bright sun. LIZ *is on stage staring front, obviously down the barrel of a gun. She is terrified.*

LIZ: I don't know where she is. Honest to God I don't know. I just left her at the bus station. If you go back you might . . . Look I didn't see the gun, I didn't see you, I don't want to know, okay? I just . . . Please. (LIZ *swallows, starts to back off slowly*) Don't you think you better . . .? We're in the middle of the road here! People are going to see you! What are you going to do!? Shoot me in front of the next bus party!? (*flinches and then stays very still, when she speaks again she is almost whispering*) I'm sorry okay . . . I won't . . . I'm sorry . . . No-one thinks I wanted to get off that bus with you. They saw you. Someone'll do something. (*swallows*) Do you think . . .? Do you think you can do *anything* just by . . . (*waves a hand at the gun*) just by . . .? (*can't go on, looks down*)

Lights come up on MARIA, *she is walking forward, looking worried. She seems to be listening. She reaches for her gun.*

LIZ: (*looking off*) Oh *no*! RUN! SHARON!

MARIA *throws up her arm as if to protect herself.*

The sound of a gunshot is heard.

LIZ: No! (*gets up to run*)

Blackout.

The gun fires, then fires again.

Scene 2

A hillside, bright sun.

Lights up on LIZ *and* SHARON *lying panting in a heap, they've been running across country.*

SHARON: I canny see him. Can you see him? (LIZ *has no breath to answer*) Jesus he's mad. He's totally gone mad, he's blown his nose and lost his brains. What's he shooting at us for? He doesnae mean it. He's funny that way. Jumpy. He wouldnae mean tae hit us . . .

Would he? . . . Well he's no about . . . We've lost him, I think we've lost him. You okay?

LIZ: I'm bleeding.

SHARON: What! Dinny move! Dinny move! Where's he hit you?! Can you feel it?

LIZ: (*wearily*) It's my period.

SHARON: Jesus, Oh Jesus you . . . you . . . (*abandons all expletives as inadequate*) . . . You got anything?

LIZ: Nup.

SHARON: I'll see if I've got any hankies.

LIZ: It's come on like Niagara.[61] (*touches briefly between her legs, looks at her hand*) Have you ever tasted it?

SHARON: Eh?

LIZ: Your blood.

SHARON: *That* blood?

LIZ: Yeah.

SHARON: *No*.

LIZ: Tastes good, like it's good for you. Seems a waste. People eat placentas you know.

SHARON: Keep going, I was starving till you started.

LIZ: And did you know, did you know, that one swallow, one wee swallow of sperm is six hundred calories?

SHARON: Where'd you hear that?

LIZ: Read it somewhere.

SHARON: Six hundred?

LIZ: At least.

SHARON: Fuck me, nae wonder the diets never worked.

LIZ: I used to think about that sometimes, here's our bodies making all this heat and energy and protein. We could feed off each other and never get hungry. It's a nice theory.

SHARON: That's your solution tae the world food crisis is it? Oral sex and placenta stew?

LIZ: A symbiotic relationship. Like oaks and mistletoe.

SHARON: Mistletoe kills trees does it no?

LIZ: Then I mean something else.

SHARON: (*offers her something*) Here.

LIZ: What's that?

SHARON: It's two hundred lira in ten lira bills, it's a' the paper I've got. Well what is that? About twenty pence? You might as well.

LIZ: It's a bit grubby.

SHARON: Wrap it in something, writing paper or something.

LIZ: (*rummages in her stuff, finds a bit of paper, reads*) "Dear Mark, I'm writing this but I bet I never send it" . . . Yeah . . . well I never do, do I?

Lights down.

Scene 3

Travelling. LIZ *and* SHARON *are walking straight in the face of the sun. They pull off layers of clothes as they struggle on, panting . . . they speak to themselves. Through this scene lights come up on the "Eye of Fatima".*

LIZ: I saw earth that was red and rocks that were pink and colours that bled into each other . . .

SHARON: I remember . . . I remember when they took you away you said "Be good an I'll see you in a wee while" but you didnae. When they took you away they had to tak me an a' but they never pit us in the same place, they pit you inside as left me ootside on my ain . . .

LIZ: I saw an angel on the roof of the cathedral. He had a sword in his hand. He was pleased about it, you could tell by his terrible happy smile . . .

SHARON: I remember where they put me. I thought you were never coming tae get me again . . .

LIZ: I saw a plain where bronze age warriors beat an iron age army, they fell on the spears, row after row of them threw themselves on the iron spears till there were no more left . . . the guide book called it a great victory . . .

SHARON: I thought you'd forgotten me forever. Do you mind that, do you mind how I was greitin an clinging tae your legs? Are you hearing me Ma?

LIZ: And I saw this man leaning over me smiling with gold and black teeth and he pointed at all the land outside the window of the bus and he said "Look it's beautiful, the rock is the same colour as your skin, the land is like a woman's skin." And I thought, is it fuck, the only thing that's the same is we're both alive and you're walking all over both of us . . . Are you hearing me Mark? I don't want to be this lonely. I don't want it!

SHARON: Oh Christ, oh Christ we'll die won't we, some bam'll start World War Three an all you'll be thinking is "Where's our Sharon got to? Where's my wee . . ." (*gets choked*) You *stupid* . . .!

LIZ: I saw a woman. I saw her in a museum. The first woman I'd been able to look in the face all day. "Neolithic Venus". All breasts and bum and belly and a smile nearly rubbed off the stone . . .

SHARON: You remember!? Screaming on you!? Mum . . . Mum . . . MUM! COME BACK!

LIZ: She'd been gone for thousands of years.

SHARON: But you never came. After a while I learned you'd got problems o' your ain. (SHARON *stops and rubs her hand over her eyes*) Oh Fuck.

Lights down on the "Eye of Fatima". A lighting change, they both stop, bent over breathless.

SHARON: I canny walk anymore oer this I jist . . .

LIZ: This (*panting*) is . . . historic ground.

SHARON: Eh?

LIZ: Do you know . . . the armies that've . . .

SHARON: Do you gie a fuck, right now? Dae you? (LIZ *laughs, groans for breath*)

I'll hae tae stop. I've had it . . . (*gets her breath*) He wouldnae follow us oer a' this would he? (LIZ *has no breath to reply*) Mind you he's fit, he does one handed press-ups. (*looks at* LIZ) You okay? (LIZ *nods*) Gied you a fright did he? He's nae really like that ken? He just gets carried away, seen too many cowboy films. He wouldnae kill anybody . . . I dinny think.

LIZ: He killed Maria.

SHARON: Eh?

LIZ: Or someone like him did.

SHARON: Who's Maria?

LIZ: She's someone I met in Nicaragua. She was killed a couple of months ago.

SHARON: How?

LIZ: A Contra attack. They came in and bombed the grain silos. She was caught in her home. They burnt her alive.

SHARON: Who did?

LIZ: The Contras, troops based in Honduras. They have big camps with arms caches bought with dollars and food and medical equipment bought with dollars and men like Lieutenant John Mackenzie to train them and teach them how to kill and they went into Estelí and bombed the grain silos and burnt Maria alive.

SHARON: Did you know her well?

LIZ: Not very.

Lights down.

In the darkness the crackle of radio static as it moves through the frequencies, music, foreign broadcasts, morse.

BBC VOICE: . . . the prime minister has sent a message of sympathy to the family of British born Mrs Hilda Heller who was killed in the bomb attack on a tour bus in Ankara yesterday, Mrs. Heller was seventy-five . . .

More morse.

AMERICAN VOICE: . . . another victim has dies as a result of yesterday's bomb attack in Turkey . . .

Military band music.

BRITISH VOICE: . . . how long will this intolerable state of affairs be allowed to continue? Any government can hold another to ransom simply by threatening its private citizens . . .

A foreign advert.

AMERICAN VOICE: . . . I say we have the weapons, we have the weapons, we have the capability what the hell are we waiting for? Nuke 'em!!

More static, bring up the sound of a backgammon game, rattle of dice and click of counters, fade static.

Scene 4

Interior. A Turkish house. SHARON *and* LIZ *are sitting cross-legged on the floor with glasses of chay in front of them.* LIZ *is looking at the floor,* SHARON *is watching something in front of her – the backgammon game.*

SHARON: Oh yes! Hey he's good him eh? (*imitates a dice throw*) That's it, pal, you'll massacre him. (LIZ *does not look up*)

SHARON: Pissed off wi' me?

LIZ: How?

SHARON: You're nae saying much. (*sighs*) Well, I'm sorry. (LIZ *looks at her*) I'm sorry for the bother.

LIZ: (*humourless laugh*) Oh it's no bother. No bother at all.

SHARON: (*looks at her and then looks at the game*) Who's winning? (LIZ *shrugs. To the men*) Hey! Hey! . . . Who's winning? You yeah? Great stuff eh? (*sings*) "We are the champions my fri-e-e-end . . ."[62]

LIZ: (*trying to shut her up*) Sharon.

SHARON: What? . . . What? (LIZ *ignores her*) I dinny think he's winning at a'. Think it's the other guy. Reckon they will give us a lift? (LIZ *shrugs*) They better eh? I havenae a clue where we are, have you?

LIZ: (*closes her eyes*) I just want to go to sleep.

SHARON: (*looks at her*) Oh fuck. (*she starts to sing quietly to herself*) "We're on the road to no-where"[63] . . . (LIZ *sighs heavily*) Oh God, you really get on my tits you, liven up will you for fuck's sake!

LIZ: (*sits up abruptly, angry*) What?

SHARON: Well . . . You didnae need tae come wi' me. I never asked you tae. I didnae ken the guy thought he was Rambo[64] did I? I didnae ken I'd been screwing a twenty-two-carat lunatic did I? . . . Anyway, it's nae as if he could shoot straight. See if this was the films he'd fire one bullet – BLAM! . . . And we'd baith be deid. One bullet and we'd be deid and eight Russian helicopters would drop oot the sky and the whole red commy universe would surrender on the spot. (*imitates* MACKENZIE) John Mackenzie, he makes the world a safer place, he blasts everything that moves. (*laughs.* LIZ *does not respond*) Oh Christ. Want another cup of tea?

LIZ: No.

SHARON: I do. How do I ask for it?

LIZ: (*looks at her, very quietly*) Bir chay lutfen.[65]

SHARON: (*trying to repeat it*) Bir chay . . . what is it? . . . Liz? (LIZ *starts to cry*) Oh fuck. (SHARON *just sits and stares at* LIZ, *then when* LIZ *goes on crying, she gets up and goes and puts her arm around her awkwardly*) Hey.

LIZ: Sorry.

SHARON: Yeah . . . me too.

LIZ: I just want to go home.

SHARON: You're gonny get hame.

LIZ: I don't know where to go.

SHARON: Yeah . . . I ken what you mean . . . I was thinking aboot nae gaen back at a'. Naething tae get back for ken?

LIZ: Yeah.

SHARON: I hate it. (*she takes her arm away but goes on sitting by* LIZ) Hate it. (*takes a cigarette, lights up*) It's nae so bad if it's summer, good weather, get oot the house a bit but winter . . . I'll gae off the heid, I'm telling you, I'll do something daft. How much boredom can you brain stand 'fore you get tae eating the wallpaper eh?

LIZ: Have you not had any work?

SHARON: (*looks at her*) You serious? Naething, or as good as anyway. I did one of they schemes ken when I was oot school a couple of years. It wasnae bad, we were building this playground, learnt a' aboot power tools and that. Fucking stupid playground, wee Disney castles made oot ae railway sleepers and they metal climbing frames supposed tae look like tanks or helicopters or something, kind the bairns keep falling off of ontae the tarmac and smashing their knees tae fuck. But it was great building it, whole crowd of us, Jean and Brian and them. It was blazing hot, it was barry, see that (*pulls up her top*) that's where the tan stops, it's never faded. We had such a laugh daein it ken, I used tae get oot my bed in the morning and just aboot run doon there, must be the last time I was oot my bed afore twelve o'clock. It was such a laugh. Story was maybe one ae us would get a job at the end o' it, frae the council or . . . (*shrugs*) Aye well. Never happened did it? Week after we'd finished we sat oot at Brian's windy and watched it a' burning up. Someone'd put a match tae the fucking Disney castle and Snow White and the Seven Dwarfs were melting all oer the tarmac. We just watched. Didnae bother. It was over ken?

LIZ: Did you find out who did it?

SHARON: (*hesitates, then*) I did it. Me and a couple o' the others. It was nae use anybody. Fucking waste of time, the hale thing. (*looks up, sees* LIZ *watching her seriously*) That cheer you up did it? Aye great eh? Sharon Mackenzie, the one-woman fun house, laugh till you cry . . . You're gonny get hame Liz. (*silly voice*) "Home is where the heart is." (*sings*) "I left my heart in San Francisco, I left my teeth . . ."[66] (*points at* LIZ) Yay, her face has cracked. (*looks at the men playing backgammon*) Who's winning 'cause it's not me. (*looks at* LIZ) You winning?

LIZ: (*smiles*) Yeah.

SHARON: It'll be PMT.[67]

LIZ: Fuck off.

SHARON: Aye right.

LIZ *reaches into her pocket, takes out a photograph and hands it to* SHARON.

SHARON: Who's that?

LIZ: Maria.

SHARON: Great smile.

LIZ: She'd a wee boy about eight. She'd been in the militia since she was fourteen. She fought in the Revolution then she fought the Contras.

SHARON: (*still looking at the photo*) When were you out there then?

LIZ: Nearly two years ago. Things are much worse now.

SHARON: Bad is it?

LIZ: They haven't got anything, the whole place is held together with second hand Elastoplast.

SHARON: Seen it on the telly, least I think it was there, I dinny ken where half these places are. (*smiles*) Is that where you're homesick for?

LIZ: Maybe . . . It was real.

SHARON: What?

LIZ: I didn't think it was . . . before I went . . . I think I thought it was somewhere to collect for . . . carry banners . . . you know . . . not a real place at all. It smelt of charcoal from the cooking fires and the wind was always warm . . . and it was alive with green creeper . . . all broken to bits with war and earthquakes but alive with weeds . . . and people. (*smiles*). I get boring about now.

SHARON: How?

LIZ: Och just . . . there's nothing else worth talking about you know . . . but . . . I can't make people feel it . . . Can't do it. (LIZ *looks at her feet for a while,* SHARON *just watches for her to go on*). I saw this man. He used to be in the National Guard, before the revolution, he was in the death squad. He made terror . . . death . . . murder . . . mutilation . . . that was his job. Now he's a prisoner. He's a "prisoner" on a farm he can walk off any time . . . I looked at him and I thought – once he skinned people alive . . . or something like that, now he's planting corn and painting pictures . . . he says he's been reformed by the revolution . . . Maybe he's a chancer . . . don't know if it matters. And I met this other man . . . a refugee from El Salvador. They had a camp . . . a farm, it even had a school and stuff . . . we met his kids and . . . all the families . . . 'cause they can't stay in El Salvador, they've been driven out by death squads you see, people that would've skinned them alive . . . or something. So. They're planting corn in Nicaragua. (*pause*) We were just tourists. We just took photographs. (*pause*) What did we know anyway? It was like two . . . Possibilities. I kept trying to write letters home, and I couldn't . . . I couldn't find a way of saying what I felt, all I could find to say over and over was . . . "They've done it, they're doing it, it's real, it's the people here, just about every person in the whole place." People living in cardboard boxes, people living from hand to mouth, people of war, struggling and fighting and dying but with that one thing – the sense of being in control of their own lives, of making their own future, and I came back home and I looked around and I thought, "When were we robbed?" And I wanted to go back, I want to go back, because I don't know how much longer it can exist like that and I don't know where I'll ever find anything like that again . . . (LIZ *is looking at the ground.* SHARON *watches her for a second then gently bangs her with her foot.* LIZ *looks up. They smile at each other.*)

SHARON: (*looking at the men playing backgammon*) Fuck naebody's winning, they just keep gaen roond and round and grabbing money o' each other.

LIZ: Sharon? Why is he after you?

SHARON: I telt you, he's got a thing aboot me.

LIZ: It doesn't make sense.

SHARON: No. Well . . . nae mair does he half the time.

(*starts to giggle*) Tell you what he's like, Disneytime gone mental, Mickey Mouse wi' a fucking forty-five that's what he's like, you want to have seen him Liz . . .

The figure of a man in an American army uniform wearing a Mickey Mouse mask appears behind them in silhouette or else dim light. It is pointing a gun right at them.

SHARON: . . . he'd get his forty-five out and he'd say . . . this is the truth right? He'd say . . . (*drawls*) Wanna see a real tool, baby? and then he'd . . .

LIZ *has seen the figure,* SHARON *notices her expression, looks round.*

SHARON: How the fuck did he find us?!

Lights down on LIZ *and* SHARON. *The Mickey Mouse figure remains visible as lights come up on* MARIA. *She is standing with a piece of paper in her hands, obviously reading a prepared statement.* LIZ *provides translation.*

MARIA: Lo que queremos decirles a ustedes es lo siguiente

Regresse y digales a ellos de lo que esta pasando aqui

Ustedes son nuestra mejor defensa

LIZ: What we wish to say to you is this

Go back and tell them the truth of what is happening here

You are our best defence

MARIA: Nosotros creemos en la solidaridad con todos los pueblos en el mundo que nuestra lucha . . . (*she puts down the paper and looks up and smiles shakily, she has tears in her eyes*)

LIZ: We believe in solidarity with all peoples in the world that our struggle . . .

MARIA: Es muy bueno para nosotros verlo aqui.

LIZ: It is very good for us to see you here.

MARIA: (*she speaks without the paper*) Esta revolucion es la revolucion de Guatemala, de Grenada, ... y de El Salvador[68] ... y esta es su revolucion, e la revolucion de ustedes, tambien.

LIZ: This revolution is the revolution of Guatemala, of Grenada, of El Salvador ... and it is your revolution, it is your revolution too –

Scene 5

Lights down on MARIA, *up on* SHARON. *She is standing squinting into bright sunshine, behind her the silhouette of the Mickey Mouse figure holds up its gun. Another roadside.*

SHARON: I'm burning. I'm burning up. Mack? Mack, can I no sit down? (*she sways*) Come on ... Come on Mack this is stupid. Come on, I'll get you a cup o' chay ... or ... och shit. Let us sit down will you? This is boring. I'm bored, you're a boring wee shite do you ken that?

The Mickey Mouse figure either strikes LIZ *or else moves violently and we see* LIZ *react. She flinches and cries out.*

SHARON: Fucking stop that!

The Mickey Mouse figure gestures threateningly with the gun.

SHARON: Okay ... okay ... Aye, I understand that, it's a universal language eh? Just leave her alone okay?

SHARON *looks at* LIZ, *her face crumples briefly,* LIZ *looks back, her hand to her face,* SHARON *looks front again. About this time we first start to hear* MACKENZIE *on the sound track – at first just laboured breathing that gradually increases in volume.*

SHARON: What do you want? ... Jesus I've telt you that, how many times have I ...? *Right* ... My grandfather was called John Mackenzie and so was his dad and his dad came frae Uist. I dinny ken when he was born, I wasnae there! Jesus what do you want!? A history lesson? I don't know!

The breathing is replaced by a breathless whistle of "The Campbells are Coming", as if by someone who is in pain, or on the point of tears. This changes into a similar ragged singing of the Mickey Mouse Club, then back to whistling under the next bit of dialogue.

SHARON: My grandad, John Mackenzie, lived in Glasgow then he came through wi' my Mum tae . . . Yes, he was in the Communist party. He *was*, he *was*, wave that in my face as much as you like. I'm no lying tae you!

LIZ: (*quiet*) Lie to him.

SHARON: Okay I'm lying tae you. Big story. Big joke. We're not related anyway, its naething to dae wi' you! Fuck's sake you dinny even look like me . . .! Well I hope you dinny . . . (*closes her eyes for a second*) Look he was a stupid auld man okay? A fucking boring stupid auld bat. He couldnae even keep his food in his mou . . . I dinny *ken* what he telt me, I never listened tae what he telt me, it was just the same stuff over and over . . . He was drunk half the time.

On the sound track we hear MACKENZIE *muttering another layer of sound added to the whistling, breathing and singing. We can't make out any words.*

SHARON: Okay God . . . okay. He said "Remember who you are, remember where you come frae and" (MACKENZIE *has interrupted her*)

He *said* "Remember who you are, remember where you come frae" I mean what you . . . (MACKENZIE *has interrupted again*)

No! No that's nae what my grandad said! That's what your grandad said! It's probably no even the same guy for *fuck's sake* Mack, who cares?

The words MACKENZIE *is muttering now become audible. He is repeating several phrases over and over, these are distorted, played over each other, scratched, we hear a mess of noise with occasional phrase sounding distinctly.*

Conversationally he is saying: "I think we all have a sense of history, yeah I think you'd have to say that."

More agitatedly: "I'm just trying to understand this okay? Do you know who you are, no, NO! Look at me, do you know who you are? Well I wanna know okay. I'm just trying to understand this."

Yelling: "How'd d'you think I feel? Huh? You think I'm crazy? How'd d'you think I feel?"

All this gets louder and louder. Throughout it the Mickey Mouse figure remains motionless but its gun arm lowers, shaking as if very tired, SHARON *speaks over and finally against the noise until by the end of her speech she is shouting to be heard.*

SHARON: Aye right, it's a great country, you're so fucking lucky tae be American. (*she listens*) If you say so Mack, it's free world, anything you say. No really I mean it, every Dallas[69] petrol competition I'm there and I dinny hae a car. Yeah you're great, you're brilliant, everybody's favourite uncle . . . Aye right look what you've gied us all . . . Eh . . . eh . . . hot dogs right? And eh . . . blue jeans, Mickey Mouse, Elvis, Lassie[70] . . . *I'm not laughing at you!*

What? What do I need to dae? *Again?* (*sighs*) He *said* . . . you know what he . . . okay. Okay . . . He said "Remember who you are what you are and where you come frae and" . . . this is so fucking boring Mack!

His name was John Mackenzie, he was my granddad, his dad's name was John Mackenzie and they were baith Commies . . . okay? And he never stopped fucking telling me about it and the only party meetings he ever went tae were the parties where he could bring a packet o' crisps and drink somebody else's bottle. He was boring senile auld shite when I knew him and afore that he was a boring middle-aged shite and he never stopped calling for his tea or his bath or his shite bucket till my ma nearly wore her feet oot running after him and he broke her nose one time because she wouldnae marry my daddy and I hated him. And that's what he said! That's what his dad telt him, that's what he used tae say tae me, I've telt you!

LIZ *has reached up and taken the gun out of the Mickey Mouse figure's hand. As* SHARON *goes on speaking she stares at it in her hands then slowly raises it to point at the figure. The soundtrack is by now very loud.*

SHARON: How can you base your hale life roond something your great-granda said when he was sloshed oot his brain? How can you base your hale life roond a thing like that? You're mad you. You're fucking loony. *Yes, that's what he said!* I heard it often enough. And he was a fucking Communist. He *was.* (*shakes her head impatiently*)

Because he was a bam! Like the rest o' us! We're all bams in oor family Mack!

Well maybe you dinny remember it right! Maybe you dinny remember where you come frae at all!

As before the Mickey Mouse figure either moves violently or strikes SHARON. SHARON *screams and puts her hand to her head – there is blood on it.* LIZ *shoots. The Mickey Mouse figure jerks, tearing at its face, tearing the mask off – there is blood all over its face. There is the sound of the "Looney Tunes" theme played echoey and distorted; instead of "Th . . . Th . . . That's all folks",*[71] MACKENZIE *screams. The Mickey Mouse figure slumps forward and lies still.* LIZ *drops the gun. She stares, stunned.*

LIZ: He was real . . . He was *real* . . .!

SHARON: (*gapes at her*) Well what did you think he was? A cartoon?! A fucking muppet?![72]

LIZ: (*stares at her for a moment, then*) Yes.

SHARON: (*sways*) What do we dae? (*her head is bleeding badly*)

LIZ: He's dead.

SHARON: Get the jeep . . . Liz . . . Liz! Get the fucking jeep!

LIZ: (*hardly hearing her*) I can't drive.

SHARON: Well try! . . . Fuck it . . . I'll try . . . get the keys . . . Oh shite . . . Liz . . . (*she collapses*)

LIZ *just stands there staring at her; slow fade of screen and lights. Blackout. Bring up the sound of flames. Dim light up on* LIZ; *she is staggering across the stage with* SHARON *on her back.* LIZ *stops, puts* SHARON *down and walks back and picks up their luggage, carries it to a point beyond* SHARON, *dumps it, goes back. Picks up* SHARON *again, can't lift her, she stops on her knees, gasping, then starts to drag* SHARON *along. Fade lights and sound of fire.*

Blackout.

The sound of laboured breathing and heartbeat, mixed with radio static, foreign D.J.'s hardly audible, morse, music blaring then fading rapidly, this continues over –

Lights up on MARIA *and her* SON, *an exact repeat of the earlier scene,* MARIA *gives him a bath, as before they seem to hear something, turn startled.* MARIA *walks front, reaches for her gun, she raises her arm as if to shield herself. There is a tremendous flash like an explosion . . .*

The Mickey Mouse figure crawling along the ground, half torn mask, half bloody face. There is smoke round it as if it were on fire.

A blaze of light like fire and smoke from the place we last saw MARIA, *it is her house burning. We hear screaming,* MARIA *and her* SON.

SHARON: No!

Blackout. Cut all sound.

Scene 6

In the dark, the sound of water, a cloth being squeezed into a bowl. The lights gradually come up.

The interior of a Turkish house. SHARON *is lying on the floor, a* TURKISH WOMAN, *fully robed and veiled, is kneeling by her head, bathing it.*

SHARON: *(sits up slowly)* Where's Liz?

The WOMAN *shakes her head, gently tries to get her to lie down.*

SHARON: Where am I? . . . My heid's sair.

SHARON *lies back, the* WOMAN *goes on washing her. Fade lights, bring up the sound of unaccompanied Turkish singing, the sound of water goes on in the dark then stops. Fade music.*

Lights up. The same scene, daylight. The WOMAN *is grinding chickpeas in a bowl, bent over her task,* SHARON *is watching while shelling nuts into another bowl. The* WOMAN *points to* SHARON'*s hands;* SHARON *looks down.*

SHARON: Aye my hands are shaking, I'm no right yet, better though eh? Concrete heid, that's me. I fell oot a tree on my heid once, trying tae climb up after David, that's my wee nephew. Stupid eh? Thought I was still wee enough tae walk on thin branches. My mammy says I never grew up, I just got bigger. *(she reaches into her pocket, produces photo).* That's my Mum . . . Mother yeah? *(pretends to rock a baby and points to herself)* That's right. *(looks at something the* WOMAN *is showing her)* Who's that? Your daughter? *(makes the same rocking movement. Points to* WOMAN*)* Coventry? Aye I ken where that is, never been there mysel but . . . Evet, Coventry, evet. She's bonny. Guzel, chohk guzel.[73] *(grins)* That's a' I ken. Bet you miss her eh? *(looks at the* WOMAN, *copies a movement of tracing imaginary tears down her cheeks)* Aye . . . I bet you miss her. *(*SHARON *bows her head, goes on shelling nuts)*

The sound of radio static, a BBC VOICE *says:* "... The body of an American serviceman found yesterday in Central Turkey..." *The sound of jeeps revving up, a foreign radio advert, jets taking off,* American voice: "... President said – this war began the day the first American citizen died at enemy hands..." *Angry voices, French, German etc. ... more jets. On the same tape we hear* SHARON *as if calling from a long way:* "Mum... MUM! Come back!" *Then the sound of a shower,* LIZ *and a man laughing.*

LIZ: (*quietly out of the darkness*) Kids have nothing to do with it... I just want life, mine, yours... anybody's... a wee bit of life. It doesn't make any difference what I want... does it?

Lights up. SHARON *is sitting cross-legged on the floor.* LIZ *is standing looking at her. It is night.*

SHARON: Where have you been?

LIZ: Around.

SHARON: What you been daein?

LIZ: Walking.

SHARON: What's the score then eh? (LIZ *shrugs*) How long have I been here Liz?

LIZ: Just since yesterday.

SHARON: Did you carry me or what?

LIZ: Aye, I carried you.

SHARON: Nae wonder you're knackered. So what's the score?

LIZ: We're waiting.

SHARON: What for? (LIZ *shakes her head*) He's maybe no deid Liz, you only shot him the once.

LIZ: He went on breathing for about five minutes. His eyes stayed open. I don't know if he was seeing anything or not. His body was running down like an engine, collapsing inside. I couldn't stand it. I wanted it to stop. I wanted him to stop...

Well... He did, at last. There was a spare can of petrol in the jeep. I poured it over him and set him on fire. He looked better when he was covered in flames. He didn't look human anymore. I set the jeep on fire too. (*she picks up a petrol can*) Look, we've still got some.

SHARON: What'd you bring that for? Was I no heavy enough? (LIZ *shrugs*) Christ you're in a worse state than I am.

LIZ: I'm okay.

SHARON: so he's deid it he? Shite. What'll we dae? (LIZ *shrugs*) What's the woman here think? Does she ken who we are?

LIZ: I don't know. I don't know what she thinks.

SHARON: She'll maybe just think we're tourists.

LIZ: We are.

SHARON: Aye . . . right. So what'll we dae?

LIZ: There's a bus through here on Wednesday's. That's tomorrow.

SHARON: How come naebody's looking for us?

LIZ: Maybe they will.

SHARON: Maybe they've no found him yet.

LIZ: They've found him.

SHARON: So how come . . . ?

LIZ: Maybe they don't want to find us, not yet. Maybe they don't care now, they've got what they wanted.

Lights down.

  SHARON *is singing "Show Me the Way to Go Home" softly.*

LIZ: (*quiet*) Dear Mark, I don't know how to get back, everything's burnt and broken, I don't know how to get home. I'm sorry. I love you.

Scene 7

A bus, daylight.

Lights up. SHARON *and* LIZ *are sitting side by side.*

SHARON: (*singing loudly*) All together now! Show me the way to go home . . . (*she looks at* LIZ. LIZ *is looking front, expressionless*) What do you call a man with a car on his heid?

LIZ: (*instant, without looking round or changing her expression*) Jack. What do you call a man with a hotel on his head?

SHARON: (*instant*) Norman Tebbit.[74] What do you call a man lying in a pile o' leaves?

LIZ: Russell. What do you call a man with no arms and legs in the middle of the Atlantic ocean?

SHARON: That's bad taste, we're no daein bad taste.

LIZ: Come on.

SHARON: Bob. Eh . . . eh . . . Knock knock.

LIZ: We're not doing knock knock jokes.

SHARON: How?

LIZ: I fucking hate knock knock jokes.

SHARON: Knock knock.

LIZ: No.

SHARON: Knock knock.

LIZ: No! . . . okay. Who's there?

SHARON: Amos

LIZ: A mosquito. (*still without expression*)

SHARON: Knock knock.

LIZ: Who's there?

SHARON: Anne.

LIZ: Another mosquito.

SHARON: Knock knock.

LIZ: Yeta, yet another mosquito.

SHARON: Knock knock. (LIZ *looks at her*) Susan.

LIZ: (*suspicious*) Susan who?

SHARON: Sousands and sousands of mosquitos. KNOCK KNOCK!

LIZ: YES!

SHARON: Wurlitzer.

LIZ: Wurlitzer a one for the money . . .[75]

SHARON: Yes! We've got the jokes and we're gonny destroy them.

LIZ: There was this man that went into a pub with a pig on his head . . .

SHARON: Heard it. This gorilla goes into bar . . .

LIZ: Heard it. These two horses go into a bar . . .

SHARON: Heard it.

LIZ: This woman goes into a bar. (*pauses,* SHARON *looks blank*) And she says. "I want Nicaragua" and the barman says "I'm sorry madam we don't serve cocktails" and she says, "Never mind I'll try somewhere else" and she goes home to her man and drags him out of bed and she says, "I want Nicaragua" and he says, "Where have you been till this time of night?" and she says, "I don't know I was drunk at the time" and she goes out in the street and she sees all these people with banners having a demo and she shouts, "I want Nicaragua" and they say, "Nicaragua? Oh yeah, we did a demo for them last week" and she runs down the road and there's all these people queueing in the street and sitting on the pavement, and looking out broken windows with the rain falling on their heads and she screams "We need Nicaragua" and they don't say anything at all. So she gets on another plane and she goes away. Thousands and thousands of miles away and everything's all different colours and its all the same, and she meets a Turk, a Scot and an American, so she fucks the Turk, gets drunk with the Scot and shoots the American in the head. (*looks to* SHARON) Good eh?

SHARON: (*stony*) Aye, you're a riot Liz. (LIZ *turns and stares out the window*) Why did you bring that petrol can? It's stinking the place oot.

LIZ: Souvenir.

SHARON: Yeah?

LIZ: Yeah.

SHARON: I think you should chuck it.

LIZ: No.

SHARON: Why?

LIZ: I need it.

SHARON: What for? (LIZ *shakes her head. She sees something out of the window.*) What is it?

LIZ: Army trucks, look, they're in a hurry eh? Maybe we're going to be famous, Sharon.

SHARON: If you're gonny dae something stupid I'm no gonny chum you. No if you dae something stupid.

LIZ: I've a return ticket.

SHARON: So?

LIZ: You haven't.

SHARON: *So?*

LIZ: (*smiles*) I'll get you home, Sharon.

> *Lights down. Bring up the sounds of a panicked crowd, kids crying, people shouting.*

Scene 8

They are in an airport toilet. LIZ *is sitting on the floor, she has just finished pouring the contents of the petrol can over herself.* SHARON *is watching in amazement.*

SHARON: What the fuck are you daein?

LIZ: (*breathing very fast, shaking violently*) Go away.

SHARON: *Liz?*

LIZ: Don't touch me! (*she chucks the petrol can away*)

SHARON: Listen one o' they guys wi' the guns going tae come round that corner any minute and then you're gonny be *deid*, hear me?

LIZ: That's the idea.

SHARON: Why?

LIZ: (*takes something out of her pocket and tosses it at* SHARON) Here.

SHARON: What's that?

LIZ: My ticket, tell them some story about the names being different, you'll manage it.

SHARON: It's a' petrol! Look! You've got it a' wet! (*stares at* LIZ) You're nae going tae dae this . . . Are you?

LIZ: Don't touch me!

SHARON: A'right, a'right. Shit. (*stands back and stares at her*) You ken your brains gone dae you? You'll wish you hadnae when you dae it. Fuck it'll *hurt* Liz.

LIZ: You suffocate before you burn.

SHARON: Says who? Joan of Arc?[76] She was a bam an a'.

LIZ: Look, you'll have to tell them everything.

SHARON: Oh aye?

LIZ: Tell them I shot John Mackenzie, tell them it was a protest about U.S. foreign policy and . . . and . . . everything, you know what I mean, give them the works, tell them I was a terrorist, make it good, a real public enemy, tell them I was gay, I sniffed glue, I had B.O. Tell them I was British, very, very British . . . No, no, say English or they won't know what you mean, that's important, they've got to understand that. Tell them I had a Union Jack[77] tattooed on my bum.

SHARON: *Have* you?

LIZ: No.

SHARON: (*points to her thigh*) I've got a tattoo in there want tae see? Brian did it wi' a penknife and a biro. Went septic, nearly killed me.

LIZ: *Sharon.*

SHARON: You're no gonny dae this Liz. What you daein it for?

LIZ: Someone got to stop all this.

SHARON: And that's you is it? Dinny kid yoursel Liz. Ken what this is? It's an attention-seeking device. I ken a' aboot this stuff. Sheena's Bobby's always burning himsel wi' cigarette ends, Sheena says he's just trying tae get attention, I says, "Bobby, if you want tae get your mammy tae notice you, set her on fire, then she'll look at you". Are you daein this 'cause she did? That Maria?

LIZ: Maria's dead. People die all the time. All over the place.

SHARON: So?

LIZ: So.

SHARON: Is this supposed tae mean something?

LIZ: I get the star prize. I get to die for a cause.

SHARON: Oh Christ. You want tae be a fucking martyr.

LIZ: Great eh? *Yeah?* Isn't it great Sharon?

SHARON: You're mental. Naebody in their right mind would dae this I'm telling you.

LIZ: Well maybe it's time a few more of us did.

SHARON: Fuck of a way tae solve the energy crisis, give me British Gas any day . . . (LIZ *puts her hand in her pocket,* SHARON *thinks she's going for a match*) No!

LIZ: (*holding it out*) It's a note. (*chucks it at her*) Give it to Mark please. (SHARON *rips it open*) Hey!

SHARON: (*reads*) Dear Mark. I don't know how to get back, everything's burnt and broken . . .

LIZ: That's private!

SHARON: What do you care? You'll be Liz kebab in a minute. "I'm sorry. I love you". Oh brilliant, yeah great, dinny gie the guy a hard time will you?

LIZ: (*scrubs her eyes, she's nearly crying*) Ow!

SHARON: What?

LIZ: Petrol in my eyes . . . (*as* SHARON *tries to get her back*) Fuck off! Look, just tell him will you?

SHARON: Get tae, I'm no gaein near him.

LIZ: Okay, okay. Just see you get the rest of it right, don't let the army get you, grab someone who speaks English and start yelling for the press and . . .

SHARON: Get tae. I'm no talking tae anybody. I'm getting the fuck oot ae here.

LIZ: You've got to tell them, Sharon.

SHARON: How?

LIZ: *Please.*

SHARON: Nup. Gonny stop this now? (LIZ *shakes her head, she moves away from* SHARON, SHARON *edges trying to grab her*) Liz? You stop it . . . Stop this right now . . . (LIZ *is plumbing in her pockets*) No Liz! Liz!

LIZ: (*freezes*) Sharon?

SHARON: What?

LIZ: Have you got a light?

Lights down. We hear military jets radio static, the BBC VOICE: "... reports are still coming in . . ." *more jets, more static,* "Estelí" *echoey and distant, the sound of someone hammering on a door.* BBC VOICE: ". . . tension in the area is growing the Prime Minister said tonight . . ." LIZ *throws up. More hammering on the door. Fade other sounds.*

A faint light comes on the "Eye of Fatima". LIZ *retches again.*

Scene 9

Lights up. They are in the airport toilet. LIZ *has just been sick.* SHARON *is cleaning her up.* LIZ *has taken off most of her clothes which are lying in a sodden heap beside her; she is shivering violently.*

SHARON: (*shouting at the hammering*) Okay, okay hud on will you. Dinny bother Liz, we're taking a' the time we need. (*she takes a damp cloth and starts cleaning* LIZ'*s face*) Watch your eyes now.

LIZ: Oh fuck.

SHARON: It's okay. (*wipes gently round* LIZ's *eyes*) Now your hands. (*takes* LIZ's *hands and cleans between each finger*) Got the shakes eh? Dinny bother. It's a' right. (*starts to sing in a silly voice*) "Time to go home, time to go home, Andy and Teddy are waving goodbye" Mind that? Andy and Teddy and the Lobby Loo, that's you, Loopy fucking Loo.[78] What am I going to dae wi you? Here ... (*pulls her jersey over her head*) put that on, it'll be warmer. Okay? (LIZ *struggling into the jersey*) Any clean troosers in your bag?

LIZ: Yes ... I think.

SHARON: Okay. (*looks in her bag*) Go I bet there's a line o' women peein on the flaer oot there (*finds jeans*) Here we go. (*sings*) "Here we go, here we go here we go" ... smile, come on.

LIZ: (*grins at her*) I've thrown up half my stomach.

SHARON: Quickest way tae diet. (*holds out trousers*) Oh here these are barry, can I get a len of them sometime?

LIZ: Okay. (*tries to put them on,* SHARON *helps her*) God everything stinks of petrol.

SHARON: Leave it, they'll think a jet engine's come in for a slash. Right, socks next, hud on I'll clean your feet up (*goes on her knees, wipes* LIZ's *feet with the cloth*)

LIZ: What do we do now?

SHARON: Get on a plane. That's what you dae at airports. Go hame.

LIZ: Yes.

SHARON: How long since you were hame?

LIZ: Two weeks.

SHARON: (*helping* LIZ *on with socks and shoes*) No I mean right hame.

LIZ: I left Scotland five years ago.

SHARON: You want tae come back, it's getting pretty bad, you want tae see it. Listen I'm telling you, you want tae set the world on fire Niddrie's the place tae dae it.

LIZ: You laughing at me?

SHARON: (*grins*) What do you want me to dae?

The sound of hammering on the door.

SHARON: Away you go! We're busy! Well we'll hae something tae write hame aboot will we, if we live that long eh?

LIZ: I'm ready.

SHARON: Right, hud on a minute I just want tae fix my hair. (*fusses with a comb*) I've got tae smarten up, I'm going to be travelling first class ken? (*pulls a wad of money out of her pocket and waves it at* LIZ)

LIZ: Where'd you get that?

SHARON: The speed of the hand deceives the eye.

LIZ: You'll never get away with that!

SHARON: How not? He'll be eight hours in passport control (*takes a passport out of her pocket and chucks it away*) Anyway naebody'll notice in a that, it's mental oot there, half the world's trying tae get hame. (*checks herself in mirror*)

LIZ: Maybe I will . . .

SHARON: What?

LIZ: Come back for a bit.

SHARON: (*looks at her, nods*) You do that . . . I'm not. I'm getting oot. We dinny hae a problem her an me, no if we could get taegether, we could dae anything . . . Aye well nae chance o' that, way things are . . . I'll need tae sort it oot myself . . . I'll go back and say cheerio . . . (*looks at* LIZ, *grins*) *If* we get hame . . . (*her smile fades*) What? You think we canny. (LIZ *shrugs*) You think we're fucked.

LIZ: (*pulls a coin*) Call. (LIZ *goes to toss the coin, blackout*)

SHARON: (*in the dark*) I dinny *believe* it!

END OF PLAY

THE WAY TO GO HOME – GLOSSARY

The gloss of Scots terms here does not include words ending in *-in*, the equivalent of *-ing*, when the meaning of the word can be deduced from forms shared with English, e.g. or *makin* 'making'.

a': all
a'bady: everyone
aboot: about
ae: of
afare, afore: before
ain: own
aint: aren't
an: and
anymair: anymore
around: around
auld: old
aw: all; oh
awa: away
awfy: awful; awfully
aye: yes
B.O.: body odour
bairn: child:
baith: both
bam: idiot
barry: fine; smart-looking
bevy: beverage; alcoholic drink
bog: toilet
bonny: pretty
brae: hillside; slope
burn: stream
caff: café
cannay, canny: can't
cauld: cold
chancer: opportunist; someone who regularly seeks his own advantage
chum: accompany
claes: clothes
couldnae: couldn't
dae, daein: do, doing
dead: (intensifier) very
deid: dead
didnae: didn't
dinny: don't
doesnae: doesn't
doon: down
dug: dog
flaer: floor
flooer: flower
frae: from
funnys: comic strips in a newspaper
gae, gaein, gaen, gaes: go, going, gone, goes
gie, gied, giein, gies: give, gave, giving, gives
go go: 1960s dance style
gonny; gonny stop: going to; are you going to stop
granda: grandfather
greitin, greiting: weeping:
hadnae: hadn't
hae, haein: have, having
hale: whole
hame: home.
hankies: handkerchiefs
havenae: haven't
heid: head
heiland: highland
hersel: herself
himsel: himself
hingin: hanging
hoor: whore, prostitute
hud: hold
hud on: hold on, wait
hurpling: limping, hobbling
jist: just
ken, kent: you know; know, knew
knackered: exhausted
lassie: girl, young woman
len, get a: borrow
mair: more
maist: most

mak: make
mebbe: maybe
mind: remember
mou: mouth
mysel: myself
na, nae: no
naebody: nobody
naething: nothing
no: not
nup: no (emphatic)
oer: over
ontae: onto
oor: our
oot: out
ootside: outside
pinny: pinafore-style apron
pissed off: irritated
rabbiting: talking garrulously
raj: radge, wild
roon, roond: round
rair: sore
shit, shite: exclamation
shouldnae: shouldn't
skirl: shrill sound on a musical instrument such as the bagpipes, here extended to the rhythm produced by such music
slash, for a: to urinate
sloshed: drunk
tae: too
taegether: together
tak: take
totty: tiny
tranny: transistor radio
troosers: trousers
wanker: contemptuous name for a male; literally one who masturbates
wasnae, wasny: wasn't
wee: little
wi: with
wifey: familiar term for mature woman
withoot: without
wouldnae: wouldn't
yoursel: yourself

THE WAY TO GO HOME
– NOTES

1. A city on Turkey's Mediterranean coast.
2. Lyric of a popular song, 'Show me the way to go home', written in 1925 and recorded by various artists.
3. Turkish alcoholic beverage.
4. The capital of Turkey.
5. Istanbul, the largest city in Turkey.
6. Beginner's Turkish: 'No, no not America, Scotland . . . Scotland. In England . . .? Yeah? You know that? Well, I'm no English. I'm Scottish, never mind never mind.'
7. Beginner's Turkish: 'Autobus? Yes?'
8. *Midnight Express*: 1978 film drama set in a Turkish prison.
9. Beginner's Turkish, roughly 'What about . . . one . . . want . . .'
10. Portobello: coastal suburb of Edinburgh.
11. Thanks.
12. Leningrad: name of the city of St Petersburg during the Soviet era.
13. Nicaragua: Central American country, which in the 1980s endured a sustained conflict between the ruling left-wing Sandinista government and US-backed Contras.
14. Spanish: 'Comrade'.
15. A residential area of Edinburgh.
16. Campbell, Scottish clan name; 'The Campbells are coming' – a rousing Scottish martial song about Clan Campbell.
17. American film actor (1931–1955) associated with rebellious youth.
18. Highland Clearances, a period of time (1750–1860) when Gaelic crofters in Scotland were evicted from their homes, many being exiled to North America.
19. American cartoon rabbit, created for Warner Brothers films in the late 1930s. The pig referred to is Porky Pig, another cartoon character, who has a distinctive high-pitched voice and a pronounced stutter.
20. Mispronunciation of Uist, a group of islands in the Outer Hebrides.
21. Somocistas: supporters of the Somoza family dictatorship that ruled Nicaragua from 1936 to 1979.

22 Frente Sandinista de Liberación Nacional, the Sandinista National Liberation Front, which overthrew the Somoza regime in the 1979 Nicaraguan Revolution and governed the country from 1979–1990.
23 Spanish: 'We would like to build more but we spend a lot on defence.'
24 Spanish: 'Do you speak Spanish?'
25 Phonetic German: 'Do you speak German?' ('Sprechen sie Deutsch?')
26 French: 'French? Ah good [Sp.]. I mean good [Fr.], can you help us, sir? We are lost.'
27 French: 'Yes? Ah thanks.'
28 Sivrihisar: town in central Turkey.
29 French: 'Can you take the bus to Ankara here? Thanks.'
30 French: 'Liz, I'm called Liz.'
31 French: 'Sharon, she's called Sharon.'
32 French: 'She says go to . . .'
33 French: 'No she is not married yet, she works . . . what job?'
34 French: 'It's very beautiful, the country is very beautiful, everyone is nice, very nice and . . .'
35 English singer and songwriter (b. 1956), who had a popular solo career in the 1980s.
36 English pop group formed in 1983.
37 American rock band, formed in 1975.
38 English pop singer and songwriter (1947–2016).
39 English pop group, globally popular in the 1960s.
40 French: 'But they are all American films. Ah well? . . . But no, we are not English'.
41 French: 'No, we are Scottish, Scottish, you understand? To the north of Great Britain. You understand? Yes, yes, that's right.'
42 French: 'She says that you dance very well.'
43 French: 'She's tired. You are a soldier, right? For how long?'
44 French: 'You count each day?'
45 French: 'Dream, yes, of what?'
46 French: 'And how old are you?'
47 French: 'Why don't you love your country?'
48 French: 'No, I misunderstand . . . Ah, yes, okay.'
49 French: 'And what do you think about 1980, about what happened in 1980. The coup and all that?'
50 French: 'No thanks.'
51 Turkish: 'Okay, a tea.'

52 Turkish: 'A Pepsi, please.'
53 French: 'Sir. Can you translate this? When was it? Yesterday? There is much death? All American?'
54 OAP: old-age pensioner, senior citizen.
55 Libya: a country in North Africa, bombed by the USA in 1986; Syria: a West Asian country bordering Turkey; PLO: Palestinian Liberation Organisation, a nationalist coalition representing the Palestinian people; Abu Nidal: nickname of Sabri Khalil al-Banna (1937–2002), a Palestinian militant leader.
56 Central Intelligence Agency, an American intelligence agency that monitors and evaluates information from overseas that affects the security of the USA.
57 Honduras: country in Central America.
58 Song by Nicaraguan musicians, Carlos and Luis Enrique Mejia Godoy.
59 Spanish: 'Comrade!'
60 Contras: right-wing militias that fought a campaign of guerrilla warfare and terrorism against the Marxist government of Nicaragua in the period 1979–1990, some with the backing of the USA.
61 Niagara: group of large waterfalls on the Canadian–American border.
62 Refrain of a 1977 pop song by Queen.
63 Lyric of a 1985 pop song by Talking Heads.
64 Rambo: a fictional character who first appeared in the 1972 novel *First Blood* by David Morrell, but later became more famous as the hypermasculine lone-wolf soldier protagonist of the film series, in which he was played by Sylvester Stallone.
65 Turkish: 'A tea, please.'
66 Partial lyric of a 1953 song popularised by Tony Bennett.
67 PMT: pre-menstrual tension.
68 Guatemala: country in Central America whose government was overthrown by a US-backed coup in 1954; Grenada: island nation in the Caribbean, invaded by the USA in 1983; El Salvador: a Central American country which suffered a civil war from 1979–1992 in which the US government backed groups opposing the left-wing government.
69 Dallas: television soap opera set in the Texan oil and petroleum industry, which originally ran from 1978–1991.
70 Various American icons. Mickey Mouse: cartoon character, co-designed by Walt Disney in 1928; Elvis: rock and roll singer and

film actor (1935–1977); Lassie: a fictional dog which featured in a number of US films and TV series from the 1940s onwards.
71 Usual sign-off at the end of Looney Tunes cartoons.
72 Muppets: American puppet characters created by Jim Henson, which appeared in their own television series and films from the mid-1970s.
73 Evet: 'Yes' (Turkish). Chohk guzel (*çok güzel*): absolutely adorable (Turkish).
74 British Conservative politician who served in the Cabinet from 1981–1987, most prominently as Secretary of State for Employment (1981–1983). Tebbit was injured in the 1984 IRA bombing of the Grand Hotel in Brighton.
75 Wurlitzer: American manufacturer of musical instruments and jukeboxes. 'Well, it's one for the money . . .' is the opening line to the 1956 rock and roll song 'Blue Suede Shoes'.
76 Joan of Arc: religious martyr (c.1412–1431) and French national heroine, burned at the stake by the English.
77 Union Jack: national flag of the United Kingdom.
78 Lobby Loo, Loopy Loo: Looby Loo, a female puppet who appeared in *Andy Pandy*, a British children's television series from the 1950s, also featuring the puppets Andy Pandy and Teddy Bear.

THE ASSOCIATION FOR SCOTTISH LITERATURE ANNUAL VOLUMES

Volumes marked * are, at the time of publication, still available.

1971	James Hogg, *The Three Perils of Man*, ed. Douglas Gifford
1972	*The Poems of John Davidson*, vol. I, ed. Andrew Turnbull
1973	*The Poems of John Davidson*, vol. II, ed. Andrew Turnbull
1974	Allan Ramsay and Robert Fergusson, *Poems*, eds Alexander M. Kinghorn and Alexander Law
1975	John Galt, *The Member*, ed. Ian A. Gordon
1976	William Drummond of Hawthornden, *Poems and Prose*, ed. Robert H. MacDonald
1977	John G. Lockhart, *Peter's Letters to his Kinsfolk*, ed. William Ruddick
1978	John Galt, *Selected Short Stories*, ed. Ian A. Gordon
1979	Andrew Fletcher of Saltoun, *Selected Political Writings and Speeches*, ed. David Daiches
1980	*Scott on Himself*, ed. David Hewitt
1981	*The Party-Coloured Mind*, ed. David Reid
1982	James Hogg, *Selected Stories and Sketches*, ed. Douglas S. Mack
1983	Sir Thomas Urquhart of Cromarty, *The Jewel*, eds R. D. S. Jack and R. J. Lyall
1984	John Galt, *Ringan Gilhaize*, ed. Patricia J. Wilson
1985	Margaret Oliphant, *Selected Short Stories of the Supernatural*, ed. Margaret K. Gray
1986	James Hogg, *Selected Poems and Songs*, ed. David Groves
1987	Hugh MacDiarmid, *A Drunk Man Looks at the Thistle*, ed. Kenneth Buthlay
1988	*The Book of Sandy Stewart*, ed. Roger Leitch
1989	*The Comic Poems of William Tennant*, eds Maurice Lindsay and Alexander Scott
1990	Thomas Hamilton, *The Youth and Manhood of Cyril Thornton*, ed. Maurice Lindsay
1991	*The Complete Poems of Edwin Muir*, ed. Peter Butter
1992	*The Tavern Sages: Selections from the 'Noctes Ambrosianae'*, ed. J. H. Alexander
1993	*Gaelic Poetry in the Eighteenth Century*, ed. Derick S. Thomson
1994	Violet Jacob, *Flemington*, ed. Carol Anderson
1995	*'Scotland's Ruine': Lockhart of Carnwath's Memoirs of the Union*, ed. Daniel Szechi, with a foreword by Paul Scott
1996	*The Christis Kirk Tradition: Scots Poems of Folk Festivity*, ed. Allan H. MacLaine
1997–98*	*The Poems of William Dunbar* (two vols.), ed. Priscilla Bawcutt
1999	*The Scotswoman at Home and Abroad*, ed. Dorothy McMillan
2000*	Sir David Lyndsay, *Selected Poems*, ed. Janet Hadley Williams
2001	Sorley MacLean, *Dàin do Eimhir*, ed. Christopher Whyte
2002	Christian Isobel Johnstone, *Clan-Albin*, ed. Andrew Monnickendam
2003*	*Modernism and Nationalism: Literature and Society in Scotland 1918–1939*, ed. Margery Palmer McCulloch
2004*	*Serving Twa Maisters: five classic plays in Scots translation*, eds John Corbett and Bill Findlay
2005*	*The Devil to Stage: five plays by James Bridie*, ed. Gerard Carruthers
2006	*Voices From Their Ain Countrie: the poems of Marion Angus and Violet Jacob*, ed. Katherine Gordon
2007*	*Scottish People's Theatre: Plays by Glasgow Unity Writers*, ed. Bill Findlay
2008*	Elizabeth Hamilton, *The Cottagers of Glenburnie*, ed. Pam Perkins
2009*	Dot Allan, *Makeshift* and *Hunger March*, ed. Moira Burgess
2010*	Margaret Oliphant, *Kirsteen*, ed. Anne M. Scriven
2011*	Allan Cunningham, *Traditional Tales*, ed. Tim Killick
2012*	*A Song of Glasgow Town: The Collected Poems of Marion Bernstein*, eds Edward H. Cohen, Anne R. Fertig and Linda Fleming
2013*	*From the Line: Scottish War Poems 1914–1945*, eds David Goldie and Roderick Watson

2014*	David Pae, *Mary Paterson, or, The Fatal Error*, ed. Caroline McCracken-Flesher
2015*	*Poets of the People's Journal: Newspaper Poetry in Victorian Scotland*, ed. Kirstie Blair
2016*	*A Kist o Skinklan Things: an anthology of Scots poetry from the first and second waves of the Scottish renaissance*, ed. J. Derrick McClure
2017*	Susan Ferrier, *Marriage: A Novel*, ed. Dorothy McMillan
2018*	*Edwin Morgan: In Touch With Language*, eds John Coyle and James McGonigal
2019*	*Corona Borealis: Scottish Neo-Latin Poets on King James VI and his Reign, 1566–1603*, eds Steven J. Reid and David McOmish
2020*	*Dràma na Gàidhlig: Ceud Bliadhna air an Àrd-ùrlar (A Century of Gaelic Drama)*, ed. Michelle Macleod
2021*	*Jacobean Parnassus: Scottish Poetry from the Reign of James I*, ed. Alasdair A. MacDonald
2022*	Helen Craik, *Poems by a Lady*, eds Rachel Mann and Patrick Scott
2023*	Dorothy K. Haynes, *Haste Ye Back*, ed. Craig Lamont
2024*	*Setting the Stage: New Wave Scottish Drama from the 1970s and 1980s*, eds Steven Cramer and John Corbett